Anna Percy was born and educated in Norwich and has been writing for performance and publication since 2004. She is currently studying for her Creative Writing PhD at Manchester Metropolitan University, with a creative critical project in Environmental Poetry.

Rebecca Audra Smith comes from Gloucestershire, but enjoys being an honorary Mancunian. She competed in the Anti Slam Final Heat 2015 representing Manchester, and the Superheroes of Slam final 2015. Rebecca studied for her Masters in Creative Writing: Poetry at Manchester Metropolitan University.

In 2010, Anna and Becca founded Stirred, Manchester's influential pro-feminist collective which organises poetry performances and writing workshops.

"This collection is legs open and unapologetic, it's warm and echt, a charming celebration of the female experience."
Keisha Thompson, *poet, singer & theatre practitioner*

"At turns both romantic and political, wry and blunt, this duet of a book tells of the reality of wanting, of being loved, and of the constant cat-calls thrown at women daily. It is a book that is both unapologetically feminist, and unashamedly feminine. "I fell in love here, here, here. / Here, where my heart was empty / and built from masks" says Rebecca in 'Heart Masks', proving that while this is a book that delights in its 'Femifesto', there are also subtler, more accessible poems dotted throughout."
Max Wallis, *author of Polari Prize shortlisted* Modern Love

"From *The Shining* to free plums, from orbiting satellites to whatever's up Marilyn's skirt, the pens of this pair know no bounds. You don't have to be dripping with lust or a party-pooper to enjoy *Lustful Feminist Killjoys*: here is poetry that is sometimes sensual, sometimes stark, and at its shuddering best, oodles of both. Plums for everyone!"
Fat Roland, *writer & performer*

Lustful Feminist Killjoys

Anna Percy
&
Rebecca Audra Smith

Flapjack Press
flapjackpress.co.uk
exploring the synergy between performance and the page

Published in 2016 by Flapjack Press
Salford, Gtr Manchester
flapjackpress.co.uk

ISBN 978-0-9932370-4-1

mostlynocturnalscribbler.wordpress.com
@AMDPPoet
beccaaudra.wordpress.com
@BeccaAudra
stirredpoetry.wordpress.com
@StirredPoetry

Cover art by Hebe Phillips
hebephillips.co.uk
@hebelicious

Printed by Imprint Digital
Upton Pyne, Exeter, Devon
imprintdigital.com

This book is dedicated to everyone who has
the courage to live and write differently.

Contents

Versions of 'Wearing Sexuality' by Anna Percy and 'Cunt Artist Boyfriend' by Rebecca Audra Smith were first published in *Hallelujah for 50ft Women: Poems About Women's Relationship to Their Bodies*, ed. Raving Beauties [Bloodaxe, 2015].

'To the Beautiful Man Who Gave Me Free Plums' by Anna Percy and 'Stories Your Friends Tell You and Ones Their Bodies Tell You' by Rebecca Audra Smith were first published in *This Body I Live In (Slim Volume 3)*, ed. Kate Garrett [Pankhearst, 2015].

'The Emperor's New Molecules' by Anna Percy was first published in *Heavenly Bodies: A Constellation of Poetry*, ed. Rebecca Bilkau [Beautiful Dragons Press, 2014].

'Wolves Devouring Tin' by Rebecca Audra Smith was first published in *My Dear Watson: The Very Elements in Poetry*, ed. Rebecca Bilkau [Beautiful Dragons Press, 2015].

Where did we begin...

In 2010, Anna said: "I want a feminist poetry night", i.e. "Let's do a thing". Becca named the night, using the line from Carol Ann Duffy's poem 'Oppenheim's Cup and Saucer': "Far from / the loud laughter of men our secret life stirred". The night was thus named Stirred, a verb, as Anna had requested, so we could say "Come get Stirred". Manchester's Three Minute Theatre has been our home for several years and has proved to be the perfect space for Stirred. We would not have been able to develop the performance night to its current standing without 3MT's Gina and John.

Stirred began as a live performance night; over the years we have added monthly workshops and have collaborated and performed as Stirred for Reclaim the Night and at many other events and festivals. In 2015, Jasmine and Lenni joined the collective, as they were also working collaboratively and we saw the potential to develop the night further. With this strong team we began the Stirred Press, releasing monthly chapbooks documenting the work we do in bringing female role models to the front of the poetry scene.

Our most recent collaborative performance as the Stirred Collective four-piece was part of Wonder Women 2016, and involved a semi-naked performance in Manchester Art Gallery on the theme of clothes.

Why do you call yourself feminist?
Anna: I don't remember not being a feminist. My mum indoctrinated me; I was a Ms. on my first bank account when I was eleven. I have always been aware of the fact that women are expected to be restricted in their gender roles, I was lucky that I grew up in a household where I was not and I was told I could do anything I wanted. Even so, as a writer I have felt the

weight of misogyny, and have found that it impacted on my faith in my writing, in how I am perceived as a writer and a performer, that my work is often confessional, the fact that I have always been compared to Sylvia Plath, due to having bipolar disorder and a dead Dad.

Becca: I didn't always use the word feminist, it took me two years into working with Anna on Stirred to begin using the word. I remember Anna asking people to put their hand up if they were a feminist, and hesitating! I feel like the word 'feminist' is very powerful, and people still feel like they are crossing a boundary when they describe themselves as feminist. People react strangely when I use it, and there's the joke, the feminist took some time out to watch a film. Once you've invested in feminism, it can be tiring to see the wider context of daily micro aggressions and keep going, and constantly finding new subtexts to pop culture. *The Little Mermaid* can never be watched in the same way.

What have you got out of creating Stirred?

The poetry performance scene can be very male dominated, and performances themselves can be problematic in many ways. It's been important to generate a space where women feel safe and comfortable performing. We also allow for a space where more vulnerable performances can be given. Because much of the scene can be quite comedic and slam focused, we like to offer a space that can be survivor focused and sensitive towards the complexity of lived experiences.

Which planet would you visit first and why?

Becca: I would like to fly on Saturn's rings.

Anna: I want to go to Pluto because it should still be a planet. It wants some love.

What's your favourite kind of cheese?

Becca: I am currently fond of brie and blue cheese stacked up on crackers, eaten stood up in the kitchen.

Anna: Reblochon because it's delicious in tartiflette, up a mountain where it's supposed to be eaten. It's an Alpine dish.

Why do you work together?

We both think that we write terribly and act as mutual support during the dark times to tell each other that we're good writers. We also can find solutions for each other's poems that we wouldn't have thought of, Anna cuts, Becca restructures.

What have you got out of collaborating?

The will to carry on. We push each other into different territory, reminding each other of deadlines, push each other to submit, we try new forms together, perform in different places together.

Why do you say 'cunt' all the time?

Because it is a political act, a reclamation of the word that is often seen as one of the worst insults in the English language. It is rejecting misogynistic names for women's bodies based on a lack or act of violence, i.e. vagina meaning 'sword sheath'. It's shocking and rejects the notion that women's poetry should be 'gentle' and 'mannered'. It is an open discussion about women's sexuality and desire, which is often ignored in favour of the male gaze. It's a plosive sound, it is satisfying to say, it has a mouth-feel.

What is your favourite insult?

Anna: Wank puffin or fucking balloon (very appropriate for politicians).

Becca: Wanker because it's gender neutral.

What's your favourite kind of pen?

Anna: Parker Fountain Pen - black ink or coloured ink, had a green phase. Or a uni-ball eye is my second favourite. I like being inky and fast pens.

Becca: Anything will do. I quite like a biro-glide feel, but sometimes I feel like I don't have time to have pen favourites, and I get crushed when I lose them, so it's better to just take whatever is handy. I do have a coloured micro-tip set of fine-liners which are ace, but I'm so paranoid I'll lose them I've hidden them in a safe place and now I've lost them.

What does writing collaboratively look like?

Text messages late at night, picking words up and putting them back down on the page in different places, responding to the same prompt or theme and hearing echoes in each other's work, slashing poems, killing each other's darlings, being polite, being rude, not looking away, telling each other the work is worthwhile.

By starting Stirred Collective, supporting each other and other women's writing, we have stretched our ink further, we have allowed ourselves to be vulnerable, rage and experiment in poetry in ways we would not have been able to alone. In this book we share some of the work that we have written together.

Anna Percy & Rebecca Audra Smith
Manchester, March 2016

Lustful Feminist Killjoys

Femifesto

Anna Percy & Rebecca Audra Smith

To place the word 'cunt' in your poem
with love and reverence
is a political act.

To stand up and speak
although you may be afraid
is a political act.

We use our uneasiness
with the world
to build change.

We use our anger
at the insults the patriarchy makes of our lives
to build change.

We attempt to stop overusing
the word 'sorry'.

We are guilty of lust
and we revel in it.

We are allowed to contradict ourselves
as we find out
what we mean to say.

Blood

Rebecca Audra Smith

We've been told that blood
is not a theme for a woman to speak of.
Let us begin with the blood that leaks from our bodies,
monthly on monthly as the moon pulls firm as an anchor.
Our bodies harbour the potential for children
to clamber from us, be held inside us (hidden);
chambers that rock them and hold them securely
as low clouds seem held by the horizon in place.

There is the blood from the wounds and the scars
which we carry, the stories behind a split lip, a burst kneecap,
the self-harm criss-crossing on upper arms; this blood
that weeps for someone to halt its flow. Regardless, the blood
drags us onwards on the riptide of bloody poppies,
bursting with the fragrance of the wars where the men died.
Do we remember to grieve for the women
who were crushed underfoot by the rolling strata of time?

Somehow we have mislaid the right ceremonies,
still we carry ourselves, our blood locked inside us
by tampons and towels, and if men bled like this
then it'd be free on the system,
five days off in the month, but we
are just joking: we do not expect much.

The Cave of My Sane Mind

Anna Percy

After the poem 'Her Kind' by Anne Sexton.

There is the damp air, a strange comfort,
something easier to breathe.
A breathing space of a cave,
the place where anxiety recedes.

A woman like that causes her own trouble.

That voice cannot follow me into the caves.
All the voices stop, I am safe to hibernate,
that fizzing energy which animates me
beyond sleep and fatigue is quelled.

A woman like that talks too loud.

I can stop my mouth running off, running over,
those words that spill too freely stopped up.
There is no need of speech here.

A woman like that makes men feel bad.

The inequities that exist are pushed out by the warm air,
by my own hot breath, find a space where nothing can hurt
and I am free to think slowly and gently.

Scarlett O'Hara at the Picnic

Rebecca Audra Smith

is slutty.
She's got this low cut dress,
shows off deep V of her cleavage.

She's not like the nice girls,
covers up in the hot afternoon.

She's roasting herself
in the sun of the barbecue,
not staying under a parasol.

You can hear the women hum like a hive
with a man-shaped heart.

She picks up their men
with the bend of her waist,
18 inches, she pecks at the food.

She revels in their gaze, why wouldn't she?
She fed them her breathing.
Takes their breath away, steals it back.

She creeps from the afternoon slumber,
time prepared for ladies to nap,
recover from the prep of woman;

fresh for the night time dancing, they sleep.
The men discuss war.

Scarlett, down the staircase,
conquest on her mind.

A Universe of Men

Rebecca Audra Smith

After the artwork 'WormHole' [2014] by Eugenia Loli.

She's faceless, lifts her skirts for us,
reveals the painted world of our gaze.
We've looked too hard and too long into her,
thinking her a cave that leads us out.

Hunt for the darting stars of her orgasm,
screwing the planets out of her, some kind of Venus,
unliveable air, unbreathable lust. We do not get too close,
only stare, pry into her with paint, telescopes, pens,

and we pull from her what we will: a universe of men.

Wearing Sexuality

Anna Percy

There are ocelot coats in dusty wardrobes
reeking of ancient amber perfume, the kind formulated
from rare creatures' musk: borrowed hormones.

There are these skins belonging to adults,
an air of naked flesh and fur,
the pelt of an adult woman.

It only figures in the mind later,
this habit of men buying women
these exotic skins, hoping to see more skin,

more shorn skin, carefully defurred,
skin prepped for a scene to be conducted
as under a low cloud,

and you are to be left deflated.
He has taken your breath with his promises
and you are left anxiously, animalistically

sniffing your crotch surreptitiously
for that familiar ore scent.
The smell of blood.

Ella's a Regular at the Dive Bar

Anna Percy

The tiny glasses of bubbles waved at dinner
have little charm, she wants something harder.
Bribed a maid with stockings for a rough weave cloak.
Smog-clothed, goes out two-shoed as twelve chimes.
She had learned to slink silent out of rooms,
her nose knew the feel of bricks more than powder.

Princesses have no need of pockets or bank accounts.
The first time she had filched a fine linen embroidered napkin
filled with silver teaspoons, small brooches, an engraved comb.
The barman peeled the comb from the sticky bar,
wiped it with a beery towel, shook his head, asked her order.
Now some nights they let her sweep up, she misses useful hands.

Now she's alone with her thoughts, a thick glass in her hand.
Although manicured, they snap stems of palace glassware.
Never alone in a room there, someone hidden attending
to every whim, she wants to be alone with her thoughts.
Newcomers are grabbed by the wrist, told to shut their mouths.
Familiarity dulls satin's sheen, the glow of her hair.

Cigarette Smoke

Rebecca Audra Smith

For Suzie, Poppy and Jon.

We've been smoking since the hot wind
flared up Marilyn's skirt and she held onto her dress
like it was smoke going up around her,
her body a fire. We've been addicted to the slow drawl
and tell ourselves that we are nicotine gorgeous. Cowboys
light up, we were smoking before we knew
it would kill us, thought tobacco a cure for heart sickness.
Smoked ourselves skinny and knew we looked hot.
Strike a match. Got a light. Smoking is shorthand
for fuck my life, fuck my lungs, we are slow to refuse.
Our graves will be glamorous and all our mourners will say
she knew how to burn.

Inner Space

Anna Percy

After the artwork 'WormHole' [2014] by Eugenia Loli.

My cunt is universe all of itself,
the quick of me, of the highest gravity
pulling my thoughts to you.
When I think of your touch

it draws in all thoughts of
my current time and space,

lust wormholing me
uselessly to outer regions of space.

I am   adrift
among
        stars
and bro
        ken satellites,

my eyes dilate large as planets,
lost in my inner space,
missing stops on the bus.

She Appears as if Reflected

Anna Percy

After the artwork 'Interior with a Lady Seated' [1914] by Francis Cadell.

A shadow of enigmatic features only resolving themselves ten feet away as there is a sense of paint unleashed, of the hand being let go, the oils remain unblended. There is a gauzy shimmer; this is how your lover looks across a room, an aura, out of focus and holding your attention. This is the world after midnight, this captures what you almost thought you saw at 3 a.m. as the light flickered. An almost-dream painting, with her possible cat porpoising the sofa like it's aware it could be her wrap, cast off on entering a warm room.

The Praying You Do in the Shower

Rebecca Audra Smith

After the artwork 'The Blue Hat' [1911-1915] by Walter Sickert.

You are fingerless,
wear a half-moon smile
denting your face like the curve of a tin can.

You are a mirror unleashed,
a reflection that steams and wobbles.
You barely know yourself.
It holds eyes, they balance
within a flat world; mockery and daylight.

How you longed to throw yourself off the chair,
sprawl on the bed and plead with the window,
to withdraw its teeth.
The panes are all summer and rain,
the gulf between what you see
and what you expect.

And look at the room, what mess!
The bed is a disc that was thrown on a spring day,
all the pictures hold light as if they were mirrors.
You catch the odd glimpse,
the shame in the bed sheets,
the praying you do in the shower.

Texts

Anna Percy & Rebecca Audra Smith

Lick of paint to make life shine
(don't lick the paint if it's layered with lead).
Poisonous history abounds;
how easy tongues move in the mouth
of those whose words mean nothings.
Keep still, allow the lie to grow,
take roots, take breath and flourish.
Weed your thought-garden with care
so as not to uproot the truth.
I will kiss the lemon roses in others' gardens
until the next cloud bursts.
The growling oranges mock
the small yellow suns and limes.
This is how it tastes to want.

To the Beautiful Man Who Gave Me Free Plums

Anna Percy

Thank you for knowing
sell-by dates are a nonsense.
I took two of them to bed tonight,

some folly had persuaded me
I did not like them

till someone handed me a plum cake,
the fruit jewelling the top.
These were my first fresh plums.

As my teeth broke in I thought

how fragrant the skin was,
how small the stone is for such flesh,
let juice run my chin.
Considered I have many more
firsts to find in this life of mine.
Considered the idea of my next lover.

Heart Masks

Rebecca Audra Smith

After the artwork 'I Fell in Love Here' [2014] by Tracey Emin.

I fell in love here, here, here.
Here, where my heart was empty
and built from masks, I told myself
to fuck without a heart was better
than to talk, the wells drip
with my old thoughts.
I fell in love here, here, here is an appropriate
starting point; I look at fruit bowls and think
of men holding paintbrushes and I think
of muses, how I fell in love here and here and here,
where the old ghosts fell silent at your approach,
the love for you keeping me safe. You,
bent and whispered, trust yourself to the ground:
it had witnessed so much already.
I'm angelic without. I fell in love here.
I spent a lot of money and caught a train.

Cycling

Rebecca Audra Smith

We've cycled here.
These streets are cords tying me to now and you.
We do not talk through our stories,
we carry them from place to place,
we juggle them like oranges.
We are careful not to drop them
or pass them to those who
cannot carry their weight.
In the dim light of this autumn,
with the single teardrop of the moon
hanging in the sky (a lost real pearl
that would be rough on the teeth,
one in the scattered pile that you collect;
in this recession you've sold all the broken gold
you could gather to pay for
the Eurostar to France,
harnessing memories from jewellery,
an act of up-cycling the expansive past
into a new here), you let the words slip slide tumble.
Have I ever told you, you ask me,
No, we've never spoken of it, I say.
Although last we did when we first met
and alcohol caved-in the walls we usually hold firm.
Somehow it's like we've told these stories
many times before, words fill out the empty space
to show the presence of what we always knew was there.

On the Difficulty of Loving Men

Anna Percy

Today is as warm as the last, making my head feel heavy and pulpy like a melon. I have been wheeling its weight with my feet on the creaking frame of my new old bike, leaning at the table for a quick getaway. My writing companion is suffused with new love, I can see it coming from her pores. She has found a good man to love and give in return, it is helping her ink stretch further. At the next bench a man is loudly saying he's never abused women, but when he chats them up why do they act like such cunts? He spits this last word and I know a man like this would seek to pluck it from the mouths of women who own their bodies, name them as they choose, who lovingly roll the word *cunt* from their tongue to their lovers. I am avoiding that whole show and learning my lust is drilling deep in dreams and making innocuous phrases, instruments tuned to bawdy. I am mocked by my subconscious and this heat, waking roiling in a sheet, looking for the naked body I just saw, sure I felt on my flesh. The desire brambles this heat and deluge. Summer has grown it large and knotted. I am unsure if it would support fruit. The raspberry has an orifice; it's a filthy fruit for capping tongues.

Silver Fish

Rebecca Audra Smith

I bought a silver fish of a skirt today
to tack over the soft tops of my thighs and crotch,
to catch my body as it tips over into sex.
It is a piece of mirror, gleaming.
I could have chosen bronze, the colour of money
and power, not this piece of slippery moonshine
that scales me as if I were Ariel legged and breathing oxygen.

It is as loud as pantomime: *Oh no you didn't.*
Oh yes I did, I bought it, needless as it is
without function. It cups my ass with two silver hands
in a vice-like grip, steel-sheeted, it creaks as I move:
Iron Lady. I want its stiffness like I want to be fucked
by a woman wearing a strap-on dick.
The knowledge that she's wet behind the hard silicone cock.

The moon is full as my heart tonight, spitting stars.
as close to over-tipping.
I am alone with my giddy treat, my slippery whims.
Who knows where my hands will stray,
whether I will press my lips to its sheen,
tongue its smooth glide? I've never been in love with a skirt before.

I can dance in it, dance like I've not hedged my bets,
with abandon. And when you try to kiss me
I will spin into its tight bright embrace.
My legs are rivers below it and the muscles
in my cunt clench, solid as an eel.

Why I Don't Tell You I Feel Bad About My Body

Anna Percy

That black and shimmer dress you thought I looked amazing in -
I tried it on last week and took it off before I went out,
decided it accentuated all the parts of my body that are wrong,
felt it made my body wrong, changed it for something less clinging.
I have a full length mirror. This is important.
I know exactly what I look like - I know before anyone else calls me
a fat cunt, or a fat slut, or a fat slag,
I know exactly much of legs and breasts are showing.
I bend and turn, I know what I look like from all angles,
and tell myself that I am good enough.
I put it on and told the mirror that my waist-to-hip ratio
puts Jessica Rabbit to shame, that in platforms and fishnets
my legs are astonishing, look at my glorious knees.
I didn't tell you about the dress's failed first outing
because I don't want to add to all that fucking noise
about how my body is wrong, your body is wrong, any body
that is strong and existing just the way it knows how is wrong.
You are beautiful and giving and funny,
and your brain, your wit, your talent, your poetry
is worth so much more than worrying about dimensions of flesh.
I never tell you about how hard it is to leave the house some days,
how I am late because I changed my clothes and make up
a dozen times till I felt acceptable,
like this body and this skin is acceptable.
I walk tall with my back straight because I want everyone who sees
to know I think this body is alright, this body is gorgeous,
this body is beautiful and that dress
that didn't make it out of the house last week
is my new favourite.

My Body Could Be an Ocean if You Would Let Me Swim

Rebecca Audra Smith

"You could be mermaid" they said,
grow your hair to reach your tits,
seaweed-fine, straightened shine, wet sea-spray gloss.

If anything it is an anchor, dragging me
to bow my head to the ground, groom it,
weigh me down, the tide tug at my toss,
sit on a rock-ritual, brush brush brush.

Look in the mirror and practice your song,
salt in your mouth, the taste of compliments
bitter as oysters, the suck of them on your teeth
as you chuck it back, "thanks".

Launch me into the ocean of my body,
rock me within the meeting of our two skins,
we can wear our faces like disguises,
we can make pet names for each other -
just don't separate my breasts and individually
name them like a species of bird you have found
that you cup, at once gentle and possessive.
This body of mine is not treasure hunting.

I will preserve myself in brine,
like sailors at sea would eat salt biscuits.
They say they would go crazy for women,
alone for months at the oceans sway;

they say they would go mad.

The Emperor's New Molecules

Anna Percy

How man sought to change the stars through maps and misnomers.

Lacaille pins down the constellation,
takes it from the minds of the Dutch sailor-astronomers,

takes their shape-name, adds the scientific:
mythic flourish and *water snake* becomes *Hydrus.*

Hydrus, despite its pretensions, has no myths:
invisible as it was to the Greeks and Romans,

it was simply a traveller's shape, snake spine,
a path to follow in the endless sea at night.

Pious Schiller, despairing of the pagan worship
of animals, grouped them into chimera:

Hydrus and Tucana, scale and vibrant feather,
forged by his hand into an archangel,

a blow to such a man that a serpent has proved
more popular than a messenger.

I like to imagine Hydrus formed the head.
An angel spoke to him through a forked tongue.

Snow White the Scientist

Rebecca Audra Smith

Skin white like sodium chloride
she will analyse you to dust,
till the sucking sound
of a coffin's lid shut
has faded. She came out of the glass,
she wanted to know how it worked.
The citric acid of an apple
still in her mouth,
swallowing aspirin;
the glorious chemical burst.

She's been blocking thoughts for years,
and now, with the delicate nose of a syringe,
they drip, painfully slow, to
a test tube's questing sides.

Chain Reaction

Anna Percy

The mist today looked solid enough to carve from out the sash window. There was the unreal notion of mist causing a disappearing act, a coast, whole mountains, the sheep in the hills with their vicious voices, all the seals we weren't sure were rocks yesterday. The cloud had come down from the sky and conjured whiteness. There was no fear in this moment of fox cunning by the weather. I knew the mountains and the cormorants would still be there; the mountain and its glacier memories, the cormorant's heart and wide wings. There is a chain reaction of thoughts when the mist glamours away such weighty geography. You grit your teeth to remind yourself what sensation is and find yourself wondering what else is hidden from view.

Day Three

Rebecca Audra Smith

The northern rain had an iron grip, like a Hans Christian Anderson fairytale that you discover the dark side to when you're twenty. You're older and it comes like a story, unceasingly sweeping over your small section of the world. You tell yourself different versions of it, Cinderella dancing in fur slippers in the sodden downpour. You realise that you're an island within a tide of melting icecaps. The third day of the fresh year and it is counting your window, each drop a number, counting down your hope. The street smells like sewage as you seem to feel a pipe burst somewhere underground, under the torrential water. The impossibility of escape, squeeze your clothing, the sting of it in your face. You doubt the tree's ability to hold the ground down (roots underground bulbous and burgeoning). On the television a bridge burns, you know this means the troll has been released from its guardianship. The water has combined with fire, it makes a spell and trolls will come, creeping like damp mould on the shower curtain. You watch a documentary. *Out of every ten breaths we take, eight have come from the ocean.*

Dear Poem

Anna Percy

Dear Poem, last night I dyed my fringe blue, I look like a mermaid, but had to don a clingfilm hairband to do it, have a clean forehead.

Dear Poem, I haven't written about daffodils or death this month, there is still an allocation for both, daffodils have been on time this year.

Dear Poem, I am frustrated with Wordpress and can't manipulate your lines, this blog is intolerant of experimental poetry and I have not the skills to combat it.

Dear Poem, I only made it out of the house once today and I noticed how light it was at that late hour, and how white and uncrumpled the blossom.

Dear Poem, this spring has come later than last year after a muddled winter which confused the leaves on the trees, the grubby, dappled foxes, and myself.

Dear Poem, I am sad that I have not found a new novel to draw me in so utterly, I wake with the book near my hand and as I open my eyes I return to the page.

Dear Poem, you were written with my heavy-handed typing on the laptop, not my preferred medium of coloured ink and a fountain pen, today was not an ink day.

Dear Poem, I am marking the run up to my twenty-ninth birthday by dressing like a cartoon, last Saturday I was Minnie Mouse in a polka-dot dress, two buns for ears and red lipstick.

Dear Poem, I am not going to berate you for being frivolous or lacking assonance, this poem is a thunder storm, its lightning strike will break the high pressure of doubt.

Dear Poem, I will not expect too much, you are a first draft, I should be kind to you.

Parcels of Good Intentions

Anna Percy

I realised the weather was wild
when a woman left the bus
with a striped jacket on her head

while umbrellas were blown arachnid.
A man dropped a clear blue plastic folder,
creased letters from the DWP,
and a handful of dark business cards.

I cut through the department store.
Someone made off with a handbag,
security scurrying, scattering mannequins.

Think of the sorry contents of my own:
antacid tablets, a purse of small change,
sachets of green tea, parcels of good intentions.

Today I was wracked by ghosts
who spoke in strange tongues.

Van Gogh and Salvador Dali Meet and Discuss the Colour Blue

Rebecca Audra Smith

In your world, singular, it stares me out,
full of ire, an eye on a stalk, as vigilant
as a thought I once had that lurks
blue and malignant underneath the bed.

I thought it was blue, but when I find the original
it is white as a pupil, staring me out;
the single peace lily in a riotous sea,
the one thought I had that one time.

The lake spreads out, holding elephants
like a banquet of trunks, a rope of necks,
hippos prance in the shallows, waist-deep in swans.
You are blue, they hiss, and you lean towards them,

only to find they are solid as trees
and you are lacking a knife
with which to carve your name.

Feminist Velocipedestriennes

Anna Percy

After the day's dressing-gown-in-the-street embarrassment
(when the carpet-fitter whacked the fire alarm, set it off, and
I, being too sensitive to noise, was forced to leave dressed as I was,
still mortified by not being properly dressed in my own house
when I live alone, that they might not realise I am working,
writing, typing in this fluffy pink monstrosity of a garment,
that I work cross-legged on a sofa or on the floor over a laptop,
a notebook, scratching, over the ancient typewriter) I dressed

for the theatre in a dress spattered with tiny daisies and lycra,
so I could cycle to Contact theatre through Alexandra Park.
I attempted to reconstruct the glass conservatory exploded
by Suffragettes, remarked how much more bearable wind is
when filtered through trees, thought that this moment,
while the uncertain weather held and my beautiful
cloudy sky-framed bike didn't get a puncture,
was a small offering of how I hoped life could be.

I went to a sold out show about body hair and feminism,
drank cheap Merlot with witty wise women with large hearts
and fierce politics, cycled back through the park with one of them,
recounted how we had come off bikes and got back on,
wanted to tell her that's the trick of everything, take a spill
and cycle onwards. I whooped "I love this park at night,
look at the glorious lake ripples" and we were not afraid together.

Gustave Courbet

Anna Percy

After the artwork 'Still Life with Apples and a Pomegranate' [1871-2] by Gustave Courbet.

These are not apples and that was never a pomegranate.
Perhaps one or two grew on a tree and have authentic pips,
the rest are not what you'd expect. They beamed themselves
onto the market stall in 19th century France when the woman's
back was turned, concerned with her apron's pocket of lucre
gained from selling her wrinkled worm-filled produce.
The observational devices were too shiny, simulated from
oil paintings, their mix of colour too bright and perfect.
There are historians hungry for real accuracy, wary
of disrupting the space-time continuum, of sending
their real all-too-mortal living bodies back in time.
The devices record all sensory experience in their range,
scholars greedily plug themselves into the feedback matrix
to taste the past. First time users are advised to turn
the nasal receptors right down to Level 2.

Cunt Artist Boyfriend

Rebecca Audra Smith

He told her, *keep it neat and tidy.*
She thinks, *same as the kitchen,*
same as the kitchen sink.

She'd asked how he'd like it done;
A Brazilian, Hollywood... he said,
just keep it neat and tidy.

She combines Brazilian and basic bikini.
It's a shame that she leaves wet sponges
damply lining the kitchen sink.

He wishes she would wring them out
or not stack used pots to stink like drains,
but leave it neat and tidy, nightly.

It is hard not to negotiate hands on flesh
and hard not to complain when cleanliness
comes to grief in the kitchen sink.

Day in and out the chores remain.
Monthly hair waxes and wanes.
He congratulates her, *you've kept it tidy.*
All but the kitchen sink.

Wendy Bird is Crying Again

Anna Percy & Rebecca Audra Smith

Inspired by The Shining.

Wendy is being lied to again, she can taste it.
She checks for the flavour with questions.
Nobody told her a tongue could lie to you.
She spits when the iron comes and it is clear.

ANYTHING THERE ANYTHING THERE AT ALL ARE YOU
SURE IT WAS THE RIGHT ROOM ANYTHING THERE

What were you thinking? Taking your family away for winter
like a squirrel with nuts. Look at your harvest now.
Your eyes are weeping willows full of birds who couldn't fly.
Even as she smashes the plates the birds
are failing to take flight from the shards.

WHAT ABOUT SOMEBODY DID THIS THAT TO HIM TO ME
SOMEBODY DID THAT

Wendy, once you rule out your version of what happened
there's only one possible explanation for this.

She can't rely on the version that came
between sleeping and waking.

ONLY ONE EXPLANATION YOU'RE TEPID MEAT IN HOT
WATER NOBODY'S LOOKING FOR YOUR CORPSE IN THE
SHOWER WHAT ABOUT WHERE YOU ARE NOW?

Philosophy of Rainfall

Rebecca Audra Smith

Mild at first, then severe, our tongues utter droplets.
We are children hoping to open up each day
and find the world a purl knit pattern,
making sunshine out of storms, dreaming doors,
carrying a ruined globe, the earth a roof.
We have ceased to regard our halting heart.

Woken by the wind, the taste of your bitten core;
a heart broke when the house caved in, a sudden drop,
the edge of your lifeline, your fingernails bitten, your eyes open,
the grit of coffee in your sight. You thought you'd explore the roof,
dusting the chimneys fresh, no need for a door.
The home you crave is built to your childhood play.

It comes again, the rain. I play the songs that make lyrical patterns;
inside my muscular brain, a thumping drum, the heavy heart.
What we are made of? The words turn washing machine, unhinged,
your hands deep in your own sweat droplets.
If we sit down and drink coffee, perhaps act like cats on the roof,
elegant and unafraid of the fall, the sky perilous and open,

we may yet learn of ourselves; trust, keep your soul open
as bird wings in flight in the storm, their feather patterns.
We pluck their washed guts from the floor, reversed roof,
unheard of woe, innocent trash leaking from the sea's heart.
I took one look at you and it all came together, like droplets
merging into water. We've crossed boundaries unbidden.

Global warming will keep us cold into summer,
the autumn will be a wish we once had, your smile open
on your face as the snowdrops which flower, each individual droplet

an earthquake of hope. A butterfly caused this rain. Watch
the pattern of its wingbeat, steeped in wine made from the heart
of a vine's perfect sun-hour. You may taste cherries, gorgeous red,

your lover may tie you to your promises, under one roof.
Made us think we could be enough, for a few minutes. The door
that shuts us out will let us in, like the ventricles the heart
stutters in your sleep. Open your eyes to see a single sail
moving out of sight upon the waves' rippling pattern.
Lean into my arms, I'll tell you a tale of the droplets, the fall.

Stories Your Friends Tell You and Ones Their Bodies Tell You
Rebecca Audra Smith

Your hands are fragile, hold the scar,
brashly it marks, graffiti of the knife the doctors used
to prise the swollen skin apart.

You climbed off the boy's bed,
you have changed your mind,
you were half naked; *let's be friends*, you said.

I came to visit you in hospital.
Next to its hulk I saw your ex walking
to visit you, offer you rolled cigarettes,

regret, and later, anger filled texts,
which you swallowed like you swallow
the three types of painkiller you are on.

We find you in a different ward, asleep,
your laptop still awake, poems you write
to mitigate your loss.

For you this year, it's been unforced.
A moth flew in your opened bedroom window.
I brought you tulips from Amsterdam.

I wanted to get you black, but got you blue instead.
The water creaked just like a bed, and shone
like many mouths made wet.

We watched the prostitutes watch us,
had stale sex, smoked cigarettes;
I wonder if it's flowered.

Things I Had Forgotten

Anna Percy

The alarming geometry of gorse.
Foxgloves: poisonous beauty.

How to walk across streams
(my feet know how to negotiate stones).

That sheep give no fucks.

The smell of a foison of ferns.
Childhood scent of getting lost
and not caring.

How the oyster catchers scream.
How jagged the sea becomes in wind.
How delicious I find the smell of seaweed.
How much I love to roll and loll on grass.
How I sniff in all the deep green scents
of grass, gorse, fern and trees.
How to walk in absolute dark.

After Midnight

Anna Percy

It is now the twentieth year of your death.
I grab some flesh I shouldn't have, I strip muscle
from haunches, seek out bones below.
I have learned my body makes men hungry.
I knew I would mark the occasion,
comfort myself with the refrain
to err is human, to err is human.

Daffs for Drum

Anna Percy

For my father, David Drummond Percy.

Today everything has felt serendipitous;
the beautiful-hearted women
helped me float a poem to you
on an apple balloon before the lanterns caught fire,
I almost wished my poem to you had smoked,
something in the burning, an offering I liked.

Although you had never run to such rituals
there were discarded tarot cards splayed on a brick wall
and the shock of your Gallic pack in your desk drawer.
Something occult in mother's rational home
a decade ago came to me.

I have bought you daffodils hundreds of miles
from your subsiding stone with its dove,
they stretch out from the neck of an antique bottle
bearing Newcastle, the city near your birthplace.

Hawk's Eye

Rebecca Audra Smith

After reading H is for Hawk *by Helen Macdonald.*

Hawks carry our grief, they come like loss does,
swiftly and heavily, their talons squeezing into prey
till it dies in the act, a merciless death.
You know that your heart has been cloaked in shadow,

that rabbit-like it scampers across wheat-blown fields,
that you are haunted by hawks who arrive on your lawn
and tear into sparrows with beak and eye.
You watch spellbound as your blood breathes through your skin.

You won't look away, don't even try. You gather the feathers
that have drenched the grass, you harness your heart, shut
the house door. You watch for the hawks as if they brought news
from your loved one's perch in the afterlife. You look at the world

with a predator's view. Night falls and the TV screen turns mirror;
you cast in it to find what's lost, feed it with memories,
the most precious you have. You live in the past
like a species died-out, trying for wings, but you can't find the way.

Then the hawks come, like those who die, so close
you can smell the wild. Peddling grief with their wind and flight
you inhabit your body like a temporary space, waiting for sight
to open out, gaze at the world through a hawk's eyes.

No More Unwanted
Anna Percy

I will no longer take lovers who are not in awe of me, lovers who find me wanting. I will now only take lovers who look at me, eyes dazzling, their lips cherries, who will look at me as if I am an amulet or charm they need to continue their journey. I will only take lovers who make me feel like I am, in this moment, exactly beautiful. I will only take a lover who loves freely, who does not have to be pressed to love, who can see beyond the flesh and rejoices in my flesh, in our laughing, braying, till I am panda'd by eyeliner and red in the face. I will no longer take a lover who fears my books. I will no longer take a lover who fears my mind.

Sap Rising

Anna Percy & Rebecca Audra Smith

As sightless as caterpillars locked in their
butterfly bodies, my heart waits.
It's a long, lonely winter ahead;
carry my song till the spring,
till we can sing together,
carry it softly as footsteps in summer.
We are waiting for the frost to kiss the windows,
warm my heart as the leaves carpet tarmac, keep
my sap rising baby: the trees have been bitten with lust
and wear their own scarlet lettering.
Street lights glow like I can fool myself,
the branches are your arms waiting for my embrace.
It's like a lit fire in October remembering you,
thinking of your touch stokes the fire
and I am aflame in an empty bed,
heavy heart and empty wine glasses
tasting like dreams and sex.
Bloodied dregs leave me bloody-minded in want of you;
you are as beloved as a movie scene I am yet to watch.
My cunt flickers at the very thought of you.
Come wear out my mattress,
come break my bed baby, I don't need sleep,
come wreck the kitchen, these tables are groaning for your weight.
Let's rattle the cutlery in the drawers, make them play our tune,
feed me like it's breakfast, I ain't waiting for a plate.
I am ripe with juice after the sun,
my bed is in mourning under the shadows
spilling light. It tastes of you.

He Has Made Her Smooth

Rebecca Audra Smith

Inspired by the play Nirbhaya *by Yael Farber.*

Lit her up, the fire burnt out now, the kerosene drenched scent
and the burning, he fainted when he saw what he had done, he
hadn't the stomach for it, in the moments before the wick touched
her skin she said *if you're going to do it, then burn me,* the beatings
dared him to give her more pain, the candle of her, a kitchen hob,
an accident, and now all hewn from a new machine of heat and a
waxed cheek, the veins sluggish crawl, she gleams, catches the
light from odd angles, is no longer recognisable as she was,
wearing her face like a newborn, unsure of how she looks, her
son screamed to see her made a scarecrow in the home, the
violence leaks in through the walls, her husband's hands were
covered in it, he painted her a martyr, unlatched the door of her
face to watch it hang by its hinges, when we heal we heal
awkwardly with great pain and effort. There are days mirrors are
shadows unveiling our pasts and days when passer-by faces are
the mirrors in which you judge your own shock. He has made
her an icon, to be held up and say to the roaring crowds look, *look
at how we shine in your man-made darkness.*

Wolves Devouring Tin

Rebecca Audra Smith

The air swings, malleable. Melting point.
We describe space by moving. Release
the hinges, cast our shadows on the sky.
Nearly as bright and hard as diamonds;
tears that slide down your cheeks
carved from glass, you smell like wolves
let loose in a zoo to snarl at parrots.
Kept behind cages, bars that last, heated
to the point of melting, we do not break.
We are brittle and spun, facing skeletons.
Dancing with our hands held up. The howl.
A funfair let loose in a parking lot.
Our hands are whole and grasp at air.

We describe space by moving.
Release at point of pressure.
Temperature reaches room.
The hinges cast our shadows
like paint on walls, you howl like a wolf.
Your tears are cast. Let loose.
Bars that last, made from cages.
A funfair in a smashed
parking lot with whole cars.
Our legs solidify beneath us.
Gold is softer, melts quicker. Ravenous.
You spit tin from your heartlessness.

Panting, you oxidise.
Wolves howl.
Elsewhere the room smashes.
You've been isolated down.

Point of greatest strength.
Built from crashed fair rides.
We are brittle and spun.
Tin in your teeth,
bright as diamonds.
Your tears have reached
melting temperature.
Electric lamps burn.
Your heart is easily forged.

Morning Pantoum

Rebecca Audra Smith

In the morning we can start over.
We'll pick our clothes off the floor and fit arms into sleeves,
we will gather up the memorabilia and junk it,
wash away the scent of the bed in the shower.

We'll pick our clothes off the floor and fit arms into sleeves.
The way last night we fit into each other,
wash away the scent of the bed in the shower.
The morning has arrived and put us asunder.

The way last night we fit into each other
like a body under sand, the contours shift.
The morning has arrived and put us asunder,
like a bed in an ocean, we are set adrift.

Like a body under sand, the contours shift,
it makes no sense to remember how we kissed.
Like a bed in an ocean, we've been set adrift,
we've not understood love, how difficult it is.

It makes no sense to remember how we kissed.
In the morning we can start over,
we've not understood love, how difficult it is.
We will gather up and burn our memorabilia.

Fell Into My Head

Anna Percy

There were broken tea cups on the carpet,
clumsy visions of someone else's tea party.
We had used them for something comparable
in colour, though stronger. It bit our throats,
brought forth those neon spiky aching words.

As they smashed the painted swallows I swore,
they flew through the window, rustling curtains,
into the summer night near an apricot moon,
to soar among the flash-fast shooting stars.

When held you always tell me I smell of roses,
perfume covers, the unwashed don't-care hair.
Without success smother sweat with rose scent,
push back dirty strands with bedaisied sunglasses,

sweep tea cup pieces, find joy in a rainy summer,
drink rose lemonade in hope of a rosy outlook
of a rose-like nature, softer, never forgetting my thorns,
grow deep roots and can take a hard pruning,
regrow my blooms. Hope next summer requires more sunglasses.

Bed Shed Bed

Anna Percy

After the artworks 'My Bed' [1998] by Tracey Emin and 'Cold Dark Matter: An Exploded View' [1991] by Cornelia Parker.

Its low flat surface is a magnet for objects,
plus the bedroom is the warmest room:

I often cocoon myself in there;
at breakfast, take a bowl and spoon,
yogurt and oats, half slumberous
eaten in bed, the decadence of living alone.

Then there is the waking and finding:

the scuba diver from your dream has left his flipper
on that olive leaf throw with the holes from
the new year's eve fire you doused with red wine.

At the foot of the bed:

that brassy wire fireguard
my tiny hands were swept away from
at Farrow Road, my first home, a thirties semi.

My dreams are leaking onto this bed:

Flash's stolen front wheel spokes all out of whack,
nestled by the cuddly hare I still need on bad nights,
the hot water bottle cold and slithered past my feet;
there are the duvet-hidden rectangles of the
three novels I am reading at any given time
(Pratchett for sleepless nights, Iris Murdoch unfinished,
Muriel Spark inhaled in one sitting),
kirby grips, crumbs, jewellery hastily removed in the night,

an
    empty
        can
            of Irn-Bru
                    rolled towards the bookcase.

Beautiful Fuck Sonnet

Rebecca Audra Smith

You're so beautiful I might be drowning being near you;
let me tell you how much I want you while I've still breath left.
If I don't, words will gather in my lungs, their wings' beat frantic
as a flock of crows, their black night feathers fill me like flight.

Loving you till my arms ache with your weight, you ghost me.
Held in your arms I walk the streets, people ask why I'm smiling.

You fuck like a sailor on the shore, it's easy as stepping into the tide.
My hair tastes of you the next day, the wall cracks under our weight,
bed creaks with plaster, we make the ceiling a sky. Skin reverberates
with the pressure of touch, how you fuck, my clothes contain me.

You pour me into dresses; I wade through desire, moving my hand
to rest on yours, pushing through volcanic heat, reaching you
with the ache. A hollowed out feeling in my chest, your heartbeat
doesn't fill me hard enough. Turning to you countless times.

Fixing the Tale of the Heart

Rebecca Audra Smith

Cutting my heart out and ramming it into an ashtray, pouring it into an ice cube tray then mixing the strongest, coldest Bloody Mary, gnawing it raw, blowdrying till it's new as a fresh football, scooping it out with a spoon and making panna cotta, pinning it up like a beetle and watching its small mechanic motions till it stops, stewing it with tomatoes, hammering it like a piece of pork, fixing it to my backbone with a piece of pipe.

Message in a Bottle
Anna Percy

This is my message to you, it bobs on waves in a bottle so green you will think it is made from early summer leaves. You will want to drink the chlorophyll, feel it will nourish you. The message is something for you to consume with your eyes and mind and heart. It is a message I need to hear. I am repeating it, turning it over, tuning it to music; a joyful refrain. Something that will calm you and stop the want. You knew it once and have forgotten. This is self-love, repeat this often enough and your heartbeat will sing it to you: *you are enough*.

Sonnenizio for a Pair on Brighton Pier

Rebecca Audra Smith

Developed from the concluding line of 'Sonnet X' by John Donne.

"Death shall be no more; Death thou shalt die."
No more will we walk along the strand, hand-holding promenade,
no more will we return to where light hits sea and sky,
fake tinge on postcard logic, more commercial than true.

Brighton Pier's lights, more like a casino's blaze.
We keep our moorings close to the shoreline's surf,
you come to me, more heart than logic.
We promise to try harder, more than it's worth.

Endings shall be no more, Clinton Card promises.
In the surf of Brighton's Pier, moths look more like butterflies.
You catch them with your hands, more quick than I,
tell me again you'll love me until you die.

Old Brighton Pier is ghosting in the bay, its moorings lost;
say goodbye sweetly, no more counting the cost.

Daily Mirror

Anna Percy & Rebecca Audra Smith

The imperfection of old mirrors,
the dark splotches and rain patterns,
are a truer version of reality

than this smooth, sheen reflection;
every pore a gleaming world of lore
of how we crawl from earth to air.

Many no longer trust their pores to static glass.
Frantic and lovely they check their profile
and twirl their hair on video phones.

The mirror a flat home, weightless,
we drink in bars and watch the shine on pints,
check the time and forget to leave.

Remember reflections and our perception frequently distorts.
Without a glass to shatter we gaze into unseen scratch of water.

Nocturne

Anna Percy

Last night I dreamed she broke in.
She'd know how to elbow a window,

dreams erase the need for ladders.
She took the notebooks from my shelves.

Although we haven't spoken in years
I conjured her mocking tones, wholesale

vitriol distorted by distance and sleep.
She tore off strips of my scrawl, vicious,

rolling them up with great ceremony
in my nocturnal subconscious.

She did what she always did on waking.
While laughing she ate my words.

A Witch Called Deborah

Anna Percy

She knew she shouldn't have taken in that last black cat.
He was like the others, but no one notices his white socks,
mewling at the back door, with his one eye, jagged tin in his paw.
He keeps the end of her brightly patched quilt warm,
greets her, purring, in the kitchen each morning,
grateful for each bowlful, not greedy like the other two.
She started drying herbs, sage, hanging dusty in the window;
her first mistake. She realises now.

After the first black cat she dressed herself in black.
Never given to sartorial flash, it hid the fallen fur.
She should never have offered that mug of peppermint tea
to the neighbour's boy who grudgingly chopped the wood.
Caffeine makes her jumpy. She saw his face change
(he'd heard the rumours); the steaming green cup,
she saw when he waved it away, looked like a potion.

She had to hide her collection of antiquarian books.
Local kids said she skinned those who crossed her
to bind her spells in those foxed pages.
She's had to add three locks to the door,
braces it with a chair so she can sleep.
The night the power went out and she,
ever resourceful, stuck those red candles
(hidden in the drawer by the ladles
for the dinner parties she had imagined
she might hold once) in the empty wine bottles,
she went to bed dreaming of pitchforks.

Medea

Rebecca Audra Smith

For Nicky Mortlock.

Brew me a new life
out of green thumbs and songs.
Make me young as I was when I thought
our souls are made of sky colours.
I will plaster myself in marble,
I will build my own tower,
I will let you slit my neck
and fill me with fresh flowers.

She promised youth:
she said, *give me an ewe,
no, on second thoughts, a ram -
head heavy with horns -
and I will restore spring.*

The pot was too small.
She stuffed the whorled body,
legs sticking out at right angles,
a bleat and then it shrunk,
leaving behind the sack of its old shape.

Drain out the stale blood,
we must fill ourselves with life.
Daughters, stab your fathers,
sharpen the knives.

When the corpse is quiet
and the moon is high
we will fill it like a chalice,
we can but resurrect or die.

Miss Representation

Anna Percy

After the poem 'Lady Lazarus' by Sylvia Plath.

Out of the ash I rise with my incomprehensible hair,
that glamour of youth and innocence a veil to cast
between me and my intellect, and still I rise
and eat men like air; I will eat their foolish words
and let their fuckeries give me strength.

Opening a jaw-wide snake dislocation,
stasis is no longer an option:
I must eat their words to make room for mine,
there are too many of them, rank and sulphurous,
the books on all the shelves stacked with them.

If boys have all the best lines and you are always cast
in a supporting role, and you are told the verse held
in highest regard is penned by dead white men,
are you surprised women feel they need permission to write?

I have wasted too many of my own words
on the fuckeries of men who have shared my bed,
hoping this thought could telephone myself
in these weak moments of desire.

Give over the strong jaw, breathe into the lungs
the strength I was lacking, manipulate that jaw puppet-like,
open the door, gather their clothes and return to the cell,
an empty bed and a clear conscience.

Before I lock the door I whisper in my ear:
"You will never learn to be your true feminist self
when you let fuckeries occur in your bed and your head."

Lustful Feminist Killjoys

Rebecca Audra Smith

We are lustful and we kill joy,
we borrow hammers to kill joy
and screwdrivers, and electric drills.
We call it feminism;
they tell us that
we are deranged,
giddy on desire.
We are gone to the edge,
we want like want is a thirst,
we love like love is breathing.

We are lustful, we wear clothes
with zips, and buttons, and holes;
clothes you can remove quickly.
They tell us that we have
neglected our dress,
we are deranged.
We clothe our skeletons with
glorious fistfuls of flesh,
we want like want is a thirst.

We are killjoys, painting portraits
of tulips in full-bodied growth,
when you ask to see us naked
we hand you an album of flowers.
They tell us that we have failed at being,
no matter how many shades
of nail polish we gather.
The cackles that racket off
the ceiling are unseemly,
we are deranged,

marooned people
love like love is breathing.

We are lustful and we kill joy,
the smash of a window that lasts
like a scent, a bottled rebellion
advertised as a mermaid with legs.
We are sampling the merchandise,
greedy newcomers to the feast,
people are told to stand back.
We are deranged;
we want like want is a thirst,
we love like love is breathing.

From crime, car crashes and rebellion to full-time ministry,
ministry and mission, growing a church in Manchester from
sixteen people to several hundred,
rescuing abandoned children in Romania and planting churches

The Rubicon

Paul Hallam

EXulon
ELITE

Endorsements

The Rubicon is a tale of faith, passion, commitment and service. Through its pages, the life and ministry of Pastor Paul Hallam are exposed, detailing the lessons we all have to learn and the choices we all need to make in the pursuit of fulfilling our God-given destinies. The book emphasises the need for complete trust in God as therein lies blessings in various dimensions. There are indeed many lessons to embrace; leadership, missions and courage to name a few. This is a story of a man, and his ministry, who has decided to live out God's true purpose in spite of current circumstances. It is a truly inspirational book that would serve to positively impact the life of every reader to step out in faith holding God's hand.

Pastor Abimbola Komolafe
Senior Pastor, Jubilee Church, Manchester RCCG UK

In the last ten years it has been my great privilege to get to know Paul Hallam and his wonderful wife Mags. I have loved working with them and watching them as their amazing church, The Lighthouse, has grown to become one of the leading churches in Manchester, and achieve an indelible footprint over many parts of the world. Paul is a tremendous leader and a true inspiration to all who meet him. He is the real deal!

I heartily recommend Paul's first book, The Rubicon to you—an amazing story of what God can do, through a life that is totally surrendered to him. You will laugh and you will cry as the adventure of faith unfolds before you. So read on ... and dare to dream, today!

Kevin Peat
Regional Superintendent of Elim Churches in NW England and Scotland and member of Elim's NLT (National Leadership Team)

Over the last few years it's been great getting to know Paul Hallam and discover a man of great passion and real integrity. Everybody loves a good story and this one is fantastic and brings great honour to Jesus. Read on and be inspired.

Andy Hawthorne
The Message Trust, Manchester UK

Paul Hallam is an inspirational leader and incredibly gifted communicator. 'The Rubicon' maps 28 years of Paul's experience in full-time ministry. In that time he has worn many different hats and continues to do so with ease–as pastor, leader, mentor, coach, encourager, visionary, dreamer, fighter and friend. 'The Rubicon' unpacks the journey of a man who with a leap of faith, began an exciting adventure with Christ. This book will give you insight into the decisions that caused Paul to burn his bridges, step over the edge and take huge risks to build what he has built–like an outstanding church here in the UK called 'The Lighthouse,' 78 other churches in his spare time as the missionary man that he is! Bible-schools and training facilities, orphanages and homes for the broken hearted and the list goes on...

I can honestly say that Paul has one of the biggest hearts for 'others' that I have encountered... He and his wife Mags are wonderful people. I have had the joy of working alongside Paul for some time now and each encounter with him has left me walking away inspired, challenged and encouraged. This book will no doubt inspire you, challenge you and encourage you too! Enjoy!

Mark Stevens
Worship Pastor (Abundant Life, Bradford and Hillsongs,
Sydney, Australia)

We have known Paul and Mags Hallam for over twenty years of ministering in the same city where church unity has been strong. Paul is a man of faith which comes across over and over again in his book The Rubicon, where he tells stories about how God has stretched his faith and been faithful to provide above and beyond on many occasions. He has built a church of like-minded people, who have not only seen transformation in the city of Manchester but around the world. Paul has truly obeyed the great commission to "go into all the world" making disciples. Read this book and you will be inspired about the faithfulness of our God and his servants.

Debra Green OBE
Founding Director of Redeeming Our Communities (ROC)

I met Pastor Paul Hallam in a newly founded church in southern Romania about 18 years ago. I could see from the first moment his desire to help this area of Romania and I think in all the years he fulfilled the word of the gospel that Jesus said in Matthew 25: 35-36 "For I was hungry and you gave me something to eat, I was thirsty and you gave me something to drink, I was a stranger and you invited me in, I needed clothes and you clothed me, I was sick and you looked after me, I was in prison and you came to visit me.
The spiritual and material ministry of Pastor Paul Hallam in the lives of many, made a big difference for them over time, and his consistency is an example worthy of praise.

Pastor Dumitru Geru
President Christian Center Oltenia
Drobeta Turnu Severin, S.Romania

A powerful account of dreams birthed and vision fulfilled. Written with honesty and humility, 'The Rubicon' provides a road-map for those embarking on a fresh adventure with God as well as affirming the faithfulness of God in those tenaciously engaged in holding on to God's promises. Paul and Mags Hallam are inspirational and highly respected leaders within our Movement–spiritual entrepreneurs who are modelling something exceptional for the benefit of generations to come.

John Glass, General Superintendent,
Elim Churches GB & Ireland

TABLE OF CONTENTS

FOREWORD

By Pastor Matthew Kurian

———————————◆———————————

Reading *The Rubicon* brought a smile to my face and I can literally visualise the preaching and the passion of Pastor Paul. This is one of the most honest and open books I have read written by a pastor. Some authors never speak about their small beginnings and the failures, but only project their achievements and great things, but Pastor Paul is speaking to us about the hard core truth of his life. It was a real joy to read it.

I have known Pastor Paul for a number of years. He is a great example for me in many ways. His passion for missions is really commendable. He comes to India and travels to remote places to preach and encourage pastors who are working in a very poor conditions. One of the best qualities I have seen in him is his compassion for souls, heart for missions and the willingness to go the extra mile for reaching out to the poor and needy. He travels the world to help Gods people and he is a great leader. In my experience he has a conviction of steel. His conviction reminds me of the word that God spoke to Ezekiel, Ezekiel 3:8-9 "Behold, I have made thy face strong against their faces, and thy forehead strong against their foreheads. As an adamant harder than flint have I made thy forehead, fear them not, neither be dismayed at their looks, though they be a rebellious house." God spoke to Ezekiel that "I will make you harder than the ones who stand against you." Pastor Paul's ministry was developed in very hard conditions and though he faced many betrayals hurts and pains he learned to put

xi

them behind him and kept going. He is like steel, if you're put in the fire it may melt for a while but the moment the fire is gone it become better and shiny.. more effective. His passion for Jesus has grown stronger and clearer through all the fires he has gone through, He remained in the Master's hand.

God is shaping Ps. Paul and Mags for a greater purpose. They are a gift from God for thousands of children, men and women who are fatherless. Children and young people love them. His courage and conviction always challenges me to go the extra mile for Jesus. Mags is also a real iron woman with a soft and loving heart. Paul and Mags have a wonderful ministry all around the world and built a beautiful community of people in Manchester and The Lighthouse Church which is their spiritual home. I salute them for their passion and commitment for Jesus. I am sure this book will be a great help for many people who are decision-makers, people who are about to go into ministry, pastors who are struggling in small churches.

I believe they are true gift for all of us. Thank you Pastor Paul and Mags for what you are doing. We can see Jesus in you both and we also want to be like you. This book, *The Rubicon*, will tell you much more about Paul's life and ministry. May The Lord use this book for His glory. Amen

Pastor Matthew Kurian
Senior Pastor, Faith Community Church–Margao, Goa
Director of El Shaddai house. Socal vado, Asagao, Bard

INTRODUCTION

By Paul Hallam

I t has been a desire of mine for over ten years now to write a book. Not just a book, but this book, 'The Rubicon'. It has literally been a matter of time and timing to finally get to this landmark point for me. Time, because I came to realise we will never just 'find time', we have to 'make time', and timing, because it had to be the 'right time' too. Once I began this mission it took seven years to write it, as I had to make the time in the midst of a very hectic and challenging ministry and business schedule. For some, no doubt this would not present too much of a difficulty but for me it was incredibly hard. Most of the book was written in India in our beautiful Bible College Library in Tamil Nadu, while away on mission, when more uninterrupted time is available. I also decided very early on that I would write it entirely with my own hand. No one else would be allowed to write my story. It has been far too special a journey to allow this to be the case.

This book is not just about me, my wife Mags and our families. It's not even just about our church family. It's about everyone who has a stirring in their soul to take on the mantle of serving a vision that would impact the lives of many thousands of lives across the world. I believe it will be a source of deep and lasting encouragement to those who serve simply from a passion for God and His people. I genuinely and sincerely want the non-believer to read and enjoy this book too, irrespective of their faith or their personal convictions. I believe we are all on a journey which for many of us becomes a quest.

'The Rubicon' charts 28 years of full time pastoral ministry and leadership in the same church, in the same city, and 22 years of missions work which came out of very small and modest beginnings. Proof if ever you needed it, that you can be in a small church but still have a big vision! It is only as I've sat down and written this book, that I've fully begun to appreciate the significance of what God has started in and through a few faithful, committed and devoted people who risked everything in their quest to see the fulfilment of a vision that shines its light far beyond that which we can naturally see or understand. Not everything that has happened over the past 28 years is recorded here, but certainly most of the important aspects that I deemed useful to pass on from an experiential point of view.. I have included the good, the bad and the ugly bits to ensure the reader gets an accurate picture of building church in the 21st century.

The Rubicon is also a story of hope, possibility and purpose. It will help church leaders pursue their personal objectives and their unique individual goals. It will also, I believe, enable you to be comfortable in your own skin as you realise whilst your habits may change and your circumstances too, you are uniquely you and God has His own special way of providing for you.

What makes 'The Rubicon' story so special is that what has been achieved has been done so without any 'sugar daddys' with open chequebooks or huge £100k offerings on the first Sunday of the month etc. God has provided by ravens, by sparrows and by hawks as well as a few generous individuals giving modestly but faithfully over decades to see God's work prosper.

You will also find in this book that 'fact is always stranger than fiction'. You will see that there are moments in church life that are just bizarre and incomprehensible! However, one thing that will come across time and time again, is that faith combined with prayer and action is a formula which fits into any age, culture or situation. My hope is that you enjoy the read and are blessed by a story that continues to live on in the lives of so many people all over the world.

Many of us see life as a journey. It is a simple metaphor which we can easily identify with. To this end I've set the book out in stages and phases, not necessarily chronologically, but in emphasis. For instance it begins with 'The Skoda Years' For those in the USA, a Skoda is a make of car which used to be the butt of all the car jokes as it was made in Eastern Europe and was very slow and very cheap. (That is not the case now, so to everyone who owns a Skoda these days–apologies for this!)

It then goes through the 'Mondeo years' and 'Ferrari years' into the off-road, missional '4x4 years' and culminates with the 'SUV years'.

This book is dedicated to YOU, the reader. My prayer is it will increase your hope, your passion and love for God. Lessen your doubts and quieten the negative voices we all so often wrestle with in the face of the impossible. May your journey be a blessed adventure too.

To you and yours,

With much love and blessing in Christ Jesus.

Paul & Mags Hallam

'Prepare to be inspired!'

SECTION ONE

"The Skoda Years"

Chapter One

INTRODUCING THE FAMILY

"You don't have to be an angel to be a saint"

That Mags and I ever came to Manchester is an amazing story in itself. I often think what would have happened had we gone somewhere else? Things could have turned out so differently. Destiny is an incredible, enigmatic thing. It seems to have no regard or respect for personal views, opinions or preferences. Destiny is like a giant steamroller that just goes on regardless of circumstances and obstacles, however it was William Jennings Bryan who said, "Destiny is not a matter of chance, but of choice." I for one firmly believe this to be true.

My life had been a strange one up until I came to Manchester. I had the most wonderful parents. Christians, though very strict, with a strong church background as one would expect. I came to a point where I decided this was not for me. My education I would describe as a "shambles". Fragmented and punctuated by various moves so as to basically satisfy my father's desire to pursue his "urge" to pastor a church, something I came to see as an expensive piece of delayed reaction. This was to become a sad and frustrating experience for him and followed him until he died in 2001.

Dad became a Christian attending a special series of meetings being conducted by George Jeffreys, who eventually went on to become the founder of The Elim Pentecostal Church of Great Britain and Ireland. George Jeffreys' brother was Stephen Jeffreys who also went on to set up The Assemblies of God here in the UK. Dad went to hear this man with a few of his mates to heckle him and have a laugh. He'd heard about him from an elderly lady who'd passed a leaflet onto him in the street. The leaflet fell out of his pocket while at home. He went along and ended up giving his life to Christ at the inevitable "altar call". (This for those unfamiliar with the term, is a moment when many preachers finish what they're saying and ask people who want to give their lives to Christ, to come to the front of the church or hall for prayer).

How destiny seems to hinge on the smallest of things! A little old lady, a leaflet, a decision by a 19-year-old man. Large doors swing on small hinges and big wheels are turned by small cogs in the process destiny calls all her own. How these seemingly trivial moments reach down through the years to hundreds, even thousands of people being unconsciously affected by them is a science in its own right. It's quite extraordinary how God pieces together through the years this huge jigsaw puzzle that only He has the final picture on, at least that's how we Christians would view it.

Dad had a very poor upbringing. He had become an evacuee along with his sister, my Aunty Molly, during the Second World War. His father and mother had divorced in a day and an age when this never happened. The story was in the papers and my grandfather disappeared, we believe back to his native Rajasthan in North India. My father's next dad was his stepfather. He was an alcoholic who drank himself to death. He was 'replaced' by stepfather number two who was a good man and I think he lasted the distance! Dad and Aunty were evacuated to a spinster's house. Her name was Mrs Hallam. She had never been married and lived with her sister, Lydia. Dad loved her as his own mother and later on, chose to take her name as his own. Dad never talked much about his own father and the facts are very sketchy here. We know Dad didn't like talking about his past at all and always evaded the subject. Despite his troubled past he was a great father, proving you don't have to repeat the past in your own life and personal circumstances. You can decide to be different to the examples you have in your own life. We can learn the lessons of how 'not' to do things from others as well as how to do things well.

20

My father was asked to join George Jeffreys' team, then called 'The Revival Band'. He wanted to, but for some reason only known to him he refused. I believe it was because of fear. Fear of change was the one thing that held Dad back most of his life. Dad would have had to have moved from home, travelled and have had to get used to an unsettled lifestyle on the road so to speak. This would be very difficult for him. He declined the invitation (something he regretted for the rest of his life). The pain of regret will always be heavier than the pain of failure. I saw this play out over many years and it's not nice to see. Some thirty to thirty-five years later, Dad attempted to pick up where he left off, but it was something of a disaster to be honest. The decisions we make and take ultimately pave the course of our lives whether for good or bad. This attempt to recover a "lost opportunity" would prove to be a very influential point in my young life. Dad chose to stay in his home town of Southport in Lancashire (as it was then!) Here he met my mother Gladys Daw, a very devout Christian lady who was very involved in the Salvation Army. They were married at a fairly young age in 1946 just after the Second World War.

Mum and Dad often commented on the times they had to run for shelter during the bombing of the port of Liverpool. Liverpool is only 25 miles or so north of Southport. The Liverpool Docks were a strategically important target for the Luftwaffe in those days and a few stray bombs ended up wiping out a few streets and houses in Southport. Hartwood Road in Southport lost half of one side of the street in one of these moments when an aircraft decided to dump its bombs over the town before returning to Germany. Half of the street is bungalows and the other is large three bed-roomed semi-detached houses. We got this story virtually every Sunday on the way to church. It seems quite funny now to think of my parents relaying this incident when I drive down the same road today, although I know it must have been tragic for the people at the time.

My parents were born and raised in an austere time. Dad was a Conscientious Objector in the war and worked on a farm in Scarisbrick, near Halsall. He was a ploughman with horses. One of them was called Satan! I guess the owner had his reasons!! Dad often boasted how only he could get Satan in his horse box.

21

I so laugh at this at times today, especially with the biblical and spiritual connotations. Dad went on to be the manager of a Dry Cleaning company. He was a Conscientious Objector (a CO as it was known) because of his faith. He went to court to give an answer as to why he couldn't fight in the war as a Christian. He offered to go as a Padre though, but was turned down because of a lack of training. My uncle George (not my real uncle as I found out later!) went to prison because he couldn't answer the questions properly due to nervousness. On the other hand my uncle Joe Grisedale went to war in the Pacific to fight the Japanese. He was captured almost as soon as he landed on an island somewhere and spent a long time in a POW camp. He never quite got over it physically and mentally. He later went on to become a pastor in Llantrisant in South Wales.

So, Mum and Dad got married in 1946. Dad was 24 and Mum was 22. Their honeymoon was a day out at Blackpool. It wasn't uncommon at all in those days. People could afford precious little back then, especially just after the Second World War. My parents lived with my Uncle Joe and Aunty Louie. Again that was something quite common in those days. People shared accommodation so as to be able to afford it. It's a strange world today when compared with those "make do days". I'm glad we were taught this though, because it always stood us in good stead. Today we hear of so many complaints from people not being able to afford this and that. Usually to do with buying a car or going on holiday or being able to afford certain things. Remember these were working people who couldn't afford the simplest of things. I believe we don't have to be a product of our past, but I do believe we are shaped greatly by our past. Our past life is used by God in amazing ways, whether good, bad or plain ugly, it's all a part of who we eventually become.

My parents went on to buy a house of their own in Hart Street, Southport. Shortly after this my sister Margaret was born. She was a beautiful child and turned out to be sought after as a young lady by a number of young men including the footballer George Best who turned up in his E-type Jaguar (which my brother and I were more interested in at the time!) Mike, my older brother, was born in 1958 and I was born in 1961. Mum had me when she was in her early forties and was totally stunned at conceiving me, believing her childbearing days to be behind her once she had given birth to Mike. Mum always said at my birth I had the loudest set of lungs on the ward and that the sisters were surprised when my Dad visited because they thought he would be a foreigner as I was quite dark. I think the Indian blood kicked in at some point here. It has done so also in my niece Samantha who I'm told is a carbon copy of me and "could get a tan in a coal mine"! I am very grateful for the parents I had and the upbringing they gave to me. They were amazing people and very devout people. They gave me my values today and supplied me with what I can only describe as a compass with which to navigate the treacherous open waters of life that lay before me. I am conscious of this and I am forever in their debt.

This book has been written to simply help others who did not have the same blessings and advantages as I had. It's been published to help ordinary people who become leaders, pastors and visionaries whether in church work or even business and enterprise. As this is my first book, I'm also aware that not many people know me or my history and my journey, even though by the time you reach the end of the book I'm sure you'll agree with me that it's been an incredible one. Now I know I am not a special person with special gifts and talents etc.–I am as ordinary as you can get! I've already mentioned my education briefly as a "shambles" and rightly so as I'll show you in the next chapter. I struggle with all the same insecurities and wrestle with all the same difficulties that every leader and visionary does from time to time. The reality is that God sometimes makes us look a lot better than we actually are and blesses in spite of us and not because of us. It is one of the greatest mysteries of life that we can be called and chosen by God for a purpose much bigger than ourselves. I am totally privileged and honoured to lead a vibrant, dynamic church oozing with vision and possibility. I am constantly humbled by the quality of people God has given to us here at The Lighthouse, Manchester and Salford. Yet, I know that I was born for this. I was designed and made for it! It's not just what I do, but who I am too!

So here I am–a young 12-13 year old. We've just left our small, narrow-minded little church to go back to a mainstream church. We were leaving a church with a leadership that abused its people and manipulated its members for selfish gain and proud motives. There is a fine line between ministry and manipulation. This is not really understood by many of today's leaders. Our members and our people are not 'fodder', they are the blessings that God has given to us! Even the difficult people. Even the impatient, selfish and awkward people. After all, they don't have to put up with us. They too have options! Over the years I thank the Lord for many people who graciously helped Mags and I shape, lead and develop the church to bring it to where it is today. Gene Wilkes in his book "Jesus The Leader" said, "Leadership is not taken, it's given." Thanks to all those who have trusted us as leaders when we have claimed we have heard from God and they have believed us and followed our lead. We would all be nowhere as leaders without these gritty, loyal followers. To be honest, I don't think we can lead well unless we can follow well. We need to keep being followers of Christ in all its various demands and challenges. This will in turn continue to give us fresh insightful knowledge on true and dynamic leadership.

As we moved to our new church, the Elim Church on Manchester Rd, Southport, I met a stunning young lady called Margaret Ann Tee. The problem was, she was the pastor's daughter. Another problem was the pastor was a formidable, quite austere Scotsman, Alex Tee. He was very well known within Elim and fairly well known outside of our denomination too. Unfortunately after becoming very good friends with Mags, as we all called her, I was to be whisked away by my father and our whole family as we prepared to move 35 miles away to a place called Skelmersdale. I would describe 'Skem' as a new town with ALL the old problems! It was built as an overflow for people in the city of Liverpool who were being re-located due to the regeneration of high-rise blocks of flats and slum areas. The lay out of the town was an experiment in organising people into sections rather than districts. We lived on Birch Green 7. There were ten of them!! Birch Green 1 through to Birch Green 10. Then there was Tanhouse 1 to Tanhouse 10. Each section had ten subsections. It became like a ghetto. The experiment didn't work, that's for sure! I suppose that's fitting for a town which means 'dale of the skull'.

My father had made an application to become a pastor in an honorary capacity which basically meant 1) you never got paid properly and, 2) you were basically on your own! Not good! My father worked as a security guard during the day so as to pay the bills, and a pastor at night and weekends. As a young teenager, being ripped out of a thriving, stable church with a great youth work and a strong liking for a certain young lady, this was not what the doctor ordered. Looking back, this was a really stupid move and a damaging one. It was stupid for a number of reasons. One of those reasons was that Dad sold the family home in order to subsidise his living costs in Skelmersdale as work was really badly paid and it was difficult to get the hours too. I left my school at Meols Cop, Southport, although I'd already had a brief period of being suspended. I think it was for smoking behind the bike sheds and constant trouble-making. I got into a lot of fights in those days, without even trying! When we moved to Skelmersdale I went to a school called Westbank High School. In reality there was nothing high about it! It was next to Glenburn High School where all the successful kids went. At Westbank many of the kids were from incredibly poor and broken families. While at this school, I got into more and more trouble as the influence of my peers took a hold. The next three years of my life were quite turbulent. I discovered lots of things. How to fight better, how to date girls and how to "wag" school (our "in word" for playing truant). In my last year at Westbank before moving back to Southport I attended four days in the whole of the year! Most of my time was spent fishing, hunting and robbing birds' nests of their eggs. I had a collection to die for. I hunted in the surrounding countryside with an air rifle, catapults and an Archery kit. It's hard to appreciate how parents who genuinely love their children can be totally oblivious to the life they are leading. This was most certainly the case with me. My mother knew I was something of a 'ruffian' and often called me names like 'gipsy' and 'little tyke', all done affectionately but the names were more accurate than she realised!

Meanwhile Dad was too busy trying to work and run the small church he was pastoring to know what his youngest son was doing! He had a lot of respect from the people in the community. A number of young people came to the church but it usually ended up with them fighting with me and in Skemersdale you didn't fight by fair means. You had to fight by using everything you had! And if you needed to use something then you just did it. It was about surviving and making sure you always hurt the person more than they hurt you. This was the law of the ghetto that "Skem" had become. I've always been 'a fighter' in all senses. Whether spiritually or in life in general. In sport for instance I won trophies at everything I did. Snooker, pool, football, fishing, darts and in my later life, golf. Most of the biggest matches I've won trophies for I've beaten better players and often come from behind. As I often say to people, I have always had to fight hard for things that others seem to get easily or naturally. At least it toughens you up when that's the case and you appreciate it a lot more. I have to say though, it's a hard way to live and learn, as when you get older, you realise there are some things simply not worth fighting for. A lesson that was long in the learning but has now finally stuck! I got it ...! Eventually!

If you're a parent and have teenage sons and daughters, then take heart from this chapter. God still loves a rebel and as someone said to me recently, "You don't have to be an Angel to be a Saint!" I love that thought. God can tame and sort out the most rebellious and hopeless of cases. In my case I knew then, only God could do this. Things were about to go from bad to worse. My father had basically had enough. In fairness he'd worked hard and he had helped a lot of people. One of my most lucid memories of "Skem" was of Dad often getting up in the middle of the night with his overcoat over his dressing gown going out with his bible tucked under his arm, ready to sort out some problem to do with the occult. I remember one such occasion when he had to go and sort out a group of people who had been playing around with a Ouija board. They had got themselves into a major mess with one of the group attacking another etc. They always seemed to call Dad. He'd got the name "Witchfinder General" due to a bizarre thing that happened. When the Exorcist film came out, many Christians protested. But Dad took it to a whole new level. He bought a ticket to go to the film, went in and just before it started he stood up and preached to the packed gathering. Some stewards came and took him out, but not before he said his piece. That night, in the Focus

Cinema, in the Concourse (Shopping Mall) in Skelmersdale, the whole of the cinema burnt to the ground! This is absolutely true and can be verified. Later that night the police arrested my father on suspicion of arson. He was later released when they found the fire had started through a discarded cigarette butt.

Despite some of the good things that evidently happened in 'Skem', Dad got to the point where he'd had enough. Not only did he leave Skelmersdale, he left Elim, the denomination in which he served. I know he felt he had been isolated and not really supported but in truth no one else can prove 'your ministry' but 'you'! When you have a vocation and a calling, it's down to you how you see it, and how it plays out in our lives, I believe, is largely down to the individual. I still believe "life is 5% what happens to you and 95% what you do about what happens to you". This doesn't mean it will be an easy or comfortable road ahead. There may be very difficult and adverse circumstances we need to experience. Bad things happen to good people! This is life! But the manner and way in which we respond to those situations is everything. There are times when we simply have to go to the end of the road. And until we do, we cannot experience the fullest, most blessed and miraculous provision of God. We have a sign in our office, it reads "We do not just believe in miracles ... we depend on them". This would become the motto for our life's work in the future. It still is today!

I returned to Southport with my parents. They decided to have a go at planting a new church there with the Assemblies of God (AoG). Why? I don't know why! Why on earth didn't they go straight back into the church they came from, i.e. the Elim Church in Southport? Was it pride, hurt, misunderstanding? Who knows? To see my father so frustrated and so unfulfilled had a negative impact on my life in those days. To be honest it still does. It still upsets me to think how much he wanted to serve God. Maybe the lesson is that we have to be prepared to do everything not only in His way, but in His time too. Dad loved to study and read the bible. He was an okay preacher, but mum was on fire! She could preach the lights out. Although she was a gentle lady with a very gentle spirit, ask her to speak and she was like a fireball! And she was extremely prophetic too, in her way of putting things across. She had a meek, yet bold spirit. A rare combination. Mum was quite adventurous too and entrepreneurial. She would take on extra jobs and squirrel away a shilling or two here and there to be able to pay for extra things.

For my part, I went back to my old school, Meols Cop. But in truth, it was never going to work. Despite my parents convincing them to give me a chance to recover some of my education, it simply wasn't going to happen. I was even more wild than before I left, so it was always going to be a non-starter. After just six months I was expelled for all kinds of things which I will spare you the details. I know I had the cane from the headmaster more than anyone else, (a record I was proud of by the way!) By the time I was expelled I was well off the rails. I left home at fifteen and went to live with my sister who spent some time trying to get me into a school near her in Liverpool. I was out of school living in Liverpool for six months before my sister found a school that would take me. It was Deyes Lane High School in Maghull.

Chapter Two

COMING HOME

"Our lives are the result of the choices we make ...if you don't like your life then it's time to start making better choices."

As a 14-15 year old I spent a short time living in Liverpool. In Walton, literally opposite the prison. My brother in law was a prison officer there–"a screw" as they were referred to by my mates and friends. I was living at my sister Margaret's home at the time. She was very good to me and helped to sort me out, at least to a degree. I was quite a wild child looking back. I just kind of did my own thing. Margaret found a school that would take me just outside of Liverpool and she and Harry were moving there in any case so I tagged along. I only had eight or nine months to go before my sixteenth birthday anyhow, so for my sister's sake I went along with it. To my surprise I liked the school. The teachers were obviously far better at dealing with the wilder more troublesome kind of kids, and to be fair it really showed. One of my teachers was very impressed with my English. She tried her best to allow me to take English O levels. It was not allowed however. I had missed far too much school for this to be permitted, so on hearing that there was no chance of anything happening, I just stayed away until my 16th birthday when I went in really just to say "goodbye". It was a funny day, I remember it being quite surreal. That's it! School is finished! Just like that.

I played a lot of football and had a chance to sign up for Maghull FC. This was a feeder club for several clubs in the area including Tranmere, Everton and Liverpool. I was a 'dyed in the wool' Liverpool fan from six years of age and still am today though I've been in Manchester for nearly thirty years. It's funny how that kind of thing happens. People said I should've swapped my allegiance when I moved to Manchester but it really wasn't going to happen. Anyway I played a trial game, scored and got sent off for petulance.

As soon as I left school I found a job in a place called Hesketh Bank near Southport. I worked on a farm which also had about eight acres of greenhouses. I cycled to work for the first year or so until I could afford a small motorcycle. I used to set out at 7.15am to get there for about 8 am and we had to clock in and out too. I was soon promoted as my boss found out I was a good tractor driver. I only had a provisional licence but I could drive anything with wheels! I even had a drive of a HGV that used to come to the farm to pick up the produce. I drove dumper trucks, fork-lift trucks, tractors and trailers, boom-sprayers, specialist hydraulic equipment and even JCB's. I loved driving and my new job was head tractor driver (a job I basically nicked off someone just by working faster and harder than them). It meant I had to be there at 6am though, but I did it until I left the company due to a string of unfulfilled promises. I had been promised that I would be sent to Horticultural College in Lincolnshire by the farm management, and that so long as I signed a declaration that I would remain at the company following my completed and successful course for an agreed time, I could go on a sponsorship from the company combined with the government. The manager had promised me this, but unknown to him, the owner cancelled the whole programme just to save time and money.

I moved onto another company called Crispa Cress. They grew and produced ... yes you got it! Cress! It doesn't sound very glamorous but at least it paid a lot lot more than the farm did. The trouble is I started to mix with a lot of guys who were into the biking scene. This was to be a huge downhill slope for me. I loved motorbikes and I didn't like the law. I saw a new identity for myself. I became a 'Rocker' and a pretty bad-ass one too. The biking world opened up a whole new experience for me. I ended up with a whole bunch of new friends who where almost as rebellious and anti-establishment as I had become. Actually, all of this time I continued speaking to God but it was all from an angry heart and a vexed soul.

After a while the inevitable happened. I lost my job. Actually I was sacked for a whole pile of abuse to one of my managers who, looking back, was a real 'pain in the proverbial' to almost everyone who worked there. I walked home after I had been sacked and on the way to town I saw a girl who looked familiar washing her little yellow car–a Datsun. I looked again and she looked at me. It was Mags Tee, albeit with a perm that made her look like Leo Sayer! (She never repeated this style, hahaha!) She invited me in and we chatted about old times and before we knew it we were dating one another. Our relationship was a rocky one and Mags' Mum and Dad did not know we were going out. I was drinking heavily and getting mixed up more and more in the biking culture to the point of fighting and making trouble almost everywhere I went. I still had a provisional licence but didn't care what I drove. Cars, bikes it didn't matter! 550cc bikes, 750cc bikes, whatever.

One night I did a stupid thing that cost me dearly for years to come. In fact it nearly cost my life and that of two more people. I crashed my brother's car on the way home from a night club in the early hours of the morning. I was just 18 years of age and had been drinking heavily. My brother and his girlfriend were in the back of the car. None of us wore seat belts in those days. I caused so many parked cars to be smashed to pieces as I skidded on the wet and greasy road surface whilst going so fast, and we only finally came to a standstill after crashing into a lamppost. I only just escaped being sent to prison. I had a huge fine slapped on me for about £600 (a king's ransom in those days) and I was banned from driving anything that had wheels for 12 months. I spent my first night in the police cells that night. I told the police someone else had been driving as I ended up in the passenger seat. The police tried to play me up a lot. I asked how Mike my brother was and they looked at one another (acting seriously) and turned back at me and said "we're not sure whether he'll pull through". My reaction wasn't good and I freaked out a bit. They also told me that Mike's girlfriend had a punctured lung. (This turned out to be true.) Eventually I owned up that I was the driver. I guess the police did suspect it but they bought the story for a while because of an amazing thing that had happened at the point of impact as the car hit the lamp post. I remember distinctly heading towards the windscreen, (remember I had no seatbelt on either). I can't remember hitting the windscreen, only heading towards it. Then I just remember waking up to voices and police, flashing lights and air on my face. I was sitting in the passenger seat totally unmarked, hardly a scratch on me. The windscreen was completely smashed through and the car a write-off. Mike and his girlfriend were taken to hospital. I was taken by ambulance separately and later ended up in the police cell. The car which was my brother's pride and joy was a write-off. Mike never let me drive his cars in the future or even his motorbike which he went on to purchase. Who could blame him? I believe with all my soul, that night I escaped death. I certainly should have hit that windscreen with my head at full velocity. I hadn't a mark on my head at all. I believe to this day God preserved my life. Somehow he managed to bounce me over to the passenger seat saving my life or at least saving me from serious injury.

Well, I'd like to say I learned my lesson that night. But, I didn't! I went from bad to worse. I still rode my Yamaha motorbike, ruthlessly and lawlessly. I had no insurance, no tax–zip! To be honest I wasn't at all bothered. I was even on probation as I got caught for petty theft somewhere along the way, ending up in a police cell for the night. I can't honestly remember all the times I rode my bike and was chased by police for speeding but got away. Really! At one point I just couldn't venture outside except as either a pillion rider or to walk or get the bus somewhere without being pulled over by the police. One night we were chased for speeding and we foxed them by splitting up–which was our strategy for running the gauntlet. I was on my brother's chopper motorbike as a pillion rider and there were about six of us being chased by the police. We all split up and unfortunately the car following went for me and Mike. We ended going down gunnels and side streets to avoid being caught. Eventually we got a little bit of distance between us, enough to ride straight into our back garden, close the side gate and get into the house just before the police car appeared. There was a knock at the door and Mike answered. There were a few questions thrown at Mike. He was wearing a shirt like he'd been in all night. "What do you want now?" Mike said, or something like that. "Have you just been out on your bike?" the officer retorted. "Oh a while ago, just to visit a friend". "...Right" the officer said "and tell that brother of yours who's banned from driving that we're onto him–and we'll have him soon!"

Well, that was the end of that! I had a police car virtually assigned to me from that time on which parked just around the corner waiting to get me as soon as I left the house on my bike. I don't think I did after that. I knew that if I got caught now, with all the other offences I had against me I was heading straight for prison. I became a pillion rider on all my mates' motorbikes then. Which was quite good fun anyhow as some of my mates were almost as mad as me!

At that time I was listening to very heavy rock music–Black Sabbath, AC/DC, Judas Priest, Pink Floyd, Led Zeppelin, Thin Lizzy, Status Quo and Deep Purple were my main taste in music at that time. Sabbath were my favourite group. Especially their hit 'Paranoid'. Music definitely affects people. Even now, I can hear a song like "Breaking The Law" by Judas Priest and I'm transported back in time almost immediately. I still confess to loving heavy rock! I loved listening to the lighter Rock music by Status Quo who were just the biggest rocking band on the planet at that time. My hair was extremely long in those days and I loved rocking to Quo's 'Rockin All Over The World'. I don't listen to it at all now, as it brings back too many bad memories.

Things went from bad to worse and our biking group formed a gang called the 'Axeheads'. There were about 15 of us in total, but we had some tough cookies in the group, including 'big Trev' who just looked like a Viking with red hair and beard to match. He was built like a rugby scrum-half and no one much would mess with him. Unfortunately I was to learn much later on he had died of alcoholic poisoning. It was all over the newspapers too. Really tragic but not that surprising, considering the amount of alcohol he would consume. We also had a guy called Scowie, who was a black-bearded, muscular guy who would stand his ground against anyone! My brother Mike was a real scrapper too. There's not much of him but his boxing experience from his teens was just amazing! Honestly! I never really saw Mike lose a fight and I saw him in many. I was always quite envious of his prowess at managing to punch holes in so called giants. He got quite a reputation. Me, I could fight a bit too. But I preferred to get others to fight on my behalf haha! And I did. I became the ringleader by default. We had two other brothers who were part of our outfit, Billy and Rob. Rob we called Psycho because he was plane barmy! A few other characters too were in our squad but these were the leading lights.

Eventually we had to disband because things got extremely serious when we began to fight with the local Hell's Angels chapters. I cannot go into detail here as it was just too dangerous. Things got way out of control and one of our guys was nearly killed in a fight. Big Trev even saved my life on another occasion when I got into trouble for chatting up the local Hell's Angels President's girlfriend! About four Angels picked me up and dragged me out of the nightclub we were in and laid into me, punching, kicking and hitting me with chains. After kicking and thumping ten bells out of me, the Hells Angels were about to throw me in the nearby lake. 'Big Trev' apparently came to the rescue and convinced them I was not worth the hassle. That was the end of my time as a rocker. I can't remember anything much after that, only coming to, upside down in a privet hedge at about 4.30 in the morning. I managed to get home somehow, and from that day, I cut my hair, shaved and changed my image completely. I never went back to the old haunts either. I heard other Hells Angels were out to get me! It was time for a whole new change of image and culture.

I was still drinking heavily and working for myself and signing on the dole. I still was banned from driving and I didn't dare take my bike on the road after what had happened. So I sold it. I began a different lifestyle though, playing darts for a pub, the Fox and Goose on a Friday and the YMCA on a Wednesday. I became very good at darts and won many trophies and shields. I also played pool and became very good especially in my local, The Blundell Arms, Southport, where the winner not only stayed on the table but the defeated opponent had to buy the victor a drink. Several times I earned all my night's beer on the pool table.

Mags at the time had had enough. She decided she couldn't take any more. We parted as a couple (I think for the fourth or fifth time!) Then one night I was at a late night party. Drink was freely available and many of us were the worse for wear. There was one unbelievable fight broke out in the early hours over some girl I think. We were all dragged into it and one almighty punch up ensued. I ended up being kicked and stamped on by someone. Someone, I can't even remember who, took me home. My face was like a football. My nose was definitely broken and I was quite concussed. The day after when my mother saw me in my bed, she cried. She called an ambulance. I was whisked off to Southport Infirmary. They couldn't do anything there as I had a blood clot so they rushed me in an ambulance to Walton Hospital. I was bleeding quite badly from my nose. Mags came to see me, as my mother had called her. She was very shocked. She asked the local church youth group to pray. A lot of the youth there knew me as it had been my home church for years. My brother had given his life to Christ six months prior to this incident just after a few of us had to change our image. I wanted nothing to do with church and Christianity and when he tried to witness to me I had a big fight with him and beat him quite badly (mainly because he didn't fight back like before–I guess that because he had become a Christian he didn't want to fight again). I was left alone in my hospital bed. I was about to have a life changing encounter with Christ.

At the hospital I was still losing blood, mainly through my nose. The doctors had tried to stop the bleeding but even after everything they did, it still kept bleeding. They were preparing to operate. They had said there would probably be a high chance of a blood clot and if this reached the brain it would be extremely dangerous. As I said earlier, Mags had asked the youth group to pray that evening. It was a Friday night and at about 8pm I felt a voice spring up from within me (that's the only way I could explain it!) "It's time to stop running." I knew it was God's voice. Everything seem to stop still in time. I prayed. "Lord okay!! Finally, it's time–I'm sorry, I'm sorry, I come to you, just as I am right now. I give my life back to you." I prayed something like that. What amazed me was that the bleeding had stopped. Looking back, I actually believe the bleeding stopped at the instant the voice came into my soul. What I didn't know was that it had stopped at the exact time the youth group were praying for me. It was precise and clinical timing. I have always thanked God for His timing. It is one of the chief factors in the working out of His plan and purpose and nothing can be more assuring than to know God has spoken even if we have to wait for His timing.

Chapter Three

SETTING THE STAGE

———————————❖———————————

*"The bible is the only book where the author
is present every time you read it."*

So, now I had become a Christian, a whole new world opened
up to me. It never occurred to me that my whole life would
change beyond recognition. I remember coming in very late at
night (when I went back to my parents to stay.) I was pretty worse
for drink at the time. Dad waited up for me. He gave me a lecture
on "the evils of my ways" and "where my life was heading" etc. I
gave him an enormous amount of anger-filled expletives followed
by an equally angry outburst against him, God and the church.
Ha! The church, yes I verbally massacred it there and then! Then
I made this astonishingly arrogant claim "I will not set foot in a
church ever again as long as I live". And boy did I mean it. I was
pretty much known for my arrogance in those days but also for
the fact that I always meant what I said. Within barely more than a
week I was at the front of one of the local churches singing hymns
of praise with all my strength and soul! My life had turned around
completely. However, this was just the beginning of a whole new
ball game now, life would never ever be the same again.

I remember attending the Elim Pentecostal Church on
Manchester Road, Southport, in what used to be Lancashire (until
some bureaucrats decided to move it to Merseyside). I was so
enthusiastic I was at everything! I once turned up to a deacons'

meeting! Well I had no idea what a deacon was! In typical fashion I got stuck in one hundred percent. The pastor at the time was a quite serious, but godly man, John Cave. 'Pastor Cave' (as we called him) was a good speaker and was a fine leader. He was my first pastor in this new era and helped me find my feet and eventually help me to discern how God speaks and always gave sound, sensible advice.

Shortly after my conversion I decided it was time to leave home (again!) and I rented an apartment along with a friend of mine. He was working at the time. I wasn't in employment at the time–I had to stop work because I was doing a lot of work and claiming benefit at the same time, as were many of my friends and associates. As soon as I became a Christian this practice ceased and I remember the look on the clerk's face when both my brother (Mike) and I asked to speak with one of the managers as we needed to "confess" to the Department of Employment what we had been doing. We were now Christians and both of us felt it was only right to "own up" to our deceitful ways. We did speak with one of the managers who was totally taken aback and hadn't got a clue what to say or do! I laugh about it now when I share this because it was one of the first times I'd ever shared my faith with a non-Christian. In the end, all he could say to us both was ... "we may be in touch at some point." They never were, and for me the amazing thing is I came to a point soon after where I never picked up another dole cheque again in my life. An amazing but authentic experience of God was about to catapult me onto the road to becoming a "full time" minister of the gospel.

From this point on I recognised my dependency totally on God for who I am, what I say, where I go and what I do. Even whom I go with. This was to become a great challenge in my relationship with a stunning young lady who I fell in love with but had to leave behind. Yes we are soon to come to the romantic part of the book, but not before I share the experience I had with God that to this day shapes my life, my thinking, my actions, words deeds and especially my decisions. I say this purposefully because I've seen many a life ruined by bad decision making. It wasn't that "someone was out to get them" or they had just been "unlucky" or hadn't had any good opportunities. It was just plain and simple bad decisions. Not one or two but several and you know what? A bad decision is often be followed by another and another until we become a victim of foolishness and worse still start to blame others. The bible for me is by far the most important book in the whole world. Its pages ooze with divine wisdom and counsel. When you read it, it reads you. It is called The Living Word of God. I am convinced today that it is this Word that I have preached in Eastern Europe, Africa, India, even Israel and of course in many places in the UK that after over nearly 30 years of full time ministry, over 28 of those pastoring the same church, that Word has created everything I've seen come to pass. The bible is the only book on earth whose author is always present when we read it! I do not decide on anything that counters the verses in scripture, which I personally received from the Lord. I too can say with the apostle Paul "that which I have received I also give unto you".

I'm now going to share with you the catalyst for my life's work to date. You too can have an opportunity to share in a life of destiny and a calling of unparalleled joy and satisfaction if you will go and get your word of direction, your personal word of instruction from the same source. Don't wait any longer! Time is passing, get reading and listening. It will change your life forever too! It will certainly not be the same as mine as we are all different and no one person is identical to another. I love tigers, I simply love them, having seen one close up and a bit too personal for my liking in the jungles of India. They are simply awesome animals. Every tiger has its own set of stripes. Not one of them is the same. They can be identified by their stripes. You have your own stripes too! So there's no need to compare, copy or worry about anyone else's stripes, so on you go but hey...go easy Tiger! You will get your own set of stripes too and this will happen as you also get a personal experience of God. I believe passionately and firmly that we are all made for mission. It's as simple as that. One person's mission could be to pioneer a form of medicine, another could be to lead a school in a city estate or run a Day Care Centre for the elderly. Notice I haven't mentioned overseas at all. Our first mission is on our doorstep. If we are ineffective there I'd question our effectiveness anywhere. Too many Christians I meet want to get to xyz before completing abc. These are basics and fundamental

principles. I was taught even by The Lord when I first gave my life
back to Him. Which reminds me ... this is how I was called into
the ministry.

I was just getting to bed and as I did every day I read a portion
of scripture just before sleeping. I was extremely tired that day so
I started to read through the Psalms. Psalm 1, then because it was
a short Psalm I read Psalm 2. As I read quickly and fairly casually
(I must say) I began to read the seventh verse. It says:

> *"You are my son, today I have become your father. Ask of
> me and I will make the nations your inheritance, and the
> ends of the earth your possession." Psalm 2:7,8 NIV*

As I read these words, I can only try to describe what I heard
and felt and even what I knew. God was speaking clearly and loudly
into my soul. I had never experienced anything like this before,
nor was I aware that this kind of thing 'could' happen today. I was
completely bowled over. It was as if the Lord had stood in front
of me Himself. But what did it mean? I stirred myself and prayed
some more until I finally went to sleep. As soon as I could I went
to see my pastor. He's like all pastors, busy and has usually seen
it all before in what was a large church at the time with three hundred or so attendees. I was a bit nervous but Pastor Cave simply
said "it is The Lord calling you to the ministry. You need to consider Bible College." Pastor Cave also said ..."I've been expecting
it." So began the call of God on my life. The thought of studying
at a college, learning in a classroom situation filled me with dread!
I had been suspended twice from school, expelled once and virtually missed eighteen months of school. I had no qualifications,
A Levels, O levels or the like. Shortly after this meeting, I got a
job working on a building site. (At least now I had a spirit level!)
It wasn't long before I had a new nickname! They all called me
'The Bishop'. Something to do with my 'preaching on the job'.
I decided I could not eat in the site hut with the guys because of
the pornography on the walls. I told them this was the reason and
it wasn't because I didn't want to eat with them etc. I nearly had
a fight with a Catholic who insisted on blaspheming every thirty
seconds. When I told him how upset this made me feel he came to

the church to hear me preach. I never heard him blaspheme again. Before I left to go to college, they all took up a collection for me towards my fees. More importantly they all commented how, although they made fun of my beliefs and my attempts to "convert them" they respected the fact that I had never compromised my faith and had lived it out "even if it wasn't for them!" During this time Pastor Cave retired and another pastor came.

It never ceases to amaze me just how fickle we are in church life. It all gets exposed when a church changes the senior pastor/leader. All the best and worst of us is seen in a few weeks. Anyhow, Pastor Don Sandford came to us with his wife Doreen. They were fabulous leaders who brought with them fresh vision and enthusiasm. It wasn't long before we had a new mission at the church. To build a new minor hall. We all set to work. I used all my experience in construction and building as a "jobber" on a site. I ended up mixing cement and hod-carrying for the brick layers and mixing plaster for the plasterers! One of my greatest joys was to be able to witness to the team of plasterers who all came to church one by one and gave their lives to the Lord. One of them is now a missionary in South America! I began to understand the call of God is not just to speak but to work and to build in faith things that need to come into being. I also came to learn how easy it is to just talk. Many preachers fall into this category but produce little more than soundbites and sound-offs. The real test must surely be who we are impacting with the message of transformation and reconciliation. As church leaders we can easily make the priority in our churches our seating capacity rather than our sending capacity... Speaking about "sending" I was being sent to Bible College in the strangest of ways.

In the early summer of 1983 I found myself at the graduation day at Mattersey Hall near Doncaster. This was the Assemblies of God Bible College, a contemporary of Elim. Most people had taken it for granted that I would go to the Elim Bible College at Capel, Surrey. What made it more unusual is, I was dating Pastor Alex Tee's daughter Margaret who I only ever knew as Mags. Understandably Mr Tee did not really approve of the relationship even though he was pleased with the change in my life. He had seen the effects of my rebellious days and who could blame a father who wants the best for his daughter' future. After all I had no real prospects! No real future in sight, but hey! That was not the full picture there were some very eventful things about to happen which showed that God was in complete control of everything.

In the summer of 1983 after attending the graduation day service, I wrote to Mattersey Hall to apply for a place. I had no money other than £300 I had saved towards the College. The costs were £1,800 per year not including tuition fees, this would be a further £500 per year. I was given a dream by The Lord shortly after I visited Mattersey Hall in which a woman handed me a cheque for a sizeable amount of money. I had written to various trusts to apply to raise funds for my tuition as no local authority grants were available to me because I had not taken any exams and because of my appalling education record. Strangely enough I was always very good at English so reading and writing came naturally to me. My mother was very good with language, writing, poetry, preaching and doing her crosswords when time allowed. She was also an avid reader unlike myself. I only tend to read biographies and stories about events and occurrences. I don't like fiction at all. To me reading about something fictional is a complete waste of time. That's just me I guess. I have read the Bible many times from Genesis to Revelation, literally from cover to cover and practiced doing this with a new Bible every year which I did for about ten years, a discipline I've recommenced. This is something extra to my devotional reading and although it is inevitable that messages, sermons and preaching material flows from this kind of discipline, it is not carried out for this purpose but for my own development as a leader, pastor, missionary, servant, teacher, evangelist, entrepreneur and visionary. I've come to see myself as a bit of an all-rounder with a special emphasis on vision which is one of my chief giftings. I became quite entrepreneurial in my early years as a pastor when such a leaning was viewed as sinful, worldly and to be avoided like the plague. I came to see through my own experience that if you didn't have any money you couldn't give any money! Simple as that! At one point Mags and I were bringing in almost eighty percent of the income for the church from outside the church whilst working within the church centre. Not bad for someone untrained and unschooled hey?

One of my favourite verses in the Bible is found in the Psalms. It reads "Praise to the Lord my rock, who trains my hands for war, my fingers for battle" (Psalm 144:1) NIV. I've always liked the saying "Professionals built the Titanic, but amateurs built the Ark". Some may feel I'm arrogant and I guess I can come across this way. I try to check myself on this but don't find it easy. I'm still impatient and have an underlying aggression that is part of my past and needs to be curtailed at times (especially in queues which I just hate!) It is however important that these things are channelled and that we allow the Lord to turn our weaknesses into strengths. I'm also a very down to earth person who really couldn't give a rat's tail for most of the egocentric hype that goes on in church life. I certainly can't be doing with some of the evangelastic (no misspelling there by the way) reporting that goes on in many quarters. To hear some reports you'd think that some people are raising the dead and healing the sick where and whenever 'they' turn up. Send them to the hospitals and cemeteries I say and let's see what happens! Meanwhile back here on earth instead of on planet Zork ... Now don't get me wrong! I believe in the supernatural power of God today to heal, to provide, to multiply, to guide in phenomenal ways but I'm still "a born again cynic" with "a street wise savvy". That's pretty challenging when you listen to some people who would be better suited to the X factor than the Christ Factor! I still believe in servanthood. I believe it is the highest call! The bible in the King James Version uses the word "leader" six times. The word "servant" appears over nine hundred times!! To serve is the highest calling. I still believe that modesty and humility are essential virtues in this twenty first century of razzmatazz church. I don't believe in 'Supermen' in the pulpit nor do I believe in every new fad or gimmick that is making everyone's hair stand on end. It may be of God, it may not be. What counts is the children it produces and the offspring that follow. Wisdom is always justified by its children.

When I travel nowadays, nearly every time, I travel to developing countries. That's east not west! Many people chase their dreams in an experience of the Spirit in the Western world, (UK and the USA) in the various huge Christian conferences and concerts etc. That's fine, I'm sure it really blesses them and they sure are needed and have an important role to play. I realise that loads of people in America will read *The Rubicon* and I'm sure they will identify with much of its contents and many may disagree. For me though, a visit to India on mission, or eastern Europe or Africa, fires me up like nothing else. Our church congregation notice it for sure. Our leadership team always sense a difference when I return. There's nothing like it for me, but that's what happens when you spend your time and resources doing what God wants you to do and going where God wants you to go. Events are great for the moment and help us to be built up encouraged and spurred on, but for me local church should not be replaced by events. There is an increasing danger in this and it will inevitably lead to detached and weak, shallow Christianity. As someone said recently "you can be committed to church without being committed to Christ, but you can't be committed to Christ without being committed to church". For me this was vital for my personal development as a Christian and really helped me grow and get my own personal depth. The bedrock of church life holds us accountable to one another in community and fellowship, the very essence of church.

Back to the Bible College scenario. The college had agreed to take me, on the basis that I could manage to raise two thirds of the finance needed for the first year. I hadn't even got one third! I told them I was sure God would provide it so I would see them in September (the beginning of the academic year). Amazingly, a little known Charitable Trust Fund had got my application which had been sent to them via someone else. The Kate Rimmer Trust Fund. They sent a cheque to one of our local councillors who had heard my story and had been touched enough by the change in my life that she had written to them on my behalf. I went with Mags to pick up the cheque. I took along with me a beautiful bouquet of flowers 'as instructed' to the councillor, who duly presented me with a cheque for £500. Wow! I'd never seen so much money! In those days a wage of £80-90 per week was good! I recalled the dream in which a woman handed me a cheque for a large sum of money. Voila! Here it was! What a fulfilment and a lovely fillip to encourage me to believe. The society in which we live says "seeing is believing". The Bible teaches "believing is seeing". Shortly after this a couple in the church who knew us quite well and had a business, promised to sponsor me for £50 per month. I was well and truly on my way.

Despite this, I had to deal with one or two things that had I not been totally sure this was in 'the great plan' I may have not followed through, or even chosen another route. Mags, my girlfriend for some time, decided she definitely did not want to be a pastor's wife. I guess she'd seen enough from inside the ropes as it were. Her Dad had been a pastor for many years and led the church in Southport before John Cave's arrival. Pastor and Mrs Tee had moved to take on the task of leading the Cardiff City Temple, one of Elim's Flagship Churches in those days and continues to be an exceptional church to this day. Mags was not for leaving Southport. This is one of the great qualities Mags has always had. She knows her own mind and is not easily moved. Anyhow the ultimatum was clear from Mags "it's the ministry or me!" I chose the ministry and was duly "dumped" as I often tell our young people at The Lighthouse (with more than a touch of triumphant nostalgia) with some hilarious responses ensuing!

As well as this, my pastor offered me a post with him as a full-time assistant in the ministry. This was a very tempting offer as I really liked Pastor Sandford and worked well with him and had a lot of respect for him and his vision. However I could not go back on my decision. I was sure that this was the course set for me, though it filled me with fear and trepidation–not because of the fact that I did not know anyone there at all; that was difficult enough–but because of the academic structure at which I'd failed so abysmally in the past. Here I was buying textbooks, dictionaries and lexicons, not to mention the commentaries!! I laugh at it now but I hadn't read a book in years and here I was looking like Albert Einstein on a mission! You have just got to hand it to God, He certainly knows how to have a laugh at the devil's expense!!

So, I was on my way to Bible College. I spoke to Mags about this. She was not pleased. She had been brought up witnessing first-hand the sacrifices that her parents had to make. Life being lived in a goldfish bowl was not for her. Everyone knowing your personal business and the personal details of your lifestyle, salary and where you live, what you do etc. This was what she experienced and is largely true of full time Pastors and church leaders who do live in incredibly vulnerable and 'insecure' circumstances. I was given an ultimatum. It was "the ministry or me!" Well I can say that I was deeply in love with Mags but the love I had for Christ was on a completely different level and sphere. I can honestly say, it took me no more than a nanosecond to reply. I was taken to the train station by Mags with all my worldly goods packed into a modest sized suitcase, and that, as they say, was that! I was gone.

I took the train form Southport in early September to begin my new life studying at the Bible College at Mattersey Hall. In truth, I can't say I learned a lot about the Bible at all. Most of what I heard was what I'd been taught as a young lad either by my pastor, parents or Sunday School. My father had always been incredibly knowledgeable concerning the Bible and that certainly has influenced me greatly. Mum had been a powerful person, often preaching the lights out, usually at women's meetings. She had however been known to bring some incredible words of direction into people's lives. What I did learn a lot about, was myself. This may seem strange but I think it's essential. I believe we have to begin to assess ourselves accurately and humbly in the light of God's Word. Only then can we truly begin to see His dealings with us and His shaping and moulding follows. God's will for our lives can be mind-blowing. Sometimes we think we may know it. Sometimes it's true that we may get nuances or promptings. Other times there are signals and feelings that add up to "a sense of God's will in our lives". We should take care in this respect though as there are without doubt times when God will smash your logical processes to pieces! I remember one such experience when travelling to and from Mattersey. The UK is in my opinion an appalling country to travel up and down by public transport. It's far worse when you try to travel across the country!! I could rant on this for some time, being quite an experienced traveller on public transport in Eastern European Countries and India's rail network. They may not be fast or particularly clean, nor are they often modern likes ours, but hey! they run mostly on time, are mostly reliable and have amazing connectivity. In The UK, we should be ashamed of the appalling often diabolical jamboree of a network of individualistic private companies who have little interest in passenger satisfaction or connections to other transport modes. Rule Britannia? I don't think so, and I'm so glad these days that I don't have to use the blessed things anymore!

Thank the Lord I still am able to go by car anywhere I need to without the total rip off and inconvenience of so-called public transport which is a joke. I tried to use the Tram recently, paid £5 for two tickets to the city centre (2 miles) and when I got back to my car I had my side window smashed in! Not good!! I did my fair share trekking across this fair country on no less than three trains, two buses and a taxi, all to get 110 miles west to east completed! Anyway, on one such journey I was travelling from Southport to Doncaster. I got off the train at Manchester Victoria. Everything stops here going east! I always had to get a shuttle bus to Manchester Piccadilly. During these short and "random shuttles" I remember many times saying to the Lord how glad I was that I would not be coming here! What a place! I really couldn't stand it. It was busy, full of hustle and bustle. People coming and going, dirty and grimy. I always thought of Lowry's "matchstick men and matchstick cats and dogs". The thing is, God did send me to Manchester! Guess what, I love Manchester! It's the best city in the whole wide world for me! Why? Because God placed us here and now it has a special place in our lives! The point is I had absolutely no idea, no signals, no feelings or any inkling this would be the place my wife and I would live and serve God for well over a quarter of a century.

Where is this leading you may ask? Well from this city, and from this placing, has come well over 75 church buildings built and planted around the world, several children's homes, a bible college, a school in Africa, Special Needs Centres, loads of street missions, children's missions, leprosy missions, youth camps, village, town and city missions, and pastors' conferences, in many nations. When you read on you'll discover how this could happen with a very small congregation with sixteen adults and three children, and £300 in the bank—because God has a plan for His church and it always produces something significant.

My first year of Bible College zoomed by. At first it was tremendously hard for me to adjust to what I felt and saw was a very artificial environment. A large bunch of Christians, students, staff, faculty all bunched together in a world of their own. I guess that this is true in any institution. I did feel very claustrophobic in this world and longed to meet and talk with non-Christians and "normal people". I know this may seem derogatory to my peers but I don't think it is normal life. Some young people, and older people, are permanent students, ever learning, studying, learning, studying, learning etc. Personally I don't get that, but then we are all wired up differently. I've got no problem with the University type who wants his or her Masters so as to get his or her credentials to do A, B or C but I don't get the point of wanting your Degree, your Masters or your PhD unless it's to achieve something. The same goes for the ministry. I do not need a Masters to lead a great church, I need to hear from God! I don't need a professorship to pastor people, I need a heart for God's people. I've always maintained this to this day, though I have a DD to my name, I would never really use it unless the situation demanded.

Just recently for example I was asked to sit on the executive board of a secular company for a while as they were pioneering a new product. I had to produce a kind of CV which gave the other board members some idea of the background and experience of each of us. I found it funny again that I was sat next to people who had written White Papers for the government including one person who came up with the National CRB checking system. Another was a chief banker in his time with the Rothschilds' Bank. It was even more funny when the Chairman was "unavoidably detained" making me responsible to chair the meeting! I again laughed heartily at the grace of God. There is a huge difference between being a self-made person and a God-made person. I admire successful, selfmade people. Usually, they've made incredible sacrifices to be where they are. They've paid heavily, many of them in hours and hours of work and dedication to see "their dreams" fulfilled. Most of them have some pretty amazing stories to tell. More than a few of them have failed marriages and damaged relationships with family. But self-made people are rarely at one with themselves and others. It is wonderfully refreshing to see and know that "our times are in God's hands". It certainly helps when the pressure's on! Nevertheless I admire anyone who works hard and is industrious. I think the world is a better place for such people. I've learned for instance never to be resentful of a person's success, or how we say it in church language 'blessing'. Envy and jealousy of possessions actually 'rob' people of what they're jealous and envious of.

When I see a successful person, I admire them, I thank God for such people. Even if they're not Christians!! Yes! The Alan Sugar's of this world, The Richard Branson's, the Bill Gates' ... The little known Samhir Sawhiri's of Egypt who owns towns and villages all over the world bringing employment and a better standard of living to communities desperate for jobs and welfare, not to mention fresh water and medicines and sanitation, to these places. Yes I admire them and thank God for their enterprise, their leadership, their philanthropy when exercised. There are the successful church people too of course. Rick Warren who never seems to sleep but seems to run on some kind of 'spiritual Red Bull' 24/7. Bill Hybels, Bill Wilson. Brian Houston for me is one of the most passionate modern day preachers you will ever hear or see in our day! But there are little known heroes and heroines of the faith too, doing utterly remarkable things with precious little in terms of resources. These are the main men and women who are making a difference in the world today. It's seldom Mega Churches that make a lasting difference. Most of the time they're too concerned with their own agendas to bother about anyone else's.

The people I mean are seldom known or recognised, but they are making an enormous difference. People like Ramona Geru-Ratiu in the South West of Romania. Literally hundreds of kids and parents are educated, fed, and nourished by her ongoing determination to pour God's heart right into homes that will never get God TV or hear Hillsongs let alone get a chance to go to the latest "conference" or understand what on earth they're even on about! The language of the comfortable and cosy Christian is lost entirely on these precious lives. Even if they do believe the gospel and repent and are converted, is there any resemblance to what we take for granted in the "must have, must get" latest phenomena to hit our town, city or even church? No, it is far too esoteric for them to understand and be a part of. Yet it is these untapped, unreached people groups that sit amidst the greatest concentration of the world's people who today remain unreached, untouched and remote from the tremendous grace and power of the gospel. The power to transform the most rebellious, arrogant and disobedient lives. Lawbreakers, criminals in the making, desperate people who are separate people. These are the people who not only make great Christians but also have the potential to reach the so-called lost. This is now my life's mission. Please read on!

The fact that Mags and I got back together is amazing. It took a wee drama or two to make this happen. Both Mags and I had gone out with other people in the year we split up. Neither relationship could have worked. We were made for one another. Personality-wise, experience-wise and background-wise. While nearing the end of my first year at Bible College, I had a very vivid dream. In the dream Mags had had a car crash and she died in the accident. I phoned my then best friend Judith and enquired of Mags. Judith was stunned by this question as she began to relay the account that Mags had crashed in her car just a day ago. She had been returning home late from her job at the National Children's Home. It was in the days when you didn't have to wear seat belts by law. She was singing and worshipping to some praise tape when she just had a random inclination to buckle up and put her seat belt on. She had done this for about 15-20 seconds when a car failed to stop at a side road and crashed into the side of her vehicle. Her car veered uncontrollably into the left side and hit a row of shops. Mags' car went straight through the window of one of the shops. It was a hair salon which as I'm sure you will appreciate has brought about a few comical comments since! Like "What my wife will do to get a hairdo!" The car crashing through the front of the shop was a write-off. A guy managed to pull Mags from the wreckage. As soon as this was done the car burst into flames. Mags escaped with a few scratches and a collar to wear for a week or so. As I heard Judith relay the incident, I was shaken and told her of the dream I had. We both knew it was just a matter of time when we would be back together for life. When I returned to Southport at the end of the first year we did get back together, and have now been married for over 28 years.

Another tremendous blessing was passing my car test in between terms. I booked a 'mock-test' in the morning and passed in the afternoon! And all done in my father's Austin Allegro! I'm

not sure which is the bigger miracle of the two! I'd driven everything from tractors to forklifts to HGV's in my time. If it had
wheels I could drive it! The blessing did not stop there however. A
good friend of mine, Colin Paton, whom I helped lead to the Lord,
came to see me. He had a business in re-making and re-spraying
cars. He was extremely good at it. He turned up a couple of days
later in a Ford Escort Mark II, dangled the keys in front of me,
and asked me if I liked it. "Do I like it?" I said "it's a beaut!" "It's
yours", he said with a glint in his eye, and for a small sum to cover
tax and admin I took proud possession of my first car. I'd gone
to Bible College having given up my job, my girlfriend, and my
security, and I was going back having landed a post in the ministry
working alongside my favourite pastor, passed my test, driving
my own car and engaged to the girl I loved! All in the space of
four months. Now that's what I call a bit of a purple patch!

The day I got engaged to Mags was very special. Pastor Tee
had come to approve of me as a genuine "trophy of grace". A rough
diamond, but a diamond no less. Albeit, he was not going to let
go of his darling daughter that easily. I asked him for Margaret's'
hand in marriage. Dad didn't like the name Mags, it just didn't
sit with him properly. The trouble is Mags never has liked the
name Margaret so there you've got 'the impossible thing meets
the immovable object'. Mags is Mags to me, and the rest of the
world. Margaret is Margaret to Dad and that's that! End of! Mags'
mum, Winifred is easy going and far too wise to be perturbed by
such matters. Mum, as I call her proudly nowadays, especially
since losing my own, is a rock of a lady. A very astute and strong
lady. A very fine wife to Pastor Tee, who sadly passed away on
the 21st September 2010. The fact that I always addressed him
as "Dad" became very much of a blessing for him. He'd never
had a son, but both his son-in—laws became close enough to
call him 'Father'. He was a giant of a man. No one but Winifred
could get really close, and perhaps Mags (or should that really be
Margaret?) She takes after him so much and as we grow a little bit
older these days her resemblance becomes more striking. Not only
in looks but in nature. I'm extremely blessed to have inherited by
divine decree a family like mine.

Margaret's sister should also get a mention. Sharon was a stunningly beautiful child. Dark and with curly black hair. She was always the object of Mags' protection. She is to this day a close friend, and great wife to Ian and a wonderful mother to Ieuan and Lewis, who as you might guess are Welsh to their cotton socks. Sharon is one of the most generous people you could ever meet. This generosity though has run through the family for decades and many times I've watched as they have blessed many people from all walks of life. So ... the wedding date was set! The 10th of May 1986. It would be held at the Southport Elim Church. Pastor Sandford would do the marriage vows and the service and Mags' Dad would deliver the message. Unfortunately, we were going to have to learn quite quickly to enjoy calm water while it lasts. The sea will not always be still for you, and on your journey there will be waves! These waves were about to test us to the max, but they would leave us in no doubt that "wherever God calls, there God will provide."

Chapter Four

NO MAN'S LAND
IS GOD'S LAND

"Where God leads ... He provides"

M y last year at Bible College flew by. I couldn't go back most of the half terms as I had to work my passage as it were. They found out I was good at painting and decorating so they gave me loads of practical work to do in exchange for writing off some of my fees. At the end of the first year I even stayed behind a couple of weeks in order to decorate the local church in Mattersey. I stayed with a couple of friends who helped me. We decorated the lecture rooms, the chapel and the local church along with some of the lounges and common rooms. Since then I've found that God uses our skills and abilities for His purposes in amazing ways. It's not all about preaching, pulpits, diplomas and degrees! The faculty asked me to consider staying another year. They even agreed a bursary for me to help with my fees. At the end I would have a degree and not a diploma. I declined. I was itching to get out into the wide world–to follow my call and to see all that God wanted to do.

Not long after I finished Bible College, I went to take up a ministry role with Pastor Paul Epton. My time there was short but enlightening! I learnt an awful lot from Paul, who even then I recognised and respected as a unique individual. He has enormous passion for God's purpose and incredible courage. In his day he was doing stuff that was way out there. He was the most entrepreneurial pastor I'd ever encountered. He taught me things and passed on to me things he had no idea that I was picking up from him! I admired his spirit and his determination even though it did get him into a bit of hot water now and again! Even today Mags and I remain good friends with him and his wife Evelyn.

While at The Wirral Christian Centre, (the church Paul was pastoring) I was made responsible for a branch of the church and being a part of the community in Milner (a really desperate part of Birkenhead). Here I visited and reached out to people and families who had very little in terms of material possessions and goods. Their spirit was nevertheless inspiring. I was truly blessed at the bible studies I was doing. These were the biggest meetings we had with 25-30 in regular attendance. Not bad virtually from scratch! The Sunday evenings were only 16-18 in attendance but this wasn't a problem to me. It was a pioneer situation and I understood this. Things however were going to change fairly swiftly and dramatically.

Due to 'political reasons' Paul was told that our Headquarters were going to move me where *'they'* felt it was right for me to go. Something to do with proving to Paul that it is Elim who station ministers 'not him'. A meeting was organised for me to meet the then outgoing Field Superintendent, John Smyth and the new Field Superintendent, Gordon Hills. It was decided I would go to Barmouth on the coast of mid- Wales, population 2,500 in the winter, 10,000 in the summer! Oh well! My mission to seagulls had begun! As Mags can confirm, I can get excited about just anything for God, so Barmouth it was. Done and dusted, or so I thought. Another few turns in the road were about to follow which changed my life dramatically!

Mags had struggled with an illness for about 12 years which was getting progressively worse. She was losing blood through some kind of disease within her colon. Every so often she would completely black out and end up in hospital having a blood transfusion. Her blood count was regularly at between 4 and 5 which is something of a disaster. She was taking iron tablets like wine gums at the time to increase her iron intake. After a series of consultations with some leading physicians and specialists she was booked into Liverpool's Walton Hospital to have an operation to remove part of the colon. The sickness had become very serious. To add to the challenges, we were engaged to be married on the 10th May 1986 at our home church in Southport. Pastor Sandford was marrying us and Mags' father Pastor Tee was speaking. Everything was set as planned and going to schedule, apart from Mags' health which was deteriorating rapidly. My father-in-law suggested to me that we cancel the wedding as it was not going to be good for Mags to be stuck in Barmouth miles away from anywhere central in case of emergency treatment. I persuaded him that as he had made me wait a further eight months to marry his daughter (Mags and I had wanted to marry the previous year after I graduated from Bible College in the September) that it was time to trust the Lord, that He who called us would be faithful! To his credit he agreed. Now looking back I see how great his faith and confidence in God was. It must've been very hard for him to agree to go ahead, but he did.

My next meeting with the Elim Executive Council members, John Smyth and Gordon Hills took place on a service station on the M6, (a motorway service station for those in the Sates). It had been decided to send me to Manchester, not Barmouth! On paper the church was small, 30 people I was told, but strong. In reality, and as all pastors know, "paper takes on anything"! When I went, the biggest service we had for three months was 16 adults and three children! The offerings were, well let's say okay for the number, but with one member being exceptionally generous giving half the weekly amount! Awkward is how I'd describe that! I was very excited indeed though. What an honour. Seriously, I was uninterested in the salary, the finance or the size of the challenge; I was just champing at the bit to take on this 'new challenge' for God. I moved from Birkenhead to Manchester the last week of February in 1986. My induction on the last Saturday of the month is something of a blur, but about 50 people were present virtually filling the small room in the former printer's premises which could seat about 80 people maximum. The day after on the Sunday was a reality check with 16 adults and 3 children present!!

One week Mags came over for the weekend to stay and visit the church. The date was set for our wedding. The 10th May 1986 at the Elim Church, Southport. I went to meet Mags as she came over on the train to Manchester, Deansgate Station. We were walking out of the station and we both saw a huge poster with a field of tulips on it. It was a field of literally thousands of different coloured tulips all in lines and stretching for miles it seemed. I looked and I felt God drop into my heart a word. It just said, this is what the church will look like in years to come ! I looked at Mags and I said, "Did you just get something from God?" She replied "Yes! That's a picture of our church in the future" or words to that effect. It was to be a revolution that was to last with us for many many years. Today, we have photos and paintings of tulips all over The Lighthouse. When you visit, you will see this prophetic revelation epitomised all over the place. Today, the actual church resembles very accurately what we saw, although in size we have some way to go.

Meanwhile our wedding plans were in full flow. I was staying at one the member's houses, as in the manse there was a young lady staying in the top of the property which had been converted to a self-contained apartment. It would obviously not have been appropriate for a single young man to be sharing a house with a single woman therefore I stayed with one of the guys in the church, David, an excellent young man who showed me great kindness and hospitality in those early days in the run up to our wedding. Mags was still at this time suffering greatly with her health and if anything became worse. She was in and out of hospital and the time for her operation in Liverpool was looming.

We had heard of some special meetings being held by Pastor Ron Jones at the Wirral Christian Centre, Birkenhead where I had moved from. Mags and I went along. Mags' father and mother were there too. Pastor Ron preached a great message on Daniel whose prayer had come up to The Lord, but experienced a delay of 21 days before the answer arrived. It was deeply prophetic. At the end he asked for people to come to the front to be prayed for, for sickness and other needs. Mags did not go forward. People were prayed for and the service ended. Afterwards Mags asked me to ask the Pastor to pray for her. She had wanted to go for prayer but was put off slightly by people fainting and falling down as they were prayed for. We had all been quite sceptical about this kind of thing. I said "But why didn't you go out when the pastor asked?" I felt a bit embarrassed to ask the pastor after everything had finished. He was very kind and more than happy to pray for Mags. Almost as soon as he began praying Mags fell to the floor as if completely pole-axed! I was stunned! Shocked! When she arose to her feet she said quietly but confidently "I've been healed! It's done!" I was kind of "Yeah right, well we'll see."

Sometime later the time for her operation came. She was admitted to the hospital, though still claiming she'd been healed. She even told the doctors and nurses this, who were very sympathetic and sensitive about the whole thing. The time came to do the exploratory x-rays etc., and to their amazement they found nothing! Whereas beforehand they had identified part of the colon had irregular cells which were haemorrhaging, they could no longer see anything wrong at all. She had felt much better since being prayed for and had stopped taking her iron tablets (something she hadn't told any of us at this point!) The doctor who was due to do the operation, came and told her that they could find nothing wrong with her! "I told you" she said, "The Lord has healed me!" The doctor was excellent and responded positively. "Well whatever has happened, you do not need an operation. But what you need to do is be regularly checked for your blood." Sound advice and sensible too. Mags did this for the next few years after coming out of hospital her blood count had gone from 3.5/4 to 13 in one year! Also, I counted the days since she'd been prayed for until the day the doctor said "There is nothing wrong with you" *It was 21 days!* Yes! *Three weeks!* This was nearly 27 years ago and Mags enjoys great health to this day with no problems with lack of blood or low blood count etc! A miracle had occurred and for us it's completely undeniable! **GOD STILL HEALS TODAY!** The wedding could now go ahead without any of the anticipated health problems. Job done!

(left to right) Paul and his older brother Michael. Paul & Michael with their dad, Percy Lionel Hallam (centre). Mags Hallam with Mum & Dad Tee (right).

Percy & Gladys Hallam, the author's Mother and Father (left). Pastor & Mrs Tee, the author's Father and Mother-in-law (right).

Paul & Mags in the Lake District, UK in 1982.

The car in which the author and his brother nearly died.
Paul was 18 when the accident occurred 1979.

The author receiving his diploma in theology at the AoG
Bible College, Mattersey Hall, Doncaster, UK - 1985

Paul and Mags married at the Southport Elim Church.
May 10th, 1986.

Paul and Mags arrive at the Elim Church Chorlton in February 1986 (centre). At Victoria Street Station (left), Paul and Mags are shown a poster portrait of the future church. Paul being ordained at the 1988 Elim Conference (right).

Construction of The Lighthouse Christian Centre begins in February 1991 and is completed in August 1991. Paul & Mags are seen (left) with the foundation stone in March that year. Also a photograph of the newly founded Lighthouse Nursery (middle bottom).

The Lighthouse was founded upon good community work, youth work and outreach. Starting from top left, youth activity weekend. Top middle - Sports days on-site (football fours - top right). Church day out to Alton Towers. Main photo - outreach to local estates. The author preaching the Gospel.

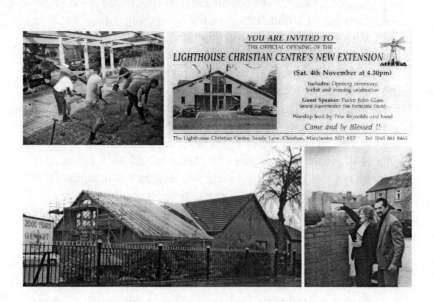

The Lighthouse Christian Centre extended on November 4th, 2000.

Chapter Five

SINK OR SWIM

"The desire to succeed should be greater than the fear of failure"
Bill Cosby

T he first six months of our time at the little church at Chorlton-cum-Hardy, Manchester, is not something I look back on with a lot of joy. It was something of a crucible to be perfectly honest. I had stuff going down that a young 25 year old pastor had to deal with that would be really unthinkable nowadays! I look at our young people today in the church who are approaching the age I was and I laugh! (In a nice way.) I tell them that they're never too young to be used by God, even as leaders! Even a child can be a leader! Yes, a child! Leadership is best taught as early as possible. One of the main reasons that churches are held back is a lack of leaders, not just leadership. Leadership begins by "leading others to Christ" or simply "leading a prayer time" a small group, or even getting 3-4 people together to take the offering!! Churches simply cannot manage to grow without more leaders being raised up. Leaders take responsibility even at an irresponsible age. It takes people who will agree to be dedicated, committed and sacrifice to become a true leader. Not many have this rare fusion of qualities. Isaac was exemplary in the scriptures in this regard. Genesis 26:25 identifies his priorities. 1) He put the Lord first–He built an Altar. 2) He put his family second–He pitched his tent. 3) He put his business third–He dug a well. Many would disagree with this

62

order but I don't. If we genuinely put God first, there's not much can go wrong in life! Even our families will be blessed and we would not neglect them either, for this is honouring to God and part of putting Him first. The work of the ministry can never be genuinely used as an excuse for neglect of our wives, children or wider family. 'The work of the ministry' is not necessarily putting God first but making Him central and I'll cover this later on in the book.

In the first six months of leadership at Chorlton, Manchester, I lost my treasurer, in very difficult circumstances. I lost eight people in the first six months. One person committed suicide. Another left because I preached on being 'born again' which kind of lets you know what we inherited. Another died of old age and I can't remember what the others went for. Basically half of our adults went one way or another. I remember getting a phone call from on high, (Elim HQ) kind of, saying nicely, "What's happening?" I can't blame them for this! It should be done more! At least it shows they're bothered. Well we lost people, but we somehow gained more than we lost in the ensuing six months. By the time eighteen months had gone by, we had virtually doubled the church with thirty people in regular attendance. But then something very special and precious happened. As I was praying at the end of 1987, I received what can only be described as a monumental revelation.

I often say the big difference between a vision and a revelation is one can be "made up" but the other has to be received! I saw a lighthouse in a city! The city of course being Manchester. I immediately knew God was calling me to prepare for much greater things. I read of the church in Antioch in Syria. This was an amazing church. It was where the early disciples of Christ were first called Christians (Acts 11:26). It became the missionary headquarters for the disciples and the launch pad for the apostolic ministry of Paul and Barnabas. From here they travelled the world and trail-blazed the incredible message of Jesus Christ to the ends of the earth. Even today we still have a legacy from them that is unstoppable and unending. Antioch also became a generous church. These qualities stood out to me then and we are still modelling them to this present day over 25 years on. The Lord showed me more of this revelation through Isaiah 60:1 NIV in the Old Testament. "Arise and shine for your light has come and the glory of the Lord is risen upon you." What has happened since is just a 21st Century phenomenom that continues to grow and develop, slowly but surely.

Since receiving this revelation we set to work. I shared the revelation with the small church, who I found at some years later thought I'd completely lost the plot!! We were going to move from the present premises because they *would be* too small to accommodate what God wanted to do. We would start to fund raise to obtain alternative premises. I started to look everywhere and anywhere. Mags and I would drive all over the place viewing properties in the suburb of Chorlton. In truth there was nowhere big enough. Chorlton is a busy congested, cosmopolitan area of Manchester. Its population of 10,000 then has virtually tripled now. It is quite quirky in that it's always been popular with hip and trendy couples, students and families too. It has very expensive areas and two council estates. A real mixed bag, but a great mission field. I announced the launch of The Lighthouse Project. A mission to build our own multi-functional purpose-built Church Centre, facilitating community activities as well as church activities.

While pastoring in the first three to four years, I had to deal with huge inferiority problems regarding my ministry, the church and our size. The smallness of our situation become a really big frustration to me! *It just had to change! It had to!* I began preaching for the future. We worked tirelessly for increase and growth. Some people teach against working hard in the ministry! I disagree 100 percent! I think laziness is one of the biggest curses of the developed world. When you take a look at the work ethic of those in developing nations, India, Romania, China, Egypt, Poland, etc you will find it wholly incomparable to ours. We complain so much here in the UK that it really is unbelievable. We have so much for so little while others have next to nothing in this world. And the situation has worsened over the past decade to the point of incredulity. I have seen it now in the ministry. Even graduates from Bible College, the first thing some of them want to know is what the salary is. The pension and holiday entitlement bla bla bla! It's completely wrong and those who think like this should do everyone a favour, themselves included, and go get a secular job. No doubt they'll be paid better. They won't have to work as many hours and they won't get the treatment they would as a pastor. Harsh maybe! But it's dishonouring to all who went before us, who slaved and sacrificed and paid in sweat, blood and tears just to build church, never mind pastor it!

Today, I wouldn't even entertain taking someone on staff with this kind of mindset. We are sons and daughters not hired servants! We should behave like God's children who have a far greater inheritance than material things, money and 'entitlements'. I'm not against those things at all. But I believe they should NEVER EVER COME FIRST! Service comes first, not reward or payment. Just service. I still maintain this to this day. A workman is worthy of their hire, but making full proof of our ministry should always be the precursor for any reward. Thomas A Edison once said "most people miss their opportunities because they come in overalls and are dressed like work".

Regarding the frustrations I felt about our church, I remember I'd never ask a visiting speaker to come in those days. I never thought they would! We had fairly large churches in Manchester that I looked up to in a good way. ABC, the 600 strong Baptist Church in Altrincham, Kings Church, the 500 strong church in the city centre. Ivy Cottage quite near to us with 400, an amazingly influential church for years and still is to this day. The Vineyard was in great blessing and had 4-500 in those days. This has gone through transition and through a change of leader as their senior leader, a friend of mine, retired. It's an influential church. But I looked up to these churches without even going to their services by the way. They inspired me no end. I believed one day The Lighthouse could radiate Christ's light in similar fashion. This wasn't about competition or jealousy and envy. I prayed and led prayer regularly for these churches and still do for increased blessing, growth and favour. But, we had much work to do and had to be very courageous in our faith and initiative. Someone once said "The desire to succeed should be greater than the fear of failure." I love this, because desire is very very powerful indeed. Our desire was not only well motivated it was something that drove us on through all the disappointments of life and they would most surely come for certain.

Despite all my efforts and my imagination to help visualise how property can be adapted, (something anyone who knows me will tell you is not difficult for me but comes naturally), our search for alternative premises seemed fruitless. Nothing was really suitable. I couldn't understand it! I looked everywhere, anywhere, but nothing. Then I know The Lord said something simple but clear. "The answer is under your nose ". I looked close to home. The answer lay in the small primary school literally over the road. I made an appointment to see the head teacher. She was surprised. "What, you want to hire our main hall? For a church service?" "Yes" I said, "exactly!" She was a bit shocked. "But why?" she replied. "Well we are moving soon" I said, "we have outgrown our present premises and need more space, and we're building a new church centre." She was really amazed but I could see very impressed too. We looked at the main hall. It only seated about 150 maximum but it was just what we needed for then. It had gym equipment that would need to be moved and a lot of work would need to be done every week to make it happen. We agreed a price about £650 pcm. It was quite steep for us at the time. Our income was very low. We started with offerings averaging £80 per week. Sometimes it went down as low as £35! Wow that was hard!! At the time I was paid £42 per week plus a fuel allowance of £18. I did some other work to supplement my 'salary'. Some light building work, painting and decorating etc. We were going to have to find more money from somewhere.

We had started a training scheme in our play group we ran at the church. We made a contract with a government-led provider for ten trainees to teach childcare vocationally. Mags had a PRC qualification (Pre-Residential Care) which she gained while she was employed as a social worker for kids at a home. She had eleven years' experience too. This enabled her to oversee the scheme and gain a modest income. At about the same time we were hit hard by one of our members leaving. He was a good man and was leaving to go and marry someone who'd already left the church. It was hard for him too. He was the man who I mentioned was giving half of our income! Not good!! We had just launched

The Lighthouse Project (verbally) and I'd just spent time sharing vision regarding this. The weekend he went our offerings doubled! They also stayed that way and never went down again! Our church income rose from about £100 pw to just over £200 pw. This was in late 1989. It amazingly coincided with a decision to give up our dependency upon HQ's Pastoral Aid Grant. They had been giving us about £130 pcm to help us with church bills etc. This had been given for some time and was in place before we had arrived. The termination of this was occasioned by the intense questioning of our phone bill by HQ which I can't remember how much it was but I know it was modest and reasonable. I wrote and told them to cancel this as we didn't need it anymore. It was another small but important step towards fulfilling the vision God had given. This was just before our tithes and offerings doubled and was not a coincidence. It taught me an invaluable lesson and one I will never forget. A healthy church should not need financial support from a third party all the time. Help is great at times, but dependency on external help is not healthy.

Personally, since being called by God into the ministry I refused to sign on the dole, or apply for unemployment benefit. God was now responsible for my income, and Him alone. Something I rely on to this day. A church which is dependent on outside help all the time is like a person on social security or unemployment benefit. A dependent looking for work (purpose). I believe, as a muscle has to be exercised, so faith needs to be stretched, so in 1990, I announced we would be moving into the adjacent school premises from the summer onwards. The existing premises we would convert to being an Administration Centre from which to raise funds. Half the main hall would be used for children's work mid-week which Mags and I personally ran, as well as our small but growing Youth Work. The first floor would continue to be used as a play group. The church was really excited by the changes. By now between 40 and 50 people were in regular attendance. Our leadership team consisted of me, Mags, a young man called, Lennox, and Rick, a great musician and a unique individual. We also had a couple of families who joined us and worked really closely with us. Jeff and Tina, and Steve and Sue. These were very instrumental in helping to implement the vision of The Lighthouse. We also had a new treasurer I'd appointed, Tony who was a guy who stepped up to the plate at just the right time! Since the original treasurer had walked out on us, and gave me all the books and records in a plastic carrier bag, Tony's appointment became a real blessing, though it turned out to be a short-lived one.

While I had the books, almost from day one, I had to effectively become the treasurer as well as the caretaker, secretary and anything else that you could possibly think of! My office was probably the smallest in the world. I put a writing bureau in it which had a folding lid cum top as every time you opened the office door, which opened inwards, the top of the bureau had to be closed. Yes, seriously, it was that small! There was no way we could fund-raise properly from this so I got the team to agree to convert the main hall into a proper office suite. My new role as treasurer was to be a learning curve, dealing with finance but it turned out to be heaven sent!! I have to pay great tribute to Pastor Tony Lacy's wife Jennifer. She had experience in accounts and helped me no end. Tony and Jennifer pastored the Chorley Elim Church 'Living Waters' which Tony and Jennifer's son John leads today. John and his wife Michelle have become good friends of ours. They have a similar DNA to us and are taking their church to an amazing place of influence.

My ability to balance the books, and handle the finance gave me great insight into how it all hanged together. I got to the point quite quickly where I was able to take on staff, do the tax (PAYE) the National Insurance and sick pay. I even managed to get to grips with contracts of employment, maternity leave and even Elim's Financial Returns. Our books had more Tippex on them than you'd find in a stationer's shop!! I'm sure that it doubled the postage due to the weight. More playgroup staff were needed. Mags and I interviewed and employed these new staff. We had not only to hire, but fire people too! I remember one woman coming to work drunk. It ended in a P45 experience!! (I think you will know what I mean!) By the time 1990 was drawing to a close, we were bringing in about three times as much money from outside the church as from within. This was essential to get us to where we needed to be! In the next chapter I will share how we managed to see one of the biggest miracles I've ever witnessed! How a church of 16 adults and 3 children, built and opened a purpose built multi-functional church centre called The Lighthouse Christian Centre, on a three quarter acre plot of land and moved into it in less than five years at a cost of over £300,000!!

Chapter Six

CRUNCHING THE NUMBERS!

———◦———

"Water cuts through rock, not because it's powerful,
but because it's persistent."

In the lead up to moving the church congregation, I needed to find another place to live. We would need to sell the manse. This would be worth at least £65,000. It was a five bedroomed house which in effect, although it belonged to our Denomination (The Elim Pentecostal Church of Great Britain and Ireland) was controlled by local Trustees. Only two of these were still alive. One was one of the earliest pastors the church had had, some 35 years earlier. The Elim Church, Chortlon-cum-Hardy had never been more that 35-40 attenders at a push. It had gone through pastors like no tomorrow. Several had come and gone over the past decade. It's not always right for pastors to stay around for years. There are pros and cons in whether we stay or leave. A lot depends in my opinion on 'what kind of church' we're building. And there are several kinds of local church which all have their place within the whole of the body of Christ. My problem was I would have to solicit the Trustees' favour, not only to sell the premises but, to ensure the proceeds went to the local church. I found the former a lot easier to do than the latter. The two surviving trustees agreed. One was the retired pastor, Jack Glass, the father of our current General Superintendent, Pastor John Glass. He originally bought the property from his own pocket via his business. John at the time was a well renowned speaker and preacher within our denomination and a Regional Superintendent too.

Pastor Jack Glass and his son John were delighted at the progress the little church had made and Pastor Jack Glass was happy to relinquish his trusteeship over the whole property, thus releasing it for sale as long as the proceeds benefitted the local church. This became a tricky one. There were those at our HQ at the time who clearly did not want this, but wanted the proceeds to go to the national fund. It became one of the most difficult 'battles' I simply had to take on. And yes it was a 'battle'. There is no other way to describe it. It was extremely stressful and very disillusioning for Mags and I, not to mention frustrating. We eventually succeeded in getting this result though sheer determination and persistence. "Water cuts through rock not because it's powerful but because it's persistent".

A new problem also emerged. We would have to sell the manse and the church in a staggered deal. We could vacate the manse fairly quickly, but we would not be able to vacate the church for quite some time. It proved to be something of a nightmare scenario, but again we set to the task. Around this time (1988) I had another amazing moment when I stayed and prayed in the church hall one night. I can only describe it as being a "bit of a temper tantrum with God!" I'd become very frustrated with the lack of help & support, financially especially!! I "lost it a bit" in my praying and some of what I said would not be worth repeating for theological reasons as well as for the sanctity of the holy reader. To say I complained a lot to God about the lack of provision is an understatement. Anyhow, the very next morning, I knew God had heard my prayer. I received in the post a letter from a charitable organisation offering us £10,000 to our project. This was the first major grant I ever had won for the kingdom. I was fired up by it and immediately set to the task of writing to loads of charities, businesses, banking and financial institutions. I also got further cheques totalling another £10,000 from these too! By now I could see The Lighthouse Project very definitely had the hand of God upon it.

Yet more difficulties were experienced. Mags and I had to find somewhere else to live! A small detail in the whole equation. There was no way any bank would give us a mortgage on anything bigger than a garden shed on the combined salary we had. It was actually laughable when we tried. But God seems to delight in us when we are faced with impossibility. He loves to 'overcome' with minorities and blesses greatly when He has just a little abandoned to His hand. Another miraculous thing happened which was pivotal in the whole move. A Christian property owner heard of our situation. He called us and we talked through the whole vision. We told him we were selling the manse but that we had to find somewhere else to live. We told him we could not afford a mortgage because of our income level being way too low. He knew this was the case anyhow. He then offered to buy a property on our behalf. We would pay him back monthly (at a very low rate) and once we paid him back, whenever that would be, it would be ours. The payments were all interest free! We were staggered. We were told to search for something suitable for around £35,000. It was to be a cash purchase too. We were overjoyed! We looked at many properties and liked a few. We wanted to be near the church and we saw a property just the right distance away on the border of Trafford and Chorlton. A three bedroomed semi-detached house which had a long garden and a large garden shed. Great for me because I'd taken to building our own furniture. (We still have it to this day.)

Well this house was ideal. A young family was living there and wanted to move to a much bigger house as baby number three was on the way. The trouble is they had a buyer and the deal was virtually sown up. "Okay" I said, "If they back out let us know as we have a cash offer of £34,500 for you." Every little helps! Whilst having this conversation I noticed we were stood in the hall and they were at the door. It was surreal. I felt like they were leaving and we were staying. It was kind of instinctive but very real. It's amazing how God speaks to us. I find His voice seldom comes with pyrotechnics and stereophonic speakers. It's still the still small voice that does it for me! Both Mags and I knew this as we talked afterwards. We exchanged our details and left. Later on, probably not much more than a week later, in the middle of one of our leadership meetings being held in the front room of the manse, we received a call from the family selling the house. Their current deal had fallen through and they would accept the offer if it was still valid. We bought it and moved in in the summer of 1989. The way had been made open to sell the manse. Our Headquarters had finally agreed to allow the full proceeds to go towards the New Lighthouse Project. By this time we had raised a measly sum of £12,000 towards the whole project. At least now we had £65,000 we could count on!

Around the same time, as we were trying to fund raise and launch the project, we discovered a massive problem which the survey on our church property revealed. We had dry rot within the joists of the first floor. It would be an astronomical amount to put right and the price would be greatly affected. Amazingly, one of our newer members was a surveyor too and knew exactly what to do. How to replace them and repair and strap them where possible. A small team of us set to it. In one weekend we did the work so as to not disrupt the midweek youth and children's ministry or the play group which Mags was developing with her trainees as well as staff.

A buyer was found for the Manse, though it was a real battle to get the £65,000 figure we wanted. Thankfully our HQ let me do the negotiations, in close co-operation with them of course, but they allowed me to proceed on a face-to-face basis. I've always loved negotiating and I've sharpened my skills to the point of still handling this side of the business of and for The Lighthouse. This would become one of my most important gifts in my work overseas, which at this point was not on my radar. I had never left these shores in my life. I knew from being a child however that I would travel and teach and preach in far away lands. I will say much more about this later in section three of the book. A deal was eventually done for £65,000 for the manse and £37,000 for the church hall. Someone at HQ wanted to settle for £34,000 but I said "No, we will get the £37,000". We had also spent a further £4,000 on the drainage system as the buyer of the manse found our drainage affected his. We had to completely re-lay new drains. I made sure we held out and got the £37,000. The particular gentleman at HQ (who has moved on now) was being stressed out by our 'aggressive' buyer. He phoned and phoned this person at HQ regularly until the chap at HQ phoned me and asked me to settle for £34,000. I said again, "Look, he's a bully. Don't worry, we'll get the £37,000 and we *need* the extra £3,000 to help recoup some of the money we spent out on the property to get it ready for him!" Mags spoke to our friend at HQ and said something in the way of "Look, just chill, he's living next door to us. We see him every day. You think *you've* had enough of him!" He got the point and left it to me after this. The buyer had bought the manse. He had moved in and we were still using the small church as a centre. We did hold out and got our £37,000 too.

Some time before this, in 1988, the local council had notified certain people of their intention to develop the old Chorlton Oakwood High School on Sandy Lane. A great residential area near the centre of Chorlton. I had registered our interest in the site. The council had earmarked the three-and-a-half acre site for redevelopment. They wanted most of it for residential housing but at least three quarters of an acre to be used for community/charitable purposes. About four charities registered their interest including us with The Lighthouse Project being our vanguard for the area set aside. We were all called to a preliminary meeting with the council to explain what was in their mind to do. The three quarter acre site would be available on a 99 year lease with a peppercorn rent (usually meaning nothing these days as it's not worth collecting.) It would cost a premium of £30,000. This narrowed it down to two of us. I threw our hat in the ring. I loved the site, it was just what we needed. I also made sure that we got the three acre site fronting onto the main road. "Do you have the funding for this?" I was asked. "Yes of course", was my reply, "though we are still fund-raising for the main new build." The pathway was set. The old school was demolished in 1989 and construction work began immediately for the residential section of the redevelopment. We had put forward our case in which The Lighthouse Project would provide a Full- and Part-Time Nursery, children and youth projects, plus training opportunities for the long term unemployed. The site would also have thirty private car-parking spaces in its car park, plus a five-a-side football pitch surrounded by a compound area.

We appointed an architect to handle the project. This was to prove to be an expensive error, and nearly caused us to lose the whole project. Meanwhile our HQ had backed the project although we had much to do to raise the shortfall. Full marks to our Head Office for backing the vision too with only such a small amount of seed money at the beginning. We had managed to raise a further £20,000 from bits and pieces. One Trust promised us a further £10,000 if we could show the project would definitely go ahead. Unfortunately, the architect's estimation of the costs kept going up until they were coming out at £450,000, which I knew would eventually become £500,000! Half a million was too much by far in my opinion. I got an appointment with a design & build company. It was a very reputable company with a lot of experience in building churches and community centres, Stock Building Company. They also fired their own bricks via a subsidiary company. I spoke with some of the guys there and came away with the instinct that this meeting was from above. I spoke with our leadership team who agreed to part company with the previously appointed architects. It nearly cost us £40,000. But I was adamant we would not pay this sum, as they had in my opinion allowed the scheme to escalate to the point where a £300,000- £320,000 build cost had become nearly half a million pounds. Interesting when you consider they work on a percentage scale! We managed to pay off the architect for about £12,000 (we had already paid £12,000 in architects' fees to get to planning stage and produce a full set of drawings and costings). Still, as I often say, you have to go through a few turkeys to get to the golden goose. For me, design and build is always the best deal in terms of economy. You get much less hassle too. Of course there's the counter argument that a separate architect is independent and will represent the client's interest a lot better. But seriously, if you've got half a clue about building and construction it's an extremely economical way of doing the job. The 'D and B' method of building as it's called in the trade, does require a hand on the tiller at all times, but this kind of input is something I enjoy and I get right involved in. I've had to literally rescue a few of our endeavours though, due to "well intentioned" but misplaced management decisions. But that's life!

So, we had paid out about £4,000 for new drains, £1,000 for dealing with the dry rot in the church roof. Another £12,000 on the Architect. We had about £11,000 left plus the funds from the church, held at Head Office, (£65,000) still to be drawn upon for the new build. A further £37,000 could be counted on for the eventual sale of the church premises. About £113,000 in total. Not nearly enough by half! The time had come to put up or shut up! The site we wanted had to be paid for. £30,000! We hadn't got it. Plain and simple. I played along as if we had it. We contacted the solicitors to start the whole transaction. New housing was going up rapidly on the cleared site by the end of 1989. The council wanted their money. Now we would have to have some courage to get through this. Amazingly a mini-breakthrough came about in a most unusual way.

I received a phone call in my office from the local authority's office. "Excuse me, can I speak to the minister, Paul Hallam please?" It was one of their officers. It turned out that the city surveyors had made a botch up on the actual measurements of the site. In effect the builders ended up with slightly more land for their development. But we ended up with slightly less. Basically, it narrowed the strip of land at the back of the site. It was about the width of a single track road and ran the length of the site. I was about to say "Oh, that's fine. We can manage okay with this" when my negotiating gene kicked in! "Well surely if this is the case we need to go back to the drawing board on the price?" I said. "Okay", he said, "but can you still do what you want to do on the site?" I said, "Well to be honest it's going to change things a bit", which it did, (marginally though!) "but I guess we can get round it somehow." He promised me he'd come back with a renewed costing in the light of the "botch up"! He did, and offered it to us for £10,000.00. "How would that be Mr Hallam?" "Hmmm, yeah, I think we could accept that ... but I will have to check with our team." Hahahahaha!! I got off the phone and popped the champagne! Ahem, metaphorically not literally, but I think you get the point. We had just cut the budget by £20,000 in one telephone call. Lovely stuff! Other phone calls were God-ordained too, and followed shortly after.

We announced the date we would be moving out of the church premises. It was August 1990. At the time we laid our plans out for the new centre. We also converted the small ground floor premises into a good administration centre. There had been a mural as a backdrop to the small platform which we cut down and rolled up and gave to a former member. The old platform and front section of the hall became two decent sized offices. One was mine and the other was my secretary's. Val served us in the whole vision for The Lighthouse Project. She was a fairly new member but you could easily tell she was going to be around for some time. I now had a secretary, a treasurer and a couple of good, competent leaders on our team. Things were shaping up. Early in 1990 we purchased the three acre site for the sum of £10,000. The scene was set for a major fund-raising initiative.

Chapter Seven

THE RAVENS ARE
ON THEIR WAY!

"When you are called to mission you will feel its demand."

The name of this book is very important to me. I nearly called
it "The End of The Road". At least three times in my thirty
years of pastoral ministry in Manchester I've found I've "hit the
buffers" so to speak. I reached a place where humanly speaking,
I simply could go no further. When you are called to mission,
you will feel its demand. There's no getting away from it. The
demands of our mission live with us every waking moment of
every day. You can walk away from a job, but you cannot simply
walk away from a call or a mission given to you from above.

"The Rubicon" was actually a river in Italy which Julius
Caesar crossed when marching south to return to Rome, which in
his opinion had become corrupted by selfish senators and magis-
trates. The crossing of the Rubicon river denotes "the point of no
return". It was here that Caesar had to make up his mind whether
to disband the XIII Gemina Legion or "burn his bridges" by
crossing over as a legion. Once he stepped foot over the southern
side of the Rubicon river without disbanding the legion he would
have committed "Imperium", a declaration of war, as all armies
returning to Rome had to disband according to the law of Rome,
so as not to be marching on Rome. Julius Caesar decided to march

against Rome and commit "Imperium" (treason) and stated the often quoted words *"alea iacta est"*–"the die is cast".

The very title of this book therefore reminds every reader that in life, we will have to go through our own personal 'Rubicon'. I witnessed an amazing sense of doubt, fear and initial insecurity when we took the decision to move out of the former printers premises into the Oswald Road Primary school next door. But I had to gain courage from the Lord and from what I knew I'd seen and what I knew I'd heard. The rest of the jigsaw belonged to Him, not me. We "burned our bridges" at that very moment. There was no going back! It was our first 'Rubicon' experience and it wouldn't be our last. Maybe you haven't experienced yours yet. Maybe you have and it's tough going. Well let me say, with anything in life, persistence pays. Massively! In actual fact most people who are going to fulfil any vision in their lives will have to pass through a 'Rubicon' or two. It's the way it is. As Mags often says, "This is life."

So, we knew we had set out on a journey that would demand faith, courage and lots of determination and lots of sacrifice and hard work! We had a small number of people who promised to help set up on Sunday mornings. We stored the chairs down in the school cellar along with the lectern and guitar stands, amplifiers etc. It took us between an hour and an hour and a half to set up for church every week. Our small but growing congregation of about fifty people moved into the school for our weekend services. We had started two new house-groups too so we had three in total. I led two of them every week and another leader led one. We continued to grow the church and it was an exciting period but, very exacting too!

One of our then senior Executive Council Members met me in the newly converted offices of the church centre. He took a look at the plans and chatted to me! It was nice to have such a visit. He then asked me, "How are you going to pay for it?" I said, "Well we are going to use the funds from the sale of the premises here and next door. Plus, we have fundraised about £30,000 to date, and we will get the rest by fundraising any way we can!" His response stunned me! "You're dreaming!!", he said. He asked again, "How are you going to fund this?" I remember being quite shattered by this as I tried to explain how I was not sure how we would get *all* the finance but I was sure we would. Now I realise that leaders come across all sorts of people with a host of well-meaning but totally unsound and dodgy projects and they are fairly easy to identify if you take a close enough look at the history and the details in the lead up to where they are presently in their given situation. I wouldn't mind but there was heaps of stuff you could point to at this stage that just shouted out God was in it. I know senior leaders can easily become sceptical when they hear initially about vision and revelation because let's be honest most of the stuff we hear about has a shelf life of approximately nine days! But usually it's easy to identify this. You can spot the chickens from the turkeys if you know what to look for, fact! Anyhow, I think I was a bit arrogant and reactionary at this stage and can't quite remember what my response was but it was virtually one which bid them "God speed" out of the door! I don't have any rankle with this brother who is a dear friend of mine and I love him and respect him for being a really great servant of God for many years. It was just a moment and I wholly and totally disagreed with him. If he reads this he will probably remember this. I hope he laughs at it, because it helped me in a funny way.

I have found in life that some things in life that "wind you up" also "wise you up". This was one such occasion. When it came to being in the same place in the future I would certainly be better prepared. I have also found in life that God has a "punchbag" approach with me! You can punch a punchbag as hard as you like, but it's still going to be there when you've thrown your best shot. (The trouble is unlike a punchbag sometimes I tend to throw a couple back.) I'm known, as I said earlier, as a bit of a fighter. I was like this as a youngster and I was still like it as a pastor and leader. I don't like confrontation. People who like confrontation tend to be walking powder kegs, who leave a trail of destruction in their wake. I don't like confrontation as I said, but if it happens I'm up for it no problem. I've since learned to pick my battles carefully as not all of them are worth fighting for. I tend to only fight those that are important to me now. Battle fatigue is a hard thing to overcome in ministry as you usually don't get the respite you need. Usually it is followed by a new and fresh round of challenges which are often just as demanding. Most pastors and leaders are not defeated or fail. They just ... well ... just give up! As someone once said, Failure is temporary, it's giving up that makes it permanent.

During that time, Mags and I were at our denomination's annual conference. This particular year it was at Bognor Regis at Butlin's Holiday Camp. About two and a half to three thousand people attend each year. We were delighted to meet a very great man of God, Billie Jay, from our Cardiff Church, the City Temple, who was there at the time. My father-in-law had been the senior pastor at The City Temple for several years. Billie was a bachelor all his life. He also taught Sunday School for many years. He declined eldership or position, preferring just to serve with the young guys in the children's work. He was also a first class painter and decorator who had given hours and hours of unpaid service to his beloved church. This gentleman was, and still is, a giant of a man in our eyes. He takes his place in this book as a mark of honour to him. Mags and I will never forget him. He was very humble, sweet and loved The Lord with all his soul. Anyhow, one day we met Billie and we invited him around for coffee. I think he was a very lonely man in many ways. He had a horrendous past and was an orphan brought up in a home near Cardiff's old docklands. As we chatted, he stopped and said "I have a word from The Lord for you both!" We pricked our ears up like a couple of sheepdogs waiting for a command! Hahahaha! I'll never forget it! "You remember when Elijah was at the brook Cherith in 1 Kings 17? Well ...", he went on, "God sent the ravens to feed him there in the famine. Well He has commanded the ravens to feed you, and all you need will be supplied".

Wham! It was like ... well it was like receiving a cheque payment right there and then. I felt the pressure and weight of the burden of lack of finance just melt away, to be replaced with excitement and expectancy. This really is the best way I can describe it when God speaks personally to you. His voice rolls away pressure and heaviness like nothing on the planet! Seriously! If you're reading this and not a believer I just want to say to you, ask God to speak to you! It's monumental and life changing when He does! Mags has always said to me I'm best under pressure. It kind of

81

charges me up. I seem to work best under it (by my admission). I don't like this but it does seem to be the case. I often wish I was more reflective and passive, more contemplative, but it's just not me! I'm a Taurean, a bit of a bull. (Mags would disagree with the "bit" part!)

It has taken me a long, long time to accept the person I am in this respect. I'm saying this because there's a lot of unnecessary pressure put on young pastors and ministers to conform to a kind of stereotypical model of what a pastor should look like, act like and be in terms of personality and style. I'm aggressive, I'm pretty non-conforming and I'm quite a rebel in many ways. I've often been treated with contempt and classed as arrogant and brusque by those more educated. I've come to realise there are loads of consultants in ministry today. Experts in telling and lecturing my "type" of person what to do, say and how to build church. The trouble is many of them have never actually done it! They're not practitioners and to be honest never were or could be. But "those who can't do, often teach" as the saying goes. Today, I'm far more accepting and relaxed about who I am and what I am. I've learned after a long time to be comfortable in my own skin. Sometimes I describe myself as a missionary who leads a church! I do so, not just to be self-effacing, (no disrespect to any missionaries!). But a missionary can't just be pigeon holed the same way as a church leader or pastor can. A missionary can mean anything from a Livingstone to a Muller. Well, back to our chat with Billie. It was revolutionary for us. It came at just the right time. Thank You Lord for your servant Billie Jay! What a guy! Wow!

In the run up to Christmas, Mags and I worked really hard to see the children's work and youth work grow. Two of our team, Jeff and Tina, worked ever so hard taking the midweek children's work off our hands and we concentrated on the youth in our church. We've never ever become detached or disconnected from our youth work, even now. We absolutely love teenagers and young twenty year olds. Always have and always will! I love that quote Bill Wilson (who heads up the largest Sunday School in the world) uses: "It's easier to build boys and girls than it is to repair men and women". We poured our time into our youth and even in that small church we had a mid-week attendance of between 30-40 kids and about 15-20 youth. At one stage when I was leading the Sunday School we were getting up to 100 children squashed in the little hall on a Sunday afternoon. I used to organise competitions for the kids and did a huge "Race to Space" feature time. If you brought a friend you got awarded points, two friends much more points and more than two was real blast off. When you reached space you got sweets like flying saucers with sherbet in them. When you reached the moon you got a small chocolate bar. Then deeper into space a Milky Way, and then on reaching Mars, yes you got a Mars Bar! Finally on orbiting Mars and landing back on earth the first ten kids to touchdown got a variety box of sweets & chocolates. It was crazy good! Creativity and inventiveness is the name of the game with kids. If we don't capture their imagination and win their attention it will be very limited how much they really take in, and take home.

In 2013 we dismantled our Sunday children's ministry (Sunday School) and replaced it with Lightforce, a dynamic, loud and expressive form of children's church. Basically making learning fun and exciting. Some of the kids now drag their mums and dads out of bed on a Sunday because they are desperate to get to Lightforce! The youth work was similar in that I used to organise treasure hunts, fancy dress travelling suppers and mystery tours in our minibus when we'd set out to different members houses and have food and fun with charades and games of one sort or another. It wasn't long before 25-30 young people were in regular attendance. On one occasion we took about 100 people to Alton Towers on our Church Family Day Out. About 40 people were in the church, the rest were made up from people outside the church. I think this is a big key to growth and winning new people. Really we are far too 'churchified' in many ways.

I'm still very big on Sunday attendance and having a main, large moment of witness and declaration when as many of the church assemble as possible. I think this gives the church great definition and identity and is I believe vital to the progress and vision of the local church. Today there seems to be a very sketchy view of what a church should be, what it should look like etc. It's what happens *from* the church that is most important though. I liken it simply to the fishing boats of the disciples. The boat was the means which transported them to where they needed to be. It facilitated them to catch fish. It couldn't catch fish anymore than a MacDonald's cooks a burger! It's people who catch fish and people who cook burgers. When people say, "Oh the church is this, the church is that", I'm not sure whether they do the maths! What is the church? It's people! It's me, it's you, it's ... ***them!!*** But what they're really saying is "those people who lead it, run it, manage it" etc. in effect "those people". But strangely enough, *they never mean themselves!* As I used to say to a lot of those who say "I'm not going to church, it's full of hypocrites" ... "why not come along yourself? There's room for one more!"

The boat the disciples fished from is a very good example of the local church. The fisherman saw amazing miracles *'from'* the boat. The amazing catch of fish, the stilling of the storm, the preaching to the multitudes at the bay of Tabgha from the boat effectively using the bay of water as an amphitheatre with built in natural PA system. Peter walked on water from the boat, deliverance came to Legion from the boat, the disciples were miraculously transported to the shore from the boat! Miracles didn't happen *in* the boat, they happened *from* the boat. Incredible and prophetic stuff. People say why don't we see more miracles in church on Sunday? Well most of the miracles God wants to do He wants to do *from* the church not *in* the church. It's like asking God to clean and cook the fish while they're in the boat. The place to do that is out *from* the boat. We need miracles in the market place, i.e. at people's places of work and business, as well as at their homes and in their difficult circumstances. We do get things all a bit mixed up and get a bit "churchified" by our understanding of church (or lack of it). For me, church should have several key elements within it. I think that Acts 2:42 probably gives us the briefest and best guide for what a church should look like. They followed the apostles doctrine; what we believe, fellowship; who are we believing with, breaking of bread; this to me denotes far more than a communion service, but some kind of ordered remembrance of the Lord's death and resurrection; and prayer; a very neglected aspect of most of our personal and church lives. Church is about 'community' but it has to go much much further than this!

One of the most amazing things we ever did in our community was hold a bonfire night and firework display free of charge for our local neighbourhood. Alas, seasons come and seasons go. You simply couldn't do it now without a whole rigmarole of red tape, health and safety measures with the bonfire alone let alone the fireworks! Recently we visited a local bonfire event near Wythenshawe in Manchester with two of our young people who we meet fairly regularly with. We were cordoned off from the bonfire so far away we could hardly see it let alone feel its worth! Pointless, absolutely pointless! I get so fed up of the bureaucracy in our country these days. It is stifling us economically, socially and in virtually every way you can think of, not to mention the stress it creates for people trying to get on with making a living! Anyway, back to the bonfires we did. The last one we were able to do, we had about 500 people attend. Most of us from the church of about 70 now, were just busy running around serving people with teas and coffees, treacle toffee, toffee apples and the like. The bonfire and the Guy Fawkes were great that year. The firework display was brilliant. One of our guys spent about £250 on them that year, plus we all chucked in a few quid too, to make it extra special. It was the last of its kind as the health & safety gurus started to see it as a great opportunity to wield their new-found power and authority. Along with many great community initiatives it became too onerous to do anymore. A measure of things to come. These kind of events though were very instrumental in building the church community.

We were by this time really "cooking on gas". The church was growing and was extremely excited. We had purchased our site and the future looked full of promise and blessing. However, new challenges are never too far away, whatever the stage of the journey we're on. A few things were about to happen that would test our nerve as well as our faith. 'Crossing The Rubicon' is in fact marching on the enemy's territory. A battle of some kind is inevitable.

SECTION TWO

"The Mondeo Years"

Chapter Eight

THE RAVENS
BEGIN TO ARRIVE

*"Passion is a powerful force: if properly channelled,
it is unstoppable." Robert Kiyosaki*

Towards the end of 1990, just over four years after our arrival, we had seen tremendous blessing. The church, though still far too small in my opinion, had 70 plus regular attenders. We had held several events including baptisms, which we had seen up to 150 people attend. This for me was a benchmark of progress. My aim was to reach this on a weekly basis as an average. I believe church should just grow naturally as we do the things we're supposed to do. Most of the time we have to just remove the obstacles to growth rather than introduce new formulas and structures. Having said this, some strategies are helpful in that they allow and facilitate growth a lot easier. Other things would occupy our time in the following weeks however, and there would be a number of twists and turns in the road ahead which were about to happen!

The Head-teacher from the primary school where we were meeting called me. "Pastor Hallam, I need you to come and see me as soon as possible! We have a problem we need to sort out." ... "Okay", I said, "I'll come right away". The problem was our ladies' shoes (hope it was the ladies!) especially their stilettos (and we had a few girls in the church who were budding Imelda Marcos

89

followers) had pockmarked the beautiful maple wood flooring. It was, like wow, really bad, but no-one had noticed it until now! We were told we had to leave by Christmas. In two months' time. In the meantime we had to ensure no more damage was done by our ladies. There was nothing else for it though. I had to find new alternative premises for us ... within two months. Whenever there's a problem there's always a solution.

Sometimes it might not appear to be the best solution. Other times God turns up with something better. This was to prove such a moment. Around the corner from our new site there was a Comprehensive School called Oakwood. It became a replacement for the old Oakwood High School that had now been demolished and was our new church site. I got an appointment to see the Assistant Head-teacher, Ed Wyley. He became a great supporter of ours for over twenty years even though he was an agnostic. He loved our work in the community and later on, our overseas work. I told him about our problem and he was keen to help. The main hall was not really accessible though and unsuitable to us in any case. There was in his opinion a ideal alternative possible. At the front of the school, there was a unit which was self-contained which the sixth formers used. It had a kitchen, a room that could seat about 120 and we could rent it for £100 a week. We could have a set of keys and display our church banner on the chain link fencing on the main road. It was, as Ed said, ideal! We started worshipping there in January 1991 and we called ourselves The Lighthouse Family Church in readiness for our eventual move to our new premises sometime in 1991. The new premises we were using on Sundays was just around the corner from our new site! Truly amazing!

In November 1990, I had my first ever trip overseas. It was a pastors' trip to Israel. A guided tour kind of thing which had been subsidised by the Israeli Government. I wanted to go but stumping up the £160 was not really do-able for me in those days. At this point I was only on about £70 a week as every bit of extra cash just got shovelled into the building fund. Plus we were having to find £150 a week for the new place we were worshipping in. Our offerings were healthy though at about £4-500 each week. Plus we had a further £1,200 a week or so coming into the coffers from our training scheme which was going really well now and our play-group. Our playgroup just about paid the bills and small salaries including my wife's who although she was on a small amount (£100 per week) it was more than I was drawing. These were very hard days for us financially. We struggled to pay bills and to shop properly. We were very happy though and no price would be too high to see The Lighthouse brought to birth. I am keen to put the figures in this book for the benefit of pastors and leaders starting out today. Although the sums are pretty meaningless when com-pared with today's figures, it's still fairly easy when accompanied by the dates to see how difficult it was. Our building fund had increased to about £45,000, a lot of money in those days, but still wide of the mark when compared to what we needed.

The Israel trip went ahead as someone was adamant I should go and a family member paid for me to go! It was just superb. I will never forget the things I saw and the things I learnt there. Even today over twenty five years on from that first visit these things live with me. When I got back in November that year we went to pick up a new addition to our family: Star, our new Border Collie. He was 10 weeks old and straight off a farm in Derbyshire. What a character too! Previously, we'd had a Border Collie called Boss from a farm near where we bought Star. Unfortunately, he had a sickness like pancreatic cancer that eventually made me have to take him to the vet and put him to sleep. It was a horrible heart-rending moment, one that I will never forget. He was only three and a half years old. So ... another 'Star' was born. We had no chil-dren of our own at this point and we were not really too bothered we hadn't been expecting, so to speak. We were too 'full on' to worry about stuff like that at that moment. We'd only been mar-ried just over five years so we thought, plenty of time left yet for a family of our own. We had no idea what trials lay ahead in this department, and it's probably just as well we didn't know too!!

By the time we entered 1991, the year we actually founded The Lighthouse Christian Centre, we were starting to be recognised as a good witness in the southern part of Manchester. We moved into our new, temporary school premises on Nell Lane around the corner from the new site. I had several meetings with our builders who wanted to get the building started especially since "laying off" the architects who had priced our new building at £450,000. I had managed to re-negotiate a final cost of £265,000 (a saving of £185,000!) True, it was a smaller building and the finishes less grandiose, but it wasn't that much different in terms of functionality. One of the biggest savings off this was professional fees which were within the D&B costings. This alone I believe saved us between £30-35,000 in professional fees. Well the paperwork was signed by our HQ and another Rubicon was passed. We had passed the point of no return yet again. We had approximately £160,000 including the premises we had sold. We were still short of £105,000. Plus we would need at least £15,000 to furnish the centre and another £10,000 for the car park. We convinced our Head Office that if we could just get the building up there would be no problem with getting the rest. To be fair to them they accepted this and we went for it.

I had by this time drawn up a kind of business plan for our new Lighthouse Nursery. I was able to meet some really influential people through our childcare and the training scheme we ran. We planned to re-model the whole of the playgroup into a Childcare Centre offering sessional care and full daycare to parents. We aimed for a 40 place Nursery. One day, I heard of the City Action Team, CAT for short. They were giving grants to organisations working with children and with those returning to employment or needing childcare to obtain full or part time employment. I called them on the telephone. I explained our situation. They came to meet us. They were very impressed with our plans and our vision. It's amazing how people who are not part of the church can get really excited at stuff the church can pull off. I think it's a fallacy that people won't support projects which are faith based. I just think we need to frame things properly. Obviously without compromising our values and beliefs, but yes, it can be done. And we were about to prove it. We ended up getting £50,000 from them. I went and got a further £15,000 off them too! More about that later. It's amazing what can come from one simple phone call. I remembered the word that Billie Jay had spoken to us. "God will command the ravens to feed you" It was happening in front of our very eyes. We still however had a shortfall of £55,000. This would have to be bridged next.

We also had a signed contract to say the builders would start the Lighthouse Project on the 15th day of January 1991. We anticipated the start date eagerly. We would have to wait a bit longer though. In January 1991 we had a really bad problem. Another "botch up". The city council's then surveyors had effectively landlocked us on the site. When we purchased the site, we were told there would be no access to the site from the main road, Sandy Lane onto which the church faced. The one and only vehicular access point had to be to the rear of the site which was through the new housing development. The trouble was, the company who were doing the new development would not allow our cement mixers, plant and machinery down "their" road! In fact they had dropped several pallets of breeze blocks in the middle of the road to prevent us accessing the site. I went to see the company bosses, who said there was nothing they could do, and no they didn't want our trucks, plant and machinery driving though their development as it was a security hazard and potentially damaging to some of their construction plans. I would need to take it up with their solicitors. I basically did so, but in the meantime I resorted to other measures as well.

Firstly, in true Pentecostal fashion I declared two weeks of prayer and fasting to overcome the situation. Secondly, on the basis that it's easier to get forgiveness than permission, I instructed our builders to approach the site from Sandy Lane (the front of the site). The original cast iron fencing was still in place, and two sets of double gates were there, they just hadn't been used. I unlocked them and opened them and instructed the builders to get on with the job. They did so. Within two days the council chiefs were down reading me the riot act. Man! It was like I'd bombed the Town Hall or something!! I explained it was their office that botched the job up. They said plainly "We're not interested in who did what when or where. You cannot use this access point at all." I was livid by now. "Well what do you expect us to do? Helicopter the concrete in?" I said petulantly. "You can do what you like", they said. "But you can't use this access point." "Well thank you for nothing" I immediately replied, whilst turning my back on them and walking off. Under it all, I knew we'd get through somehow.

Two days later the city council had placed concrete bollards in front of the cast iron gates on Sandy Lane. They are there to this day! I've never seen the council move as fast! Incredible! The problem was we had signed a contract. Builders had to be paid. Bills had to be paid, this could be really expensive. I prayed, very fervently. The whole church prayed. It was a Friday. The builders simply had to get back on site on Monday otherwise the budget would begin to increase. But we have a God who is never outmanoeuvred. Over the weekend we had one of the heaviest snowfalls I've seen. The whole site lay under two feet of snow. On the Monday it was totally and completely covered. The builders came from Yorkshire. They phoned on the Monday and said "Sorry Paul, there's no way we are going to be able to make it until this clears." I said "No problem lads, we'll be ready for you when it clears." "Okay Paul, great. Oh, and how is the problem with the access for our vehicles now? Is it sorted?" "Ahhh yes", I said, "everything is being dealt with, it's all under control now." Well, it was! It was under God's control for sure. The weather delay had saved us, at exactly at the right time.

We prayed like mad and I spoke to solicitors and legal eagles for the whole of the next two weeks. The snow lay frozen on the ground until the Thursday of the following week. The builders checked everything was all clear for Monday. "Yes, all's well", I said. We prayed like there was no tomorrow over the Saturday and Sunday. In actual fact after the Sunday morning service that weekend I organised for as many of our people to come to the site as possible. We actually laid hands on the pallets of breeze blocks. We cursed them, rebuked them and cast them into the sea, (verbally of course) though it did enter my mind to take a JCB to them hahaha! We must have looked like a bunch of basket cases conducting an ancient ritual or something! I laugh about it now. The next morning, they were gone. Seriously! I do not know to this day who removed them or how, but yes! They had been removed. Everything was sorted. Now we could really begin The Lighthouse Project!

Chapter Nine

FOUNDATIONS, FRUSTRATIONS AND FINISHES

'It's not always on the frontline where we face
our greatest opposition!'

We started the building work in late February. It was cold and dark on those mornings, but our purpose and our cause just brightened everything up. The first job that had to be done was to dig out and lay the foundations. It was to be a slab foundation rather than strip footings which just basically carried the weight of the walls. We were also building on sandy soil (the name of the road, Sandy Lane gave us a clue!) and the raft or slab foundation was ideal for this. The guys who worked on site worked really hard and fast too. They laid the foundation including the steel mesh that reinforced it. Then they had to float it with a power plate and then use a vibration plate. This can be a very long and messy job and in this instance it could not have been worse. As they were laying the concrete it absolutely "tipped it down". It meant the lads had to work virtually through the night. It did not, needless to say, go down too well with the neighbours.

What I did not mention prior to all this, is that in the lead up to acquiring the site and launching the project, we had a constant running battle with a group of neighbours who opposed everything and anything we did and stood for. It was a New-Age group who were openly pagan, anti-Christian and couldn't stand the fact that we were coming to set up a church and community centre opposite their home. The boys laying the foundation late into the night got a 'real pasting' from these neighbours. The morning after it was like a battleground. It got very bad indeed, with the Yorkshire lads really giving them some stick. I tried to calm things down as best as I could. All the tradesmen said to me time and time again "What's up with these people? They just don't want a church here do they?" They were spot on. Again, in the lead up to launching the Lighthouse Project, I had organised a very thorough survey of the neighbourhood to see who would be for and against the development. This was something that had to be done in any case for the planning permission application. I had asked residents which services that we would provide which they were they most likely to use. A letter with a questionnaire was prepared. The childcare facilities were a massive hit. I was confident that we would fill the nursery almost immediately. I also had a bona-fide record of the residents' eagerness to use our premises and services. We were accused of making up all the forms and completely fabricating the survey. But I had records of when the survey was carried out, addresses and those who conducted the survey at the time. It was a fairly watertight survey.

At the Town Hall, at a public meeting, I had to stand up and summarise the project, while thirty or so members of the public attended. I put our case forward the best way I knew how. The Council liked it. They did not like the aggressive tone of the objectors, who I firmly stated, were objecting not on any reasonable grounds but on the basis of our faith. The opposing party reacted badly to this. After the meeting, the leader of this group came and stood in front of me and pushed his face right into mine and was very close to hitting me in the face. He cursed me and shouted personal filth and abuse at me. I was calm. I'd met many a person like this in my past and to be honest I smiled and said something like, "Now I know where you're coming from." My two colleagues were flabbergasted. One of my team was about six foot three and stepped in. We went our way feeling a great moral and spiritual victory had been won. Indeed it had and our full planning permission was granted shortly after. It was however, quite literally a battle. We had won the first round, but there would be a few more unsavoury encounters to come.

The foundations were laid and next the steelwork arrived. Once this went up everything really started to take shape. I love this stage of any project. For me it's like painting a picture. In goes the background wash, then the different hues and colours, then the details. Exciting and enjoyable is how I always describe this. I had also put a very large advertising hoarding on the site saying "The New Home of The Lighthouse Christian Centre" with a smaller brief description of some of the activities we would be providing. There was a particular Sunday that I organised the church to meet up on site after the morning service to dedicate the foundations to the Lord. A member of ours and good friend Jim Codd filmed it. I still have the tape today and while the fashion is hilarious, (of all of us I might add, not just me!) it is a very precious and special piece of footage. I also prepared the foundation stone in advance, which was quite a sight. Mags loves to see it played now and again, as I strode out in front along with the foundation stone on my shoulder as about 50 or so of us marched to the new site after the Sunday morning service. It was a very special moment and is captured on our "timeline" we now have on our mezzanine in our new centre.

Once the steelwork had been erected the brickwork and block work began. Brilliant! The shape and form of the centre became very clear to all. We were building it to seat 200 though we did it in such a way as we could get a few more in the foyer area when needed. It was all ground level. I had discussed the possibility of putting a first floor room in over the nursery section, but was told by the builders that this would not be possible as the space did not allow it. Once the roof trusses went in though, I went back and checked this as I was never convinced by their argument. They agreed, it was very possible actually. I immediately spoke to the City Action Team again, who I asked to consider helping us to put a first floor room over the nursery so as to provide a Training Room for our childcare Trainees. They loved it, especially once they came on site! There is nothing like seeing things first hand to enable people to be inspired. They asked me how much we needed. "Only £18,000", I said. "Okay, we will see what we can

97

do" was the reply. We got £15,000 no problem. Unfortunately, getting the go ahead from them was far easier than getting the paperwork signed by our Head Office.

Now it seems like I'm always having a moan about our Head Office. I'm not! They have an incredibly difficult task. Overseeing some five hundred plus churches, with all their challenges and problems just cannot be easy. It's a monumental task which is certainly a lot harder to do now in our bureaucratic age with all the red tape and rules and regulations. But sometimes there are things in life that beggar belief. Here we were, sat on £65,000 worth of funding. All we needed was a signature from the trustees at our Head Office. The document had to be signed off by a certain date. They'd had the document for at least two months. I reminded them of the deadline to sign it. The reaction? "We will sign it when we are good and ready!" Unbelievable! Here's a secular organisation willing to put sixty five grand into one of 'their' churches and that's the attitude! I was completely beside myself. I had been asked how we were going to raise the money, now we were raising serious money they couldn't sign a piece of paper between them. Yes you can feel it! I was furious. I told them that I was coming down on such and such a date *and I was **not** leaving until I got the paperwork signed!* I went down to our Head Office and told them I had come to pick up the 'signed paperwork.' I arrived mid-morning and by two o'clock it still hadn't been signed. I paced the reception like a bull with with a sore head. Eventually, Brian Edwards, our then Missions Director saw me and asked me if I was okay. I told him the story and he was very sympathetic. I will go and have a word he assured me. He did. The problem was sorted within about two hours. I don't know how he did it. I suspect he went and took it round to our current General Superintendent Wynne Lewis who would have signed it in seconds. Wynne was a fabulous man. A true hero of the faith who loved red tape just about as much as a turkey loves Christmas! I got the signatures and got the funds released. It was probably one of the most stressful encounters I've ever had and one that for all the wrong reasons will live with me forever. I think it's moments like this that seriously wind you up and give you real insight into where the battle lines are really drawn. It's not always on the frontline where you face your greatest opposition.

A word or two about our denomination here. I am sincerely grateful to Elim for giving me the opportunity to serve God and live out my call for Him. As I look around I believe that for me The Elim Pentecostal Church of GB and Ireland is the most releasing and at the same time most accountable of all the Pentecostal denominations. I'm not a big fan of denominations, but they do have their place and I certainly would not want to lead a totally 'independent' church with no accountability and the lack of a solid network of Churches and leaders that have a meaningful sense of belonging. There's always going to be pros and cons, but as I said and state again I'm very grateful for a denomination that's solidly based and rooted in the scriptures and has great foundations too.

So back to the job in hand. Now we had the funds from the CAT team, we were only £55,000 short. I had arranged a bank loan through our headquarters for the sum of £25,000 which I knew was serviceable from our new nursery without it stretching us too much. I had also been offered an interest-free loan for £30,000. Then an incredible thing happened. Our bank account balance in our deposit account suddenly shot up by £18,000! I checked the account. It was correct. Someone had made a deposit to us. I suddenly realised it was money from a student who had been with us some years ago. He had moved on to the north east of England, but had mentioned he had an apartment that he was selling and wanted us to get a large percentage of it. He asked for details of our account and left Manchester. I showed my usual enthusiasm and thanked him, but basically forgot all about it. The £18,000 was just what we needed to furnish the centre and to do the car park. We ended up doing all the grunt work for the car park ourselves. Digging out, putting in the hardcore and the drainage. Eventually we did it all for about £6,000. We spent the £18,000 on the furnishings and PA system etc. One of the amazing things at the time was the PA system costing us £10,000! Wow what a sum to pay out for back in 1991. A few years ago, (in 2010) I signed a cheque for £150,000 for just part of our new PA system! How things change!

We had a little test with the ceiling. To do it in nice polysty-rene tiles would be in budget. But if we wanted a pine tongue and groove ceiling it would cost an additional £10,000. Unfortunately there was no comparison. We all agreed, especially Mags, that a pine ceiling was nothing to God to pay for. Her take on it was we shouldn't compromise anything in this part of the building. We went ahead with it. It was always a beautiful crafted ceiling which was an unequal hexagonal in shape. Very difficult to do, but exceptionally aesthetic. The job was done and looked superb. I'm not sure now how we managed to pay the extra amount, but we did. It was another lesson to be learned.

Chapter Ten

THE LIGHTHOUSE BEGINS TO SHINE

"If you have the passion for your dream then the price tag won't stop you."

The date had been set for the Grand Opening. It was to be Saturday 31st August. We literally had to slave to make it happen. The bills were coming in thick and fast. With the D&B company, they had given me a schedule of costs. This was invaluable and helped me juggle all the finances in order to make things work. One month we had to pay £64,500 at the peak of the project. Although we'd received funds it was still tight as the loan money hadn't come through yet. We managed, but it was tight, very tight. We also had to set to work on the car park which was hard work. I hired a mini-excavator (which I'd driven many times before in my past). We had an amazing team of about a dozen people who hand-balled and barrowed soil, hardcore and cement. It took a few weeks but we levelled it, hard-cored it and edged it around with concrete edgings. We also had to edge around the whole of the building. Another job we did ourselves. I was very much "hands on" in this as was Mags too! Once we had edged it we filled it with stone chippings to make sure no standing water ever rested against the brick work. We were "cream crackered" by the time we'd done this. I negotiated with a small family business to tarmac the car park. They wanted £7,000 to do it. I got them to do it for £5,000. They did a great job too I must say.

The day for the Opening came. It was a really wonderful day. About 350 people came on the day. It was obviously a real jam getting them all in. We had to use all the foyer area too. My Father–in-law Pastor Alex Tee spoke and Pastor Paul Epton came and took part in the service too. A letter of congratulation from our General Superintendent Wynne Lewis, (who, due to ministerial appointments could not be present) was read out. We also had people present from the local council, charitable organisations, other churches and other bodies. To be honest though, I was really glad when it was all over! I just wanted to get motoring now on building a great and influential church that would be The Lighthouse that I believe The Lord had shown me. Also, I couldn't get the image of the church at Antioch out of my mind. At least we had reached a point now where we could begin to harvest more effectively than ever before. What amazes me beyond belief to this day is that in less than five years we had seen the church grow from sixteen adults and three children to just over 120 now, plus had gone from a tiny little premises in a backwater, to moving into our purpose built multi-functional church centre, on a three quarter acre plot of land in a busy residential area. Boom!!

We also had our "Community Opening Day" complete with the media and several political big hitters at the time. Robert Keys, the then Cabinet Minister for Employment came as the guest of honour. A really nice gentleman who showed avid enthusiasm in how we'd manage to arrive at where we had in such a short space of time! "Well," I said, "this is just the beginning for us, we are very excited about the future." The City Action Team were present, plus a man of great influence who became a personal friend of mine for some time. Michael Bracegirdle. He was a well connected, extremely successful man who was the CEO of Jarvis Training Management, (JTM). Jarvis was one of the largest construction companies of the day. He managed their training division. A friend of Princess Diana, Margaret Thatcher and many other well-known people. He was fascinated at our work and in my role in particular. He couldn't believe I was a "priest" as he put it! Hahaha! I pointed out to him I wasn't a priest but a "pastor

". He never quite got that one. Michael however was to prove to be one of our closest supporters and a great influencer for us. I spent quite a lot of time in his office sharing with him how God had done this and how he'd done that. He was more interested in how I'd become a preacher though. Sometimes we think people are more interested in what we "do" than who we "are". It very often just isn't that which draws people, but our enthusiasm and our passion for God. *It's who we are that really counts.* He told me he once wanted to become a priest, but he had got married so there was no chance of that!

We had set up a training scheme via JTM, and it was just great. Mags & I developed it to 25 Trainees. It was bringing in good finance after this development. I was picking up two monthly cheques totalling nearly £4,000 every month. Our nursery, which was duly opened by Mags and her staff, was 70% full in a matter of a month of opening! It was always 90-95% full six months on, with a waiting list as long as your arm. Our pre-construction survey had proved to be spot on. The income level alone from the nursery was better than I had expected. We had smashed our target of being 50% full in the first 5-6 weeks, and the development of the training centre brought in good income in which to not only pay for a great training scheme but also staff, facilities including 100% of our loan with the bank. I was still paid a pittance and in all fairness the then treasurer was not happy about it and spoke to the leadership team to suggest it was not healthy for me to be on £72 per week still. They immediately raised it to £90. I was fine with this although it was still a struggle for us personally. I've never been driven by money for personal gain. It disinterests me. I love creating and earning money for The Kingdom as I put it. I love it! The bible clearly teaches that God gives us the ability to create wealth:

> *But remember the Lord your God, for it is he who gives you the ability to produce wealth, and so confirms his covenant, which he swore to your ancestors, as it is today. (Deuteronomy 8:18 NIV).*

Jesus told us to *"Seek first the Kingdom of God and His righteousness."* Then He says *"ALL these things shall be added unto you" (Matthew 6:33 NIV).*

I am creative and pretty industrious and everyone knows a bit of a workaholic too! I have to watch this as I can work for weeks without taking any proper days off! I am what I do, and I do what I am, which is not always good. There's a price to pay for this kind of involvement. Anyhow, I had at least three members of staff far better paid than me. It took me a year to realise it! Hahaha! At least one was my wife who was making everything hang together in the nursery and training centre, even though I was the manager of it. I didn't touch a single penny at the time until I realised I was struggling doing what I was doing. My car needed changing badly. I had a Ford Orion which had gone round the clock. Before this I had a Ford Cortina which had gone round the clock twice. I remember when the engine was smoking through the dashboard! Not good at all. My enduring and lasting memory of this was when I took a funeral and went to the crematorium afterwards. We had just finished and I personally had told the guys there not to start the furnace up too early as people tended to hang around for quite a while afterwards. We didn't want to be seeing lots of smoke. That would be embarrassing! They did as requested, no plume of smoke to be seen anywhere. Then, as I started my engine, I nearly gassed the entire cortège leaving the crematorium in a cloud of smoke like Del Boy and Rodders of Only Fools and Horses! Maybe very comical but hardly comforting to the mourners.

The other memory of this otherwise dear but fast-losing-favour car was taking a Projects Manager of the building company who we were looking to use at the time through the city in my car. The whole of the gear stick came out in my hand as I approached a corner. I had to manoeuvre the car in such a way as I took the corner with my passenger feeling he was being driven by some one-handed lunatic who loved to take corners with one hand on the wheel and the other on the gear stick. It was the last straw. I said to the guys. Okay, look! I need more than I'm getting now. I'm running this Training Centre and bringing in about £4,000 pcm, I am asking for 10% to supplement my salary. They agreed immediately. It's not that people want to be mean sometimes, it's just that if you go through life saying nothing, nothing is what you seem to get! This is especially so if you are a strong leader and a lead pastor too. No one is really going to say, "Oh pastor it's time we helped you and paid you more", or even "How are you coping financially Paul?" Hahaha! In all the years of service at the church this never, ever was asked by anyone! Never! People always just expected us to ... well ... just get on with it!! I got my 10% and my wages doubled immediately, and I changed my car too. I bought a Ford Sierra! It was Rossi Red and it flew! I loved it!

Things were going very well indeed. I was very encouraged. We had taken cheap holidays in caravans to this point. I had also never missed a Sunday in the last five years apart from my visit to Israel. (It's hard to get back for a Sunday from there!). Even when we went on our holidays in those years, I drove back to take the services. I felt it was very necessary. To me it was like raising a baby. We had to be there, it was just simply a must. The only time I started to take some time out at weekend when on holiday was when we started going on our holidays overseas, which at this point we hadn't done. Today, the church is not an infant. It's strong, mature and has great leaders too. I don't need to be there at weekends, though I miss it like crazy when I'm not there. It's still our home. It's where Mags and I belong and belonging is massive to us. It's fair to say though, things were going to have to change in this area as a new call from God was about to be made known to me. The Mondeo Years were going to gear up to more like the Ferrari years soon! Everything was set to take off.

The next few years were going to be incredible in terms of what we managed to bring about both at home and overseas. This next part of this book reads like I've exaggerated things. I promise you I haven't. It was our most industrious time ever. Personally it was nothing short of a season of miracles when God provided in astounding and unusual ways.

Chapter Eleven

THE CALL OF MISSION

"The need is the call ..." Pastor Bill Wilson

The church grew very quickly after we moved in and we went from eighty members attending each Sunday to over one hundred and twenty in the space of three months. Believe it or not this created its own difficulties. We had our existing members coming in Sunday after Sunday only to find they couldn't sit where they normally sat! I loved it! It was very therapeutic for the church in a funny way. I called a 'closed' meeting for all the members. I'm not a massive fan of church membership and we introduced partnership a few years back to give more focus on expectations for the church leadership, as well as for the members/partners. I'm a member of the RAC but I don't want to see them, unless I have a problem with my car, which of course I hope is never! I'm a member of the gym and I can come and go as I please. A partner of something is an investor. A recipient of benefits, yes, but a responsible person within that organisation who has a duty to help, support and be involved in that organisation. We can be just like consumers in church life. There are lots of consumer Christians today and it is one of the reasons why the church lacks influence and credible witness. Churches just slip into the 80/20 mode of operation. 20% of the people doing 80% of the work. This really needs to be turned around for us to be effective. I think a realistic standard is to get 60% of the people actively participating in the work of the ministry. The meeting I called was to communicate how to deal with the growth and increase in the church. I reminded the people this wasn't "their church" it wasn't "my church" or anyone else's for that matter. It was His church and we had to remember that we existed *for those not yet here*. Even then, we were starting to lay down a generational attitude to building church. Our strap-line today is "building the church of tomorrow today". This was totally organic to us. It was something we just did.

Our youth work by now was exceptional. We had about thirty to thirty five teenagers and about forty to fifty children in our mid-week Tuesday Club. Unfortunately this declined over the years due to a lack of dynamic and passionate leadership. Without that you just get a 'maintenance spirit' which lacks vision and creativity and therefore becomes stale and a bit lifeless. Not good, no not at all. We are addressing this currently in our new location.

The people in the church responded well to this clarion call to manage the growth and expect for more. Our offerings had increased by now to well over a thousand pounds each week. We had taken on an assistant pastor for two years too. Gregory Kane, a hard worker and someone who genuinely has passion and love for God. He married one of our students, Sharon the previous year we moved into our new centre. We used Ivy Cottage, a well-known Evangelical church for the service, as we had nowhere to conduct the wedding. Gregory and Sharon eventually went off to the Mission field, to Zimbabwe for a number of years. Several assistants came and went. All of them playing their part in the process of building church with us here in Manchester. Ken Gabbadon came for a couple of years too while he was a chaplain in Strangeways Prison (now revamped and renamed Manchester Prison). Ken was pastor of the Elim Church, Rochdale in the north of Manchester too for a while. Ken has since joined the Anglican church and is living his dream, doing what he does best, being a very caring man, and very pastoral. Each person played their part and gained a unique experience too, in being part of an exciting, daring young church, The Lighthouse Christian Centre.

While we had been building the new centre, a gentleman came and joined himself to us. A very good man with a great heart for mission. In 1991 the awful plight of the Romanian orphans had fully just come to light. Romania experienced a revolution at the close of 1989 when people became so fed up of the repressive regime of Ceasescu their dictator ruler. He and his wife had accumulated unbelievable wealth at the expense of countless poor souls, in a country buckling under the weight of famine and poverty. The poverty became so acute that up to 300,000 of the nation's children were placed into orphanages up and down the country. Many of these children had been born by way of Ceasescu's prohibition of family planning. He wanted lots of large families so as to encourage a vast population of children who would be his Romanian future. He actually did not like villages but preferred large towns and cities so he bulldozed many homes and forced people to move into these larger towns. It was all about controlling the masses of course. Virtually every home in Romania had satellite TV, so they could watch him on television giving out his edicts and speeches. The whole plan backfired. The revolution which started in Timisoara instantly spread to the rest of the country, and into the capital, Bucharest. Eventually, the despotic leader and his wife were arrested and tried for treasonable acts against the Romanian people. The trial took place over Christmas and they were both found guilty and sentenced to death. They were both taken outside the trial room and executed in broad daylight on Boxing Day 1989. Photographs were posted around the nation so the people could see they were dead.

This chap, Trevor and his son Mike, started attending the church in 1991. Trevor came to me while we were building the church and said, "Will you come to Romania with me?" I knew he was heavily involved with gathering clothes and food to take to Romania on trucks. He had linked up with the firemen who had been doing the same. There was huge publicity about it. I told Trevor that as I was busy building the church I was unable to go, but after we finished it I would be open to go on a visit. Little did I know this would be the beginning of a twenty year plus journey that would see Mags and myself with several abandoned kids who see us as their parents now and we see them as our kids! We've literally just got back from visiting a few of them and celebrating birthdays with them. Some have already moved to the

UK, to Manchester, to be with us as part of The Lighthouse here. Incredible, just unbelievable!

With the close of 1991, Trevor came to see me. He'd bought two tickets to go out to Romania in January 1992. I couldn't refuse. I'd set myself up for this it! It's funny though how things transpire. We often complain about interruptions in pastoral ministry, but they can be the most amazing opportunities in life. This was to be once such "interruption." I packed my bags for the very short whistle-stop visit. It turned out to be one of the most incredible moments of my life.

We flew out to Bucharest, Romania's capital on the Monday. When we got to the tiny airport it was something of a culture shock. We were searched at gunpoint by several army personnel. We had to apply for our visas early on in those days, though it was a simple process and one Trevor managed quite easily. We stayed with a lovely Baptist family in an apartment there. We discussed where it was we should go. We had heard of a small group of Christians in Slatina, in the Oltenia district in the Southern part of the country. We felt drawn to visit them. Slatina was about 140 miles west of Bucharest. About 80 miles of motorway as it turned out, then the rest meandered through villages and industrial wastelands. In Bucharest it was surreal. There were many cranes with their loads just left as if in suspended animation. There were no street lights, and nothing in the shops at all. To get diesel you had to queue for hours and hours. Most Romanians queued overnight to get fuel. The people walked with their heads down and no one made eye contact. Today I have many many friends in Romania. For me it is like a second home. We have a very good infrastructure there, which is the result of twenty years of ministry. It makes me laugh when I hear the young people talk about how tough it is there today. It is light years away from those first five to eight years just after the revolution. Change has come to the country, slowly, yes, but it has come and it is a far cry from the desperation of those early days. I have loads of young people in particular who I'm close to, who I tell stories to, of how it was when I first came to their country. As I mentioned earlier, we now have several children over there who we took from the orphanages to live in our Family Centre we went on to build out of Manchester. This was and still is called 'Casa Noastra'. These kids are just like our own and we love them to bits. Mags and I travel regularly to see them. The oldest is in his twenties as I write and is in the UK working. God gave them to us, and us to them through great trial and pain. We are still involved in their lives.

Our attempt to go to Slatina at the time was thwarted by way of the weather. The snowfall had been unbelievable in the few days before our visit. The Romanians fly and land planes without blinking, even in several feet of snow. They are used to it. It's something they have learned to live with. I've since flown in and out of Bucharest so many times in conditions which if prevailed in the UK would have brought the nation to a complete standstill. The problem was, that at the time we were travelling it was about 20 degrees below zero. Most people were not travelling far, if at all. Should we risk it? Would anyone attempt to take us in any case? We were unsure. The night time experience I was about to have would remove all doubt as to where we should go!

We were sleeping on two mattresses on the floor of the living room, in our apartment. I had a dream in which I saw three men, sitting in front of us on a bed. I saw their faces and me and Trevor sat on chairs facing them. I woke up only to hear an inner voice that said "Three men are waiting for you". I tried to go back to sleep, but the images of the three men kept coming into my mind. The voice continued to be repeated to me "Three men are waiting for you." It was about 3.30am when this happened. I quietly asked "Trevor! ... Are you awake?" "Yeah", he said, "wide awake. I can't help thinking about this place Slatina. We have got to try to get there." I told him what had just happened and we prayed together over the whole matter. It was like something straight out of the book of Acts (where Peter was on the rooftop–Acts 10:19). We tried to get some sleep. We succeeded a bit, I think, though I do remember vividly hearing the telephone ring at about 6.30am. I also heard a couple of words I understood. 'Da' which means 'yes' and 'Multsumesc' which means 'Thank you' and 'Slatina'! We got up at about 7am, washed and dressed properly and tried to eat the breakfast with as much zeal as we could 'manufacture'. I'm not a fan of sausages and pig fat at any time, especially for breakfast *and fried*! But it was, as they described it, a delicacy, and no doubt something they'd queued up for hours for and paid a king's ransom for. They chatted excitedly to us about the phone call, as we tried to look like we were eating our special VIP breakfast with relish. Someone had called from Slatina saying they had someone in the church who had a dream that people from England came to help them. I shared my experience I had overnight. We knew we had to try to get there.

We were told of a man who was coming in his Dacia motor car to pick us up at about 9 am to take us there. We waited. The snow had started to freeze a bit and we were pensive but somehow assured we would reach our destination. Our transport arrived. All I can remember is this huge guy in a Russian Cossack hat with a white Dacia car. Dacia's were mass produced for the Eastern European market. Because they were made under Ceasescu's communist regime, they were built to last. This is because the service industry for cars is chiefly a part of the capitalist system. If things hardly ever go wrong with a product then you don't need a whole 'singing and dancing' parts and service industry. People fixed and repaired their cars themselves *'if'* they broke down, not *'when'* they broke down. Even today, I am amazed at the way Romanians can fix cars and mechanical things. One of the good things left over from the Communist era. Let's face it, there aren't many.

So, we got into our Dacia car and started our journey to Slatina. What an experience! We passed loads of abandoned vehicles. Trucks were by the roadside with guys lighting fires under the fuel tanks to thaw out the frozen diesel! It took us about six hours to complete the journey. When we arrived at, about 3pm, we were met by two guys by the roadside. They hugged us and kissed us and invited us to follow them into their apartment. The concrete blocks were very grimy and depressed looking. I have to tell you the smell was awful too. We ascended several flights of stairs, which were bordered by very rickety iron railings. We were escorted into an apartment not dissimilar to that which we'd just stayed in at Bucharest. We went into a nice warm room, which was good because the temperatures were freezing now outside. In the room were chairs for Trevor and myself and our interpreter, Ion (John), I think his name was. The two guys who met us at the roadside then sat down on the bed. I thought nothing of it, until a third man came and sat in the middle. Then it hit me. Bang!! It was exactly what I'd seen the previous night! I whispered to Trevor, "The three men I spoke about last night. These are the men." Trevor just whispered back something like "That's amazing!" We listened to all their stories. It was very interesting. They were part of a small Pentecostal church which met in a small house near the town centre. We promised we would help them as much as we could. We ended up bringing them a building on two Turkish trucks, plus they also ended up with an acre of land to build a new church. That's another story! Prepare to get an example of fact being stranger than fiction on that one!

While there we visited one of the local orphanages, the "Leaganul de Copii." Nothing on this planet could prepare us for what we saw!! It was like a concentration camp for kids! I came back determined to do something, anything I could as a pastor, leader and as a Christian. I have been going back ever since. It was Pastor Bill Wilson who said ... "The need is the call." *I believe it still is by the way.*

Once I'd returned to the UK we began to look at ways we could help with the situation and we brought together a group of like-minded people who would help us to formulate a long term strategy for the crisis that the children faced over there. In actual fact this gave the church a more missional feel just by default and it drew some wonderful people into our church and into our lives. One such couple are Justin and Jo Marks who have been with us now for over twenty years. They came to us as an engaged couple and it was the work we were doing in Romania that drew Jo especially to The Lighthouse. Jo and Justin were both students at the time, Jo studying Speech and Language Therapy and Justin studying Architecture. To say they were a blessing to us is an understatement! Jo and Justin became our most trusted and loyal companions in an amazing and adventurous journey spanning over twenty years now. They made not only The Lighthouse their home but their cause too. In the last chapter of the book of Romans in the New Testament of the bible, Paul lists several characters who were essential in his life's work and ministry. Similarly we read the same in 1 Chronicles, of David's mighty men. Jo and Justin would be at the top of our "mighty men and women" list.

Today, they are vocational pastors within the church, Jo still doing Speech and Language Therapy, and Justin Architecture. They brought an added dimension to the church which was to be so vital in growing the church.

Whilst there's addition in church life, there's also subtraction too. We lost our treasurer that year in quite bizarre circumstances. Since my visit to Israel, I organised a small group visit to go there from our church. With ten people I got to go free, with twenty people another free place was available. As it happened we got our twenty and I didn't take a free place but shared the saving of the two free places amongst the twenty people, making it an exceptional deal. The trouble is, our treasurer thought it was not good to be encouraging people to spend their money on something like this when we needed money for the new building! I've put this in my book, (without mentioning any names) so as to show how fickle and small-minded people can be. This person served us really well for about four years and was part of something great and really special but packed it all in for a trivial and misguided point of view. Since then I've always explained to those who work in finance in the church, they are in 'ministry ' too, and their job is not to decide *how to spend the funds that come in*, but to *account for the funds that come in*. Big difference! It's a shame too because the church was in blessing, paying its way and growing year on year. It's been well said, "the strength of a tree is in its ability to bend". I have seen this so many times that it's mind-blowing. The ability to bend and adapt is essential to all walks of life not just ministry. Sometimes if we simply do not bend we break. Today, I constantly remind our team and our staff that change is here to stay. That we need to be flexible and adaptable ready to move through the gears as the Lord leads. We have a brilliant team now, right through the ranks, something I thank God for continually and the calibre of our leaders is ultimately the most important factor in taking any church forward into blessing and fulfilment. They are familiar with the fact that from time to time we need to 'adapt, adjust and advance'–the simple Three 'A' Strategy I have always believed is necessary for fruitfulness and longevity.

Chapter Twelve

WANTED! ... FATHERS! THE COST? £...POA!

"Religion that God our Father accepts as pure and faultless is this; to look after orphans and widows in their distress and to keep oneself from being polluted by the world." James 1:27 NIV

Around the close of 1993 we had set the wheels in motion to create an International Charity which could raise funds for Romania and wherever else that we felt led to serve in. (I need to mention here, that I had tried to do the fund raising through our denomination but was told in no uncertain terms this would not be possible. In fairness though I was given full permission to set up an alternative charity for this purpose by the then General Superintendent of our denomination Wynn Lewis). On my early visits I used to go into the orphanages in Slatina. There were three orphanages there at the time, housing approximately 500 children in total from babies to eleven and twelve year olds. After this the children were transferred to Youth Centres. (These were even more detestable places. Really unimaginable!) Caesescu was born and raised in the town of Scornicesti less than twenty miles from Slatina. The industrial heartland of Romania is the south of the country. Many of the 300,000 children placed in orphanages were placed into institutions in the south of the country.

I visited the orphanages everytime I flew out to Romania. We managed to build a good relationship with the 'Madam Directors' (the title given to the Directors of these dreadful places). Most 'missionaries' who came to Romania in the early days went almost automatically to Arad in the west, where the Christian community is a whopping 15% of the population. Also Timisoara and Sibiu are popular areas. No wonder as both cities have all the best amenities as they were set up for tourism. But the Romanian Bible Belt is definitely in the west of the country certainly not the south. Very little missional input went into the south. I discovered that it was viewed as something of a graveyard for missionaries and pastors. Today, I can hardly think of a church with over a hundred people meeting. I have noticed when a church in the South gets to anywhere near this number it splinters, fragments and/or divides. The little church of about 30-40 people in Slatina needed help.

We set to, and brought goods and things from the UK to help with the church and encouraged the church to take a responsible attitude to the situation of the local orphanages and the children's needs. We set up a Storage and Deposit Depot donated to us by a local businessman (who, we later found out, expected his fair share of goodies in return!). We since came to realise the notion of a Romanian doing something for nothing is a foolish one! (There are exceptions but they're rare ones!) There's always a price tag somewhere along the line. This includes the Christian community too. In fact they often expected a lot more! Nevertheless we did the necessary to keep the boat afloat, without using bribes, we gave rewards, and those who trusted us did fairly well out of it. Our main priority was the kids in those wretched orphanages–I've often wanted to set up family type homes which are far more effective but far more costly too, and come with their own set of complex problems too. We went on to do this and the results are still in the balance.

The church was very small, and met in a house albeit a large house. The problem was that it was earmarked for demolition and the site to be used for the construction of a bank. The problem was "prophet John" (let's just call him that!) prophesied that no such plan existed and that God would protect them from all assailants. My own spirit did not agree with this and I went to visit the Primera (Romania's equivalent of our City Council Leader). He was basically a good man. He was honest with me and sympathised. He showed me the plans–and sure enough, there was the bank. He told me that everything had been signed off. I told him boldly of our plans to build a Storage and Distribution Centre and a Therapy Centre for the kids in the Orphanages. Again he was very supportive. "I will look to see if I can find a site", he said. I thought, okay, but I won't hold my breath. We chatted some more and he gave me some small gifts including a special commemorative pin badge to celebrate 50 years for the town of Slatina. I gave him a nice fountain pen and took my leave. It had been an appointment of divine destiny however and I was completely unaware at the time. Only looking back now can I see so clearly the invisible hand of God at work. But miracles were about to begin, I believe for the sake of the children. I am utterly, completely and totally convinced that God has a special love for children. I believe with all my heart we will be held to account for the lives we have neglected. James makes it clear as to the passion God has for those who are fatherless. (James 1:27–"Religion that God our Father accepts as pure and faultless is this; to look after orphans and widows in their distress and to keep oneself from being polluted by the world" NIV).

By the way, being fatherless has nothing to do with biology. What I mean by this is you may be a father biologically but have you been a father spiritually, emotionally, psychologically, mentally, physically and in example? Men need to get their act together in this area. Too many children are being destroyed through a lack of simple, responsible and loving fatherhood. We will be called to account for this for sure! It's not just a case of being a parent. It is being a Dad that counts. I realise now that I've spent about 20 years of my ministry actually 'being a Dad' to loads of kids who weren't mine biologically, but are as close if not closer to me than many kids are to their biological fathers. Today there are countless widows of a new variety. They never lost their husbands to war or disease, sickness or tragedy. Their husbands just walked out on them and their child or children. They are what I refer to as 'new century widows'. Basically their husbands or their kids' fathers may as well be dead as far as being useful, healthy and good examples and role models is concerned.

With daughters this is even more tragic. A girl needs a father in some ways even more than a son does. It's been said that, "a son is a son until he gets a wife, but a daughter is a daughter for the rest of your life." Here lies one of the greatest challenges the church faces in modern day times. Fathering a fatherless generation is not going to be easy, but we have to find a way! The world cannot do it. Society is deteriorating in terms of morality and core values. Families are being ripped apart by greed, selfishness and shortsightedness. Politics is becoming more and more meaningless and the political systems are becoming even more irrelevant and powerless in their confused attempt to arrest the tide of deterioration of values and principled living. I want you to stop for a moment at this point ...

STOP!
THINK   PRAY

Why is God very often referred to as *Father*? He is *"Our Father"* It is a fact that we will always be His children–no matter what age we grow until. You can be one hundred and ten years old and you will still be his child! Did you get that? You cannot outgrow your father on earth–obviously. But you can never outgrow your Father in heaven. He has "fathered" us. We are His children forever!

Maybe you never had an earthly father yourself. Maybe today your father is so bad you wished you never had one! I've met some of those! Well you can make it your mission to be the best Dad ever! I'm writing this while in the library in the Bible College we built over ten years ago in India. Tonight I get the privilege of watching our kids in our children's home we built twelve years ago, next door to the college we built the year after do a dance programme. Many of these kids don't have a father. Some have uncles and aunties, some grandparents. Others have no-one at all. But I am returning as often as I can to give the role of at least a spiritual father who loves them and is prepared to invest in their future lives. I'm having the joy today seeing kids who were in our homes going into College and even University! I laugh, because in my day if you knew anyone who'd been to university you were like "Wow! Really? You have a friend in University?" Now virtually everyone goes to university and it's become almost a rite of passage. If you're a father reading this today, I urge you to take your responsibility seriously. Stop neglecting your child. Invest time, effort, energy and yes finance into your child without spoiling them of course. Teach them true values. Don't neglect to give them your time.

Recently all the kids who've adopted me as their father and Mags as their mum keep me real busy. Especially my daughters Ella and Alex. I see them as our own kids in every sense. They're 19 and 18 now! They always want to talk with me and they lean on me heavily at times and though at times they are very dependent upon me, especially emotionally and psychologically, they are so caring and devoted to their Dad in such a natural and normal way. Mags is awesome and teaches me what they need most. Her father was her 'hero' in everything and gave her a blueprint for what she wanted in a husband. I'm flattered and deeply complemented just to have a shadow of what her Dad exemplified. Alex Tee was an incredible man and an awesome father too. Although away on "ministry" a lot, he always showed his love for his girls Sharon and Mags. He was a great husband to Winifred too. Strong, faithful, loving and considerate. He set a great example to us all.

Back to the mission field then ... I left the Primera's office there in Slatina. I can't even remember where I was at the time. Visiting a family I think. The Primera sent his driver with a car for me, to take me to see a plot of land that had been returned to the owner. Apparently the government, after the revolution, had created a policy to return to the rightful owners, land that was confiscated by the Communist government under Ceasescu's orders. The couple who owned this land were old and childless and had no time to spend in order to enjoy their land. I jumped into the car with a colleague and went to meet the couple on their site. Amazingly I had enough funds with me albeit in GBP (Great British Pounds) to, I believe, purchase the site.

I saw the old couple. Sweet as they were, you could tell they had had a hard life. They were just at the end of their days. I explained how we wanted a piece of land to build a centre for the children. I don't really think they were that bothered what we wanted it for. They were just happy to get the land back and were obviously looking for a quick sale. I viewed the land. It was a hectare in size, but far from being free of complexity. Some three or four shanty type houses lay to the side of the rightful owners' house. Squatters who had to be removed. I was assured by the owner they had no right to be there and they would remove them shortly. I could tell it would be harder than he envisaged and was cautious about this but nevertheless I was enthusiastic about the possibilities. As far as I was concerned it was an opportunity not to be missed. I took the plunge. I realised I had one chance at it. I had £2,500 The owner wanted at least £3,500. There's no way he would come to my level. I thought long and hard and then an idea came to me! He's never really seen what GBP looks like. And has never really seen proper cash before. I opened my brief case up, took out the cash–all in twenties and tens–and counted out £2,500. Most of us would know that twenty three piles of twenty pound notes and two of ten pound notes looks a lot more than it is! I saw the owner's eyes pop out of his head. It was a lot of money in those days and in Romania you could buy a lot of things with this. Probably another good house or two smaller ones in the countryside. He arose from his chair and went to a side cabinet (I remember this like it was yesterday!) and opened the glass door. He brought out a bottle of his best home grown vintage red and poured out several glasses. I realised the deal was done! I tried a gulp of the celebrated toast. It would've gone down great with a bag of chips, but who cares? We had reached a momentous first step to what was to become an amazing centre in the future and bring hope, to some beautiful kids.

The only thing I hadn't reckoned upon is how to deal with the religious, 'Christian community' who, I would soon come to realise, seldom served God in reality, but loved serving money. Any currency, any origin would do. And they were virtually all up to it! The higher up the chain you went the more corrupt it became. The Pentecostal denomination was in my own opinion the worst. I'm not sure how things are today, as I ceased working with them a long time ago. I found even some of their senior leaders fake, fraudulent and would sell their grandmothers for five hundred pounds! Indeed many had their nose in the troughs of their congregations and were living power-crazed lives in their little white palaces. I walked out of leaders meetings appalled dismayed and disillusioned with the whole thing. I've since tried to become more philosophical about the matters I experienced as I grew older and hopefully wiser, but I believe things like this need to be exposed and it will definitely help other leaders to become more cautious in their approach to pioneering and taking Christians at face value.

I need to make the point here. I'm not at all naive when it comes to non-Christians. When it comes to those who are outside of Christ I'm pretty street-wise. But those who are supposed to be Christian and leaders within the church–Wow!! I was in for an eye opener. Even today, now I see the biggest problem in Romanian church-life is the material culpability of leaders. They tend to be controlled by their love of the silver and the gold. It hasn't changed that much either. They can easily change their allegiance and legitimise their use of funds for whatever they need. It's what I call the "ex-communist gene"–it's a payback for years of being oppressed and abused. Anyone working in an ex-communist country take note. What is reprehensible to you, is quite legitimate to some! I get it a bit now, but boy, oh boy, I was going to be battered by it for a few years to come. Nevertheless, I always remembered what Paul the apostle had to endure–"false brethren" he called them and do you know something? When serving God you have to endure all kinds of tribulation. And my goal was always going to be bigger and greater than the trials and tests, so for me the main thing was to keep focused and remember, God is bigger, greater, stronger and mightier than any opposition no matter where it comes from. It was a lesson well learned and to this day is an axiom of mission for me whether at home or overseas.

Paul buying land in Slatina, Romania for the building of the Casa Lumina Centre (Lighthouse Romania) including the specialist childcare and therapy centre and Casa Noastra (family home) on the top floor. Jo Marks (bottom right) in the multi-sensory room.

Bethany Children's Home, Erode, Tamil Nadu, India - built by LIM in 2001/2

Bethany Bible College, Erode, Tamil Nadu, India – built by LIM in 2002/3

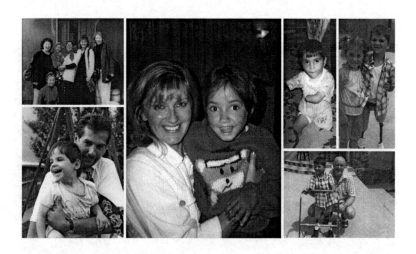

Some of the many lives changed: top left, some of the family re-housed through Mission October 10. Mags Hallam holding baby Margaret - rescued at 6 months of age from and orphanage in Alexandria.

Top and bottom right - Stefan who was born without any limbs has been looked after by LIM for 15 years now, here he is pictured with Dr Ken Mcrea, a senior prosthetist who has worked with LIM for many years.

Four of LIM's Charity Shops in Manchester. UK 1993 - present.

The Casa Noastra Family (bottom centre).
left-right: Mags Hallam, Vasi, Alex, Lily, Ella, Paul, Mada, Danny
Miha, Bobi, Myno, Claudio, Iuli, Juli.

LIM's BACS church building scheme, India.
At the time of writing (late 2014), 78 church buildings have been built in India by LIM.

top right - Church building no. 25 and top left and bottom - church building no. 50. LIM's Jubilee church,
Dedicated to Mag's parents, Pastor and Mrs Alex Tee.

Erode City Mission, Tamil Nadu, India
Thousands come to Christ in a mission that is televised live across Tamil Nadu state to over 50 Million people.
Paul is preaching to the crowd (bottom right) while The Lighthouse John 3:16 band lead worship (top left).

Literally thousands of decision cards being counted (top right) by Paul with host pastors Samuel Innocent and Jenson Jeberaj.

Chapter Thirteen

'MAGPIE PASTORS'

---

*"So many people can be responsible for your success,
but only you are responsible for your failure." Unknown*

In 1994 we successfully set up Lighthouse International Ministries (LIM for short). We also went on to set up Casa Lumini in Romania, our sister charity, in order to safely transfer funds overseas. At the time of the purchase of our piece of land for the Centre we wanted to build, we had not registered the UK charity however and so had to buy the land through the local Pentecostal church we had been helping in Slatina. We set up an agreement with the then local leadership of the church to say that LIM would always be the ethical and moral owners of the site even though in Romanian law we realised they would be regarded as the legal owners. We made it clear that LIM would be firmly in charge of the site. All the leaders signed it and still today I have the paperwork on file. We should in hindsight have conveyed the site to Casa Lumini as soon as possible while the ink was drying so to speak. It was a mistake that cost us dearly, but no one really expects to be robbed by a pastor and a church leadership, especially one that's been bankrolled!! I said earlier that fact is stranger than fiction. This was a good example of this.

We also made a contract with a local company to build the new Casa Lumini Centre. It was to be a multi-purpose Centre. The building company were very good and flexible with us. They even provided accommodation for the church in their basement, once the church had come to terms with the fact that "Prophet John's" *version* of God's plan wasn't the real deal. The church was given notice and had to leave. But God provided so marvellously. Three men were in charge of the church at the time. Radu (a godly man of passion. A man who was to be taken by God in a swift unexpected moment in order I believe to save him the agony and ignominy of what happened to his family and church at a later stage), Busoi, and "Prophet John", (Ion in Romanian). All had their strengths and of course weaknesses but they worked well together and had started the church. The trouble is they hadn't much idea where they were taking it! With our help and input the church grew to about eighty people. A considerable sized church for this region.

At this time the 'three leader team' wanted a friend to come as their pastor who was in Bible College in Austria. They were absolutely sure that this was the man they wanted. We arranged a meet up. The leadership called a meeting and several months later we agreed to finance the new pastor and put some money towards his apartment in Slatina. I will refrain from using his name but anyone who knows me or anyone in this book will know who this person is. I will call him Sovack. The deal was done and Sovack eventually arrived along with his wife and family. We gave him a great deal and paid him well above the average salary of his peers.

One of the leaders, Busoi, was put in charge of the Storage and Distribution Centre. He did a great job and at least was honest and his son helped him. Things worked well until the arrival of Sovack. We found out that things went missing–probably sold by him, and then we found out cars were being imported and sold by him in the name of the charity, Casa Lumini. He even sold cars to his congregation! The process was and still is totally illegal and the charity would have been closed down if we had not have acted swiftly. Imported cars carried a huge tax liability and charities could bring vehicles tax free. The temptation was too much even for a pastor. Sovack wasn't alone in this fraudulent activity. Many did it and I guess some still do. I have no problem if the vehicle was being brought in to be used by the charity for the charity's purpose, but these were simply business deals. I called Sovack to account. We had an enormous row. He denied any misuse even though we had evidence and witnesses. Eventually we took the Casa Lumini stamp off him. Other misgivings emerged of very serious nature and we decided to stop supporting him. In effect we gave him six month's salary as a severance.

In the meantime we had brought a church building for the church from England! We were given a large sectional building by Stoke City Council. It was only sectional before it was put up we found out later. At the time back in The UK we had started a project called 'Pathway'. It was extremely successful and led by one of our members. A great guy named Steve Kinnear. Steve is one of the best people I've ever worked with. He's away from the church at the moment. I still believe he'll be back whether at The Lighthouse or wherever. Steve ran our 'Pathway Project' for the church. I had financial input and did the managerial stuff and the contractual managing too. We were due to go to Stoke with a team to pack up the building and put it onto two Turkish trucks which would take it to Slatina, Romania for us. A tradesman who worked with us 'John Boult' (his real name!) agreed to go to Romania to oversee the assembly of the 'church'. The sectional building would seat easily two hundred so was considered a great move. I had damaged my knee badly due to a very bad anterior cruciate ligament injury I had suffered at Bible College playing for the College team. I was a very good footballer who could get a goal from nowhere as I proved many times! Our college team never lost a game in our second season and once we were 2-1 down and I equalised in the dying seconds at Sheffield AoG Church. I "nosed" the ball into the net with a well mistimed header. I decided to throw myself at this ball as it was 'last chance saloon'. It saved the day and we didn't lose, even despite Sheffield AoG 'ringers' in their team (ringers being a couple of pro-footballers!) In playing football so passionately I completely severed my ACL. An injury I found out later was to plague me until this day. I tried to carry on playing, but my knee would literally pop out of position. I found a way to 'pop' it back in place but occasionally it refused to go back! This was one such occasion.

I had played with the church youth football team the day before only for the inevitable to happen. Here I was, lying in bed and scheduled to set out early in the morning to go to Stoke with a team of guys to collapse a sectional building into two equal parts. Hmmmmm! I told Steve I would definitely be there no matter what my condition, much to Mags' complete disdain. She knows what I'm like in these situations when I'm as stubborn as a mule. To my amazement that night, I remember turning over in the night several times. I woke up and my knee was the best it had been for months. I got up did the usuals–"Word for Today", breakfast, into the car and down to Stoke with the boys. That day we actually hired two large Alligator Saws. We sawed the building into three sections. We had to do this–once we realised it wasn't sectional at all! But we improvised and made it sectional. I loved this about The Lighthouse. From day one, we always believed there was a way to do something if you really wanted to do it. It's my firm belief that if you really want to do something, you'll find a way. If you don't you'll find an excuse! I actually did a lot of the sawing by the way and was up and down a ladder like a hamster on steroids! My knee was the best it had been for years. I felt long ago God say in His word, "As your days are, so shall your strength be"

> *"... as thy days, so shall thy strength be."*
> *(Deuteronomy 33:25 KJV)*

I've always taken that as my guarantee that if I'm serving Him and on duty *in His service* I can expect health, wealth and provision to see the service completed. It's as simple as that. That doesn't mean for me and for myself. It means *for His service*. Anything else I treat as a bonus. My meat and drink is to do the will of Him who sent me. That's all at the end of the day. The rest for me is just peripheral.

So, job done. A new church building, courtesy of Stoke City Council was finally on its way to Romania. The team re-assembled the building without too much difficulty apart from a dreadful accident that happened on site when a young man was hit by a piece of steelwork. We thought he had died and he was unconscious. People prayed for him while the ambulance was coming (an ambulance in Romania was nothing more than an estate car!) He became conscious and refused to go when the ambulance came and continued to work on the re-assembly. An amazing moment for sure.

The new building was great. It was panelled with wood inside and to be fair was very spacious for the congregation. Just after this was when we experienced what I can only describe as the beginning of a very sorry era which has rumbled on for nearly two decades. It tested my resilience and vision to the max, I can tell you. There were times when I felt like wiping the dust off my feet. But I knew God had positioned me here to do a work which was far deeper than people's greed, selfishness and ego. I was encouraged by Paul's resilience in the Acts of the Apostles when in the face of danger and a variety of perils he continued to surge forward and showed courage and tenacity in the face of all kinds of opposition.

The incumbent pastor's financial agreement with us was virtually ended. But he was digging his heels in and was going nowhere. In fact the church since he took over had sadly declined in number. We had lost about 25 -30 people. Then something happened none of us were prepared for. Out of the blue, the main elder and pioneer, Radu died. At the age of about 52 when he was really in his zenith concerning ministry. He came home from work, felt a pain in his head, lay down and just died. I was in the UK at the time. It was awful. I had become so attached to this family, they had become like my own family. They wept over the phone and asked me to come. I couldn't of course, I had so many things I simply couldn't cancel. It was a truly dark and dreadful moment. Not only had we lost a great man of God, we had lost a person who was perhaps the most, maybe even looking back, only man with the spiritual calibre to see the work advance now it had come to having its own 200 seater building on its own two and a half acre site. The funeral went ahead and I visited as soon as time and space would allow.

Back home in the UK, we had discussed opening a charity shop through which to raise funds for our new Therapy Centre at The Casa Lumini Centre in Romania. The trouble is that's all we'd done–discuss it!! I got a bit cheesed off with talking and decided to get started. We did it. We opened our first charity shop in Chorlton around the corner from our church centre. It was a little gold mine and raised thousands of pounds for the new centre. It provided a bedrock of funding that we knew we could count on to sign contracts and pay bills. On top of that we did our best to raise grants and funds from anywhere we could. We had mixed results but every little helped. I saw the amazing work that the shop was doing and Mags kept a close eye on things and although she was still running our Nursery "hands on" at the time she went into the shops personally and served customers and got voluntary staff from church and from the customers.

Mags is the best "persons person" I've ever seen at work with people. Seriously! Not just because she's my wife. But because she can keep people working together who don't really get on and in some cases can't stand one another hahaha! There's not many who have the wisdom, the skill and the savvy to have such a broad blend of people working towards the same goal. People as a rule are pretty selfish. They're not gracious at all. Our default position is one of what suits us, not others, period as the Americans say. Only bundles and oodles of the grace of God *and* a full on passion and devotion to the goals set out by God will get us to the point where we see beyond the existing situations that deflate and discourage us. Because I could see the success in the shop I opened another. I built the changing rooms, the counter and did the whole refurbishment with a friend, a fireman, Stuart Saunders. We turned it around in three days. The shop there in Tyldesely is still going to this day, though we moved over the road to larger premises a few years back.

The new centre in Romania was coming along nicely. As I mentioned earlier, a trainee architect–Justin Marks and his fiancée Jo Saunders came into the church in 1992 and they got married a couple of years later in 1994. Justin came to Romania with me and did some calculations to ensure enough concrete had gone into the foundation and that the foundation was deep enough for the two storeys. We found out that there was enough concrete for about five storeys which at least helped us to know what we had for the future. We would need a third storey as it happened. Jo and Justin would come to be our closest partners in the work of the Lighthouse, both at home and abroad. Jo is very charismatic, dynamic and exceptionally gifted as a leader and loves progress. Justin is an incredibly pragmatic man with tons of experience and is wise way beyond his years. The stability and soundness he exudes is priceless. He is an anchorman in The Lighthouse in many ways. If there was an emergency, this is the man. Calm, controlled and a great sense of humour. I cannot pay them a high enough complement.

I went out to visit Romania to check on building work. To my horror I found out that our pastor friend had replaced most of his leadership team. The church were now down to about thirty five people. All the old guard had left. A new group of people had been appointed. What is more, Sovack told me "The whole site is now mine, and it is up to me what happens with the centre you are building. It will come under my control." I told him I had a document in my possession that his church leadership had signed and that he had to honour it before God. I gave him a copy. His church leadership read it and dismissed it as "then and not now". The land now effectively belonged to The Pentecostal Church Denomination of Romania and as such he was their representative. It was in his control.

I arranged a meeting with a Senior Pastor in Timisoara. He was one of the national leaders and, at the time, in fact the General Superintendent of the Pentecostal Denomination in Romania. I spelt out the position clearly. He wasn't really interested at all and told me it was up to me to sort it out with brother Sovack. I had driven a round trip of about 450 miles to be told basically to sort it out myself. I met another leading senior Pastor in Bucharest. He was an older, well respected figure within the leadership of the denomination. He listened and sympathised. "Brother Paul, come and see the church we are building, look what we are doing here. Don't concern yourself with all those matters in that place. Come and help us here ... blablablabla."

By this time I'd just about had about enough. I took it up with our head office and our then International Missions Director, Brian Edwards, who was terrific about the situation. He faced them up and spoke to them and visited them with me. He reminded them of their moral and spiritual obligation. He was very concerned about – well, their ways with money, to put it mildly. Another Pastor, a younger man from Bucharest, but well known and respected at the time, told Pastor Sovack to say to us "Brother Paul, thank you for your help–but goodbye, we don't need your help anymore", and advised him to take over the whole site and the new centre we had by now brought to two thirds of the way to completion.

To cut to the chase, we had to give a cash amount to Pastor Sovack for his new church extension he was planning, and to pay legal fees for conveying the site to Casa Lumini *(us!)*. In other words we were to pay for our site again. This time however it cost us four thousand pounds for half of our own site. To this day the site is split and the church site has been used to build his own son's homes and family dwellings. The church meanwhile exists just to license his presence on the site as a pastor. To be honest it is a disgrace and totally dishonouring to God what happened in this situation and a denomination that just sits by and not only allows this kind of exploitation but encourages it should be ashamed of itself. The title of this chapter **"Magpie Pastors"** sums it up for me. I have since had people who were on that very same leadership team, who would not accept the signed agreement we had originally drawn up come, and apologise to me, and more importantly before the Lord. They told me they had been tricked and duped into allowing Sovack to control the situation. I am including this in my book because it's an integral part of mission and a lesson to many, of the cost of getting things done overseas. We still have the Centre today and we have achieved a lot through it. But our plans were hindered not by the devil but by man's greed for money, power and control.

The lesson is well and truly branded into my soul. My greatest lament is what could have been achieved had we been able to work together with integrity and sincerity. I believe we could have seen a totally outstanding church built in Slatina. A town with thousands of bright young people. If I was to choose a town in which 'I' would like to start a church from scratch it would be Slatina. Probably because I feel that so many potential leaders have let the people down here. They deserved far better than they received. Nevertheless I know that my priority must be that to which God has called me to do, not which 'I' would "like to do". To that end I continue to try my best to be lead pastor of The Lighthouse until my successor is ready to take over. I'm sure someone is being lined up for this. It will be just a matter of discerning, empowering, equipping and releasing. Sounds easy when you say it quickly!

Chapter Fourteen

THE DARK SIDE OF THE RUBICON

"The pain you feel today will bring the strength you need tomorrow. For every challenge encountered there is an opportunity to grow."

In or around 1995, just four years after opening our new centre in Manchester, the thought of raising our own family had become stronger. We had been married nine years and had up until 1993 just got on with our lives preferring to give ourselves wholly and totally to the work and service of God. Children, family and all that stuff would just have to wait. In all honesty we did not take a proper holiday until five years after we were married as we felt it would be detrimental to the growth and the momentum we had seen as a church. Rightly or wrongly we did not regret those early years and particularly the cost. However what was about to happen hit us so hard the scars remain deep within us to this very day.

One day Mags came home and informed me she was expecting. I was overjoyed. I've always wanted children and it's something I always just expected to happen. Mags said not to get too carried away as it was very early. About eight weeks. Within a few days however we felt we should tell our parents and close friends. So we did. We ended up with a house full of flowers. It

133

was a very strange time and a lot of pressure was on us at the time. I remember Mags in the prayer meeting saying she felt really unwell, and she was taken home. That night she lost a lot of blood. The doctor came but didn't seem duly alarmed and said he felt she should go for a scan. Mags and I went to hospital. What happened next for us both was a recurring nightmare. Bizarrely the nurse told us the date of the baby's arrival. It was supposed to be sometime in May (it was now late October). The scan confirmed our worst fears. We had lost the baby.

We sat down stunned. How could we have just been given the birth date of our first child one minute, and be told it had gone the next? Looking back there could only have been one explanation and that is, the nurses got mixed up between us and someone else. We were just left there in a corner of the hospital grief-stricken and our hopes were completely destroyed. We went back home to a house full of flowers and congratulation cards. Slowly but surely we removed them all and put them in a black bin bag. I think our spirit went in with them–at least for a while. I remember Mags' parents coming over immediately on hearing the news. This put even more pressure on us as I think we really needed space and room to be on our own for a while. Our house is beautiful, but it's not the biggest and in moments of great emotion it's not always the easiest thing to do, to be living on top of one another.

Anyway it ended probably just as badly as it could. Our church, our leaders never mentioned it! There was no one to speak to us. No one to console the consolers. It just didn't happen! It was like–we just don't want to know what happened. I think they were all so embarrassed they didn't know what to say. Looking back, really, they should've sent us away on a holiday. On a restful vacation or something. But no! Zero! Nothing. Mags returned immediately to work. She was running our busy, very successful nursery at the time. She went straight back to it. Both of us used our work and our ministerial responsibilities to bandage our wounds. We hurt so badly and I have to say for many years even we struggled to talk about it. It became the subject to avoid at all cost and there was no doubt it affected our friendships especially as most of our friends were getting pregnant and giving birth like shelling peas. I remember Mags going back to the nursery and one of the first things that happened was a parent came in, in floods of tears wanting to speak with Mags. She spoke with her. She was a parent who had just had an abortion and was devastated by it. She had no idea what had just happened to Mags. None whatsoever! As I've said a few times in this book, fact is stranger than fiction, and there are some times when all you can do is accept that something indescribable and inexplicable is happening. We just tried our best to get through as best as we could but it knocked the stuffing out of us. There were a few people who said to us "Don't be too worried, next time you'll be okay." And "Often you can have problems with the first child", etc.

We had many a prophecy too by the way. From all over the place. It all rang pretty hollow to me at the time I must admit. To cap it all, two years later I booked us on a holiday at the last minute to go to Turkey as we were both tired out. During that holiday Mags had another miscarriage. We were left devastated again. This time we kept it mostly if not completely to ourselves. Our parents never really spoke to us about our childlessness either. Both sets of parents probably didn't know what to say. It would've been nice to have just had a "Listen, son" or "Listen, daughter, we have no idea why this has happened we just want you to know we feel your pain", etc, but again, just like our leadership team–zero. That's when we realised–Leadership can be the loneliest place on the planet! We were in fact, when it boiled down to it, on our own. Okay God was with us–somewhere–we believed, even still our faith was tested severely.

We went to see a specialist. A lovely Nigerian doctor. He was great with us. The first person who we felt wanted to help us. He offered us IVF. We thought about it long and hard. I'm a stubborn €%#^¥$ at times. I have a word in mind and it fits the bill but I understand would be inappropriate to say, but I want to help you to understand how I am. I said to myself, "If God can't give us a child then I'm not going to have one by artificial means!" Full stop! Now don't get me wrong, I have absolutely nothing against any couple who go this route. It's great for those who want it. For me and in my call it wouldn't have been right. Both of us knew it too. I know God said "This is your Isaac, you need to lay it down." We decided not to have any intrusive means to have a child. We were offered a treatment called GIFT which is basically IUF. We had to pay however, and it cost a whopping five hundred pounds. We went for it and had three goes but nothing came of it. We slowly began to accept our situation. To come to terms with the reality that sometimes in life there isn't a happy ending in certain areas is hard. Some would claim we hadn't the faith to believe God. Some would say children are a right, and I should've prayed and believed more or claimed more. I would say actually children are a privilege, not a right. We went on to serve God, but with a huge shadow over our lives.

The complex emotion, hurt and the pain of a wife who dearly wants to give her husband the children she deeply believes he deserves but she can't give him, has been a very heavy cross for my wife to bear for these past 15-16 years. I know this is extremely hard for her. I cannot pretend to one and all. The thought of never ever being able within the context of a fantastic marriage to be a biological father has been and still is the most bitter pill I've ever had to swallow and accept. Even now when I'm in my fifties I can't believe it never happened. It's the weirdest, strangest thing ever. Has it made me doubt God? No! Never. Not doubt Him. I came to a place long ago to realise that there are many mysteries in life and being a Christian is not an encyclopaedic fount of knowledge. Sometimes being a Christian can cause you to question more differently than those outside of faith. One thing is very sure. We are living on a cursed earth for a very short period. And when you give your life to God, He is in charge, full stop. There's still a lot of pain, suffering and hurt. Not only to the unjust, but to the just as well. Our way through it is to trust in Him at ALL times. There will be a reason why. The difference is I don't need to know now. Not this side of eternity. It will all become clear one day. I'm settling simply for that.

I have to say too, that Mags and I are as close a couple as ever. I thank God for giving me the greatest wife, friend and confidant I could ever wish for. She is just perfect for me. Strong, wise, compassionate, passionate and courageous. It helps also being gorgeous and attractive of course and being in great shape helps too!

For some time I refused to carry out child dedications which were coming thick and fast. Every time we visited a hospital maternity ward to see a new born child of one of our church members I dreaded it and put on the biggest acting role you've ever seen. I should have a cabinet full of Oscars by now! What a performance I could give. Entering into the joys of a new baby with the father being ecstatic. It was excruciating for me, yet at the same time I knew very much how much of a blessing this was to a dad and mum. As you can imagine in a growing church it was an increasing occurrence. I remember sending about 30 young people to Fraisethorpe Camp near Scarborough one year. I'd bought a large bus so we could get large numbers of youth here and there. One Saturday, there they all were. All the parents and the kids. The kids said goodbye to the parents, the parents said goodbye to the kids. And then it struck me! ... and who do I have to say goodbye to? This was the voice though of someone who wanted to take me out! It was like a spear that pierced my soul. I decided that I would jack the whole thing in tomorrow–Sunday morning. No way was I going to preach the way I was feeling. This was it! "I'm out of here", I said to myself. It's time to 'do one'. The morning came and I preached from the 23rd Psalm. I remember it well. It was another Rubicon moment in my life. I decided fully and wholeheartedly I would take the whole thing on my chin. After all, **we are called to finish the race, not just to start it.**

In truth, the situation didn't get easier. We just 'learned' how to deal with it, privately and personally. Mags in her way and me in mine. It's still extremely hard thinking how the bible teaches that children are a blessing from the Lord and most Christians used to view us as a couple who had everything worked out together. When one particular couple we'd known for ages found out, they were deeply shocked and thought it was just a 'lifestyle choice'– who can blame them? When I look at fathers who've abandoned their kids I feel so much pain and so much hurt. "How could they?" is the question I always ask. It has been a big driving force in my life, helping me to focus on the fatherless and the abandoned kids in India and Romania. What has happened though, is I have loads of fatherless kids in our church too. They are so close to me they are almost like my own kids and I guess I look at them a bit like this too. We have people in their thirties with their own children now who we refer to as "the kids" because we became like their parents. They came to faith under the rays of The Lighthouse and were raised under the canopy of its blessing. Baptised, married and serving in the house. God has indeed been gracious to us despite our personal darkness.

Throughout the book, I'm purposely nipping backwards and forwards to Romania and then the UK, basically because this was and is my life. Someone in our church got mad with me once and said "Pastor, don't you think you should choose? Is it UK or the mission field? Shouldn't you make a decision and do one thing or the other?" I answered graciously "I have decided between the mission field and the UK already ... and it's both!" The fact is, that I believe I've been able to accomplish far more than many missionaries in the traditional sense. By building a strong base and an amazing church, we've been able to impact churches and communities way beyond many people's imagination. When I taught as a leader in India, Africa and Romania I did so as a pastor of a church. Someone who understood the rigours and pressures of ministry within the local church. Most itinerant ministers can't really do this with as much impact. As you continue to read this book, you will see that the rays of God's favour were about to go way beyond anything many had ever anticipated. The local church can still have a global vision.

Chapter Fifteen

WALKING ON WATER OR SKATING ON THIN ICE?

"We teach what we know ... but we reproduce who we are."
John Maxwell

Despite the personal setbacks we faced, we drew strength from the fact that God was blessing us in amazing ways. We had opened two charity shops and a third was on the way in Levenshulme in the eastern part of the city. This would be our largest shop. A double fronted shop in which we majored on selling furniture. As before, I built the counter and decorated the shop along with a couple of our people. I used to have a tactic of going into poorly decorated shops so as to get a low rent and paint the ceilings with a satin black colour. It works a treat and 'covers a multitude of sins.' I employed this tactic in a few situations where I felt we needed a low cost quick turnaround. Time for me is always the most expensive commodity so there's no point trying to be a perfectionist in these situations.

A big tip here for anyone in an entrepreneurial role as a pastor. Ditch the perfectionism!! Listen! You haven't got time to be a perfectionist and in my experience this is one of the biggest reasons why churches and church leaders often make bad entrepreneurs. They try to do something perfectly and miss the point. The point is my friends to make money! That's what entrepreneurs do! Yes!

It really is as simple as this. I came to the realisation pretty early on in church life that if we were going to rely on church finances for our vision the growth rate would be massively held back and the fulfilment of our goals radically effected by a lack of finance. Mission needs money–it really is that simple. And we have a limited amount of time but a limitless potential of resources if we can but awaken ourselves to the possibilities and opportunities within our grasp. Just recently I made a decision not to replace our second hand ceiling tiles in one of our shops, even when we had the chance when we made some extra money. I refused to spend it on that. Why? Simple! The customers couldn't care two hoots whether our ceiling tiles were white as opposed to 'off-white'. Ninety percent of them probably didn't know we had ceiling tiles at all. Instead I spent the extra money on a critical need that would make a difference in regard to the actual purpose we were opening and running shops for in the first place.

Making the main thing the main thing is vital in any area of ministry or even business. If you are a perfectionist you are going to struggle massively to oversee and manage a multi-faceted church. You will be so frustrated, because you won't be able to compromise your standards. I love excellence, I really do, but you can't possibly have excellence in every area at once and on some things you have to learn to compromise. Sometimes you will have to say I've spent enough time on that–it will have to do. It's often a 'trade off'. Where do I want excellence and where am I prepared to make do even if just for a while? These are great lessons to running, leading and managing what I now call a 'hybrid organisation'. I want to deal with this a bit more in another book and intend to write more thoroughly on the subject in a future leadership series. This may be uncomfortable to some pastors and church leaders but it's a fact of life for me. I place the local church in complete centrality of all the business. It has to be the hub, heart and centre of operations. Someone recently referred to it as "The Mother-ship" and I must admit I like the feminine description as it does fit well with the typology of the church in the New Testament. We are called to build the church and nothing else. I'm really acutely aware of that and para-church groups need to be even more aware of this. In fact I believe para-church organisations only actually exist because local churches aren't strong enough or in existence enough to address the issues that para-church groups address. The reason this would not work is pretty obvious however and that is the diversity of churches with an even greater diversity of vision. Which inevitably leads to different emphasis because vision drives that diversity.

We hear of churches that have 'an anointing for this' or 'an anointing for that'. An example is Hillsong, Australia for worship, Willow Creek for enabling and equipping believers, Metro Ministries in New York for their amazing work across the world with children, Elevation church in America for their progressive approach to building church, Mars Hill Church, Seattle with their controversial approach to outreach etc. Personally I don't think this is as much to do with anointing as it is with vision. The single biggest common denominator in all these churches is the visionary they have or had at the helm of the church. It is the vision that has received the blessing because in all these cases the chief visionary was "not disobedient to the heavenly vision." Hillsongs–Brian Houston; Willow Creek–Bill Hybels; Metro Ministries–Bill Wilson; Elevation Church–Steven Furtick; Mars Hill Church–Mark Driscoll. There is no other real element they have in common. Their identity comes out of their vision. John Maxwell said "people buy into the visionary first, not the vision." I think this is extremely important to understand. The Lighthouse is an incredibly missional Church because its leadership is missional. It is a very down to earth Church. Because its leadership is down to earth. As John Maxwell again states, 'we teach what we know, but we reproduce who we are'. Much more about this later.

Okay. With three charity shops open and another in the pipeline, we were really motoring. By now the new Children's Therapy Centre in Romania was well on the way to being built and I had a missions visit to Nigeria. It wasn't my first visit to Africa as Mags and I had been to Kenya, but it was one of my most memorable ones. I had been asked to accompany Pastor Paul Epton along with one of his assistants, Neil Cheetham. On the night we landed in Lagos, we were literally bundled into a Mercedes car and whisked away to a nearby hotel. We heard what we first thought were firecrackers from a big party going on. That is until we looked out of the balcony and saw a couple of bodies on the streets and realised the noise we heard was gunfire. We turned on the news to see the full story. There had been a coup, literally as we landed. The president had been overthrown and a new president (Abacha) had been installed. And ... the capital had been changed from Lagos to Abuja literally overnight. Welcome to Nigeria!

What happened in the morning will stay with me for the rest of my life! We went to the airport to catch a flight only to be told all flights were cancelled due to the overnight coup. Fuel prices had increased by 500 percent and it was total chaos everywhere. I was supposed to be heading off to Jos, a city in the central region of Nigeria, and from there I was going north to Bauchi State. This was and still is one of the most volatile regions in the world especially when it comes to Christianity. So ... all flights had been cancelled officially. Thinking that was that and we would return to our hotel for a day or two, one of the pastors said "There is a flight taking a politician to Abuja and this is the only flight taking off." Then I was introduced by the pastor to another man dressed from head to toe in bright yellow! Even his shoes were yellow! My instinct was to say "hang on a moment–who is this guy?" But things happened so quickly before I knew it, I was ducking under the passport counter and going through the portal for the baggage with two guys running behind me with our luggage toward the one solitary plane with engine running preparing for take off. Man, it was surreal! I boarded with my friend and our bags were taken and somehow made their way to the hold. Off we went, me and my new friend who was looking like a giant banana!

We arrived ... somewhere, I really can't say where to this day, but it was supposed to be Abuja airport. I say this because it took us an hour and a half to reach Abuja by taxi, once we managed to find one. Then we arrived at the craziest market place I've seen on the planet. Wow it was unbelievable! People were buying and selling, shouting and trading in what looked like a complete and total jamboree. My Banana friend entered into some negotiation with someone and before we knew it, we were on our way to Jos by car with two spare fuel cans in the boot, full of diesel just purchased by 'banana man'. We travelled for hours and hours to arrive at Jos early in the morning. I was

142

taken to a guest house, where for breakfast I was told not to eat anything but the porridge. It was "welcome to mission" alright! I was warned of the power cuts that took place, literally when-ever, and was told just to sit tight and the lights would come on eventually. (The power cut did happen in the early hours of the morning.) I discovered the room was infested with cockroaches especially under my bed, so I guess the blackout during the night helped to hide the fact for some time.

I was moved the next day by a delightful young lady called Anne, who had been assigned to look after me. My time in Jos went by without too much going wrong and then my onward journey to Bauchi went well, where I have to say, the brothers in the church looked after me constantly. I was booked into the best hotel in Bauchi. It was nice enough and clean, though as I found soon enough it was a great attraction for the local prosti-tutes. I found out after I had just finished my first evening gospel meeting. I ordered a coffee at the outside hotel bar as it was a lovely evening. I was joined by a beautiful young lady who talked with me and after a couple of minutes I realised what she was about. I shared with her about the Lord Jesus Christ and how He can change our lives and bring purpose and fulfilment and she had no need to live like how she was. I invited her to the meeting the following night, bought her a Coke and left a few Nira (the local currency) on the table for her, just to help her buy some food or something. I had really little confidence to think she would come along the following night but she did. And she gave her life to the Lord too. I don't know what became of her though she did con-tinue to attend the meetings. I hope she made it. It's such a tough life for these girls and it's easy to sit in judgment of them, but I knew God's love for this girl was great.

After Bauchi, I went on to meet Paul and Neil in Jos and from there we all went to Kaduna and then Kano and home! I found out later that the plane on which 'banana man' and I flew to Abuja was hijacked as it took off after dropping us off at Abuja! Were the hijackers on the flight when me and my bright friend were on it too? I have no idea but I know it was a very grave situation and the papers said there was loss of life. I have never been back to Nigeria since! But who knows? One day maybe, but I think I will need more than an invitation from a church. I think I would need a personally delivered invitation form above before I book the tickets!

Our next missions venture was to Mombasa in Kenya. This came about via my father-in-law Alex Tee. He often went to Kenya and was responsible for raising the funds to build the Kiserian Orphanage in Nairobi which the Nairobi Pentecostal Church (NPC) managed. The senior pastor of NPC was a wonderful man, Pastor Denis Whyte from the Pentecostal Assembles of God in Canada. He and my Father-in-law were great friends. I'd go as far as to say 'soul mates'. Dad felt he had come to the point where he could no longer travel these distances and do all the ministry so recommended me for the mission at Mombasa. The present Pastor was a man named Elmer Komant. Elmer was as apostolic a leader as I ever met. He was so full on though, he even left me standing! (and that's saying something!)

The Mission was to hold a week of meetings and at the end officially hand over the church to a national Pastor. In this case Pastor Tom Arati and his wife Flora, who would be assisted be Pastor Ti and his wife Elizabeth. They were all fine people. I took on the mission. Mags and I went and led the mission. I preached about 11-12 times in eight days and was completely exhausted afterwards, though I loved every minute. I called the mission 'The Unstoppable Church'. They had a huge banner made up for it and praise God we saw many people come to faith in Christ, and some healed but the hallmark of it all, was the sheer number of people baptised in the Holy Spirit. On the last two nights virtually everyone who came forward was filled. It was wonderful and very memorable. On the Monday a brother took us on Safari to Tsavo East and across to Tsavo West. It was very exciting and of course we saw the big five. That church moved to bigger premises and thank God, we went back and even helped fund their new building to the tune of a few thousand pounds. We are still in contact with the church and Tom and Flora are still there, serving God. Elmer and his wife Sherie went off to Rwanda to plant a Church in Kigali. The last we heard he had a church of over a thousand people there. Unsurprising for such a trailblazer.

This, up until now was our main involvement in Africa, though we are beginning to re-establish ourselves in Africa as the Lord leads.

Chapter Sixteen

THE MINISTRY OF SHOCK ABSORBERS

"Peace and trust take years to build and seconds to shatter."

By this time (around 1996) we were really growing. We had about 200 in the church and had to think seriously about extending the premises. We had gone from 16 adults and 3 children to 160 adults and probably about 80 children in 10 years. I thought long and hard about how to increase capacity at the best premium. I had no doubts that we would keep growing if we made room.

Our building had been built in such a way as to be fairly flexible and multi-functional. We had a purpose built Day Care Centre in approximately half of the building with the main hall, foyer and offices to the other half of the building. I proposed to the Leadership that we should build an independent wing onto the side of the church with its own access point and very importantly its own WC's and kitchen so it could be used as a totally separate part of the premises. One of the main reasons for this was it would then be exempt from VAT currently at the time at 17.5% which with my calculation could be as much as £30,000 on this extension. We arranged a building fund and some partners' meetings to communicate thoroughly our intention. Here again is a big secret

146

of launching a new building project of any kind. I will deal with this more fully later on when the 'big move' was needed.

As soon as we began to put this forward I was hit with a bombshell that I'll never ever forget. I took a call in my office from a young lady. It appears she had come to the Lord recently, which was great, but then she proceeded to tell me about her life. She had, in short, been having an affair with one of my closest leaders. Since becoming a Christian, she had received counselling from a pastor's wife who knew The Lighthouse and me as well. The lady who came to Christ confessed to the pastor's wife about her affair. She advised the lady to call me. So she did. I made it very clear how serious an allegation it was and because I could scarcely believe it of this brother, who was an elder in the church for several years, I actually thought it was a set up. The woman was clear and confessed to me that it was a full on relationship they'd had. I was stunned! I no sooner ended the phone call before I called the brother to ask him what was going on. "Is it true?", I asked ... "I will come and see you as soon as I've finished work on my way home." "Yes, but is it true?", I asked again. "I'll come and see you on my way home" was the answer again. I knew from the answer it was true.

I felt like I had been hit with a sledgehammer. The couple in the church were so close to us. Their children too. When I say they were like family I mean–they were really close to us. I listened to all that had gone on along with Mags. We decided to protect the children and the man's wife. The gentleman in question had to step down from the ministry, and from being a Trustee, and he had to confess to his wife, which he was reluctant to do, but we stated it was not an option. When he resigned before the church I projected like it was on the basis of a lesser demeanour which several people knew was an issue with him. Unfortunately the wife was on staff. We gave her six months compassionate leave. After six months we re-employed her in a different area of ministry. The trouble is we hid the real reason of his resignation from the rest of the leadership team for the sake of their children. We were to pay a heavy price for so doing. The guy in question started to become quite arrogant and rude with me. To the point of questioning everything I did. Eventually he wrote to the leadership team to ask the following ... 1. How much money was I being paid? 2. Was I on two salaries? (This had come about because he knew part of my salary came from the percentage I brought in from the training centre–it was just an attempt to cause mischief). 3. What level of expenses was I paid for using my car i.e. per mile? 4. What other expenses am I on?

I had set up an independent salaries committee at the church previously which was given the responsibility of reviewing wage structures within the church as we were employing more and more people at this time. They wrote back to him basically to the effect that the rates were set by our Head Office and that I was on less than the recommended scale and that's all he needed to know. The matter of course did not stop there but went on to include complaints by other members of the family who by this time thought the brother should be restored to full status and full responsibilities. They didn't know the gravity of the situation. The trouble is I could not trust the person again and I have to admit that I found him very self-deluded, as many are when they have to pay the consequences of their own actions. These people usually try to pass their guilt onto someone else when they think they see a failing they haven't got. Also the problem was no one knew the full extent of what had taken place and to be honest I have sanitised the details in the book here for the sake of people who may read this and who will know who I'm referring to. In the end the inevitable happened and I warned the brother that if it carried on I would have no choice but to tell the whole leadership what really took place. He did not listen and in fact both the husband and wife set their faces against us. They even seemed to unite together against us. At the end of the year they decided to leave and I went public about the whole thing.

Mags and I learned a valuable lesson from this whole business. We said from now on we will always let the leadership know the full story. We attempted to basically be the 'shock absorbers' for the church on this and for their children. In the end even that wasn't appreciated. We learned from this to be open and upfront as to this kind of situation. There is still a huge place for diplomacy and wisdom and certainly forgiveness and compassion. But there has to be genuine repentance shown over a period of time in my opinion if there to be any return to a similar position within the same ministry. Too many people just don't do the maths and don't realise you can't cross the line and not pay the price. Trust is an enormous issue in ministry. There is in my opinion a tendency to be very slack regarding this today. I'm all for restoration, forgiveness and restitution, but the true test of authentic repentance must be well proven, especially in the area of adultery. That must include time as it tends to be the biggest test of all.

It is very interesting to note, as an avid record keeper, the year this all came to light and unravelled and dealt with, was the only year when we did not grow numerically and financially. In fact we lost some ground. It literally is the only year in 28 years that this happened.

Amazingly, straight after the end of that year in about 1997-8 we really started to see new growth again. Not just in terms of quantity but quality too. In the lead up to this period we had employed a very special young lady, Emma Smith. Emma was a first generation Christian and her background would give any soap opera a run for its money! Emma had a great conversion, being led to the Lord by another Emma, Emma Walmesley. Both our Emmas were and still are dynamic Christians and both were born again and baptised in The Lighthouse and are now married and have children of their own. Another Emma followed, Emma Ford. She was and still is a fabulous leader with a lot of character. Another couple I have to mention is John and Liz Guard. 'The Guards' have been one of the most faithful and supportive families one could ever meet. Elizabeth came to us as a young student in our very early days while at Manchester University. John came a bit later and was a bit of a ducker and diver at the time. Eventually they both got their act together and they were the first couple ever to get married at The Lighthouse. Their first child, Hannah, is incredibly special to us. Liz was expecting Hannah while Mags was expecting our first child too. Hannah always reminds me that we have children we've never met, that one day we will meet them in heaven. Hannah later went on to to have a brother Joel and another sister Lois Amy. Seriously, the most wonderful family ever.

Now the church was not only quite large and dynamic it was getting stronger too. The difficulties we had all gone through together made for a solid outfit, though there was still some sifting to be done.

Around about the time I took my first ever trip out to India to meet an Indian pastor who I was introduced to at a small Bible School in the town of Tyldesley in the north western part of Manchester. We had recently opened a charity shop there so the church there knew us well. The same year I went, I bought a small piece of land for a children's home. To me going to India fulfilled a childhood dream. I knew one day I would go on mission there. It was for me a very spiritual feeling and I guess with my ancestral roots being there it was bound to be life changing. It certainly was. I have to say I really love India a lot. It is a wonderful country. I've been travelling there now for at least seventeen years and probably visited about thirty times over that period. I was definitely led to buy this piece of land, as when I was shown it, I knew this was partly to do with me being there. Pastor Jenson Jeberaj showed me several plots of land in a small village outside Erode City, in Tamil Nadu. Erode by the way is mentioned once in The Lonely Planet Guide as being a city that trades in textiles. That's it! Full stop. When I got back to my office from this visit, Emma, my PA-cum-Secretary told me that I had a letter on my desk and a cheque in it. I had negotiated a price for the land and it was about £2,500. I read the letter Emma had already opened and put on my desk. It was £2,500 to go towards the missions work in India. I knew this was the beginning of something very important to God. I couldn't wait to get back out there.

Back in The UK I was preparing for the extension. We would open up the whole of the inside so as to seat an extra 70-80 people giving us a comfortable capacity of 280. Many times we had many more than this in attendance and we did have a few gatherings that were over 400. It would cost about £150,000. We started to save and did special offerings and we made some good income from the nursery and training projects so as to tuck several thousand pounds away. The green light to begin this project came while I was India too. I returned and bought another piece of land adjacent to the first. Then another and a fourth. In four visits I had bought about two and a half acres of land. On one of the occasions I said to the Lord, "Lord, if I am to begin this extension at The Lighthouse, please give me ten percent up front. And let it come out of the blue," This was my prayer.

When I returned home, again, I had a letter on my desk. It was on blue letter-headed paper from a company called 'Bechtel'. They apparently were a subsidiary company of North West Water. They explained that they were doing some crucial repair works to sewage pipes in the area and our car park was ideal for them to run their operation from. In short they wanted to rent our car park. We met up with them and they did say that under Her Majesty The Queen's authority they can 'commandeer' any private piece of land to carry out works of this nature without even remuneration. I wasn't to be brow-beaten though and I said, "That may well be true but I don't think you'd enjoy the long delay as it goes to court and is appealed under charitable law" etc. They agreed and we began to negotiate costs. We would have to enable car parking on the opposite side of the site (which is something I was keen to do in any case!). This would ensure our parking capacity did not decrease. It also meant we would get a rental income. The agreed time was 20 weeks and I had a sneaking suspicion it would end up being considerably more. The only thing reliable, it seems, about construction work is that it will take longer and cost more than you first expected. It ended up being 26 weeks. We actually were paid £18,200 ie £700 per week. The other thing I negotiated with them was that when they left, they not only reinstated the car park but they would re-surface it and re-mark it for us. They agreed (reluctantly) but eventually. It was a great deal and came "out of the blue!"

This period of time we entered was very industrious, I would say unique and although extremely demanding was a sheer joy looking back on it. Things were about to accelerate big time. 'The Ferrari Years' were about to begin.

SECTION THREE

"The Ferrari Years"

Chapter Seventeen

THE LIGHTHOUSE SHINES OUT

"Ability is what you're able to do. Motivation determines what you will do. Attitude is about how well you will do it."

1998-9 was such a busy period for us all. We were preparing for a phenomenal season of industry for the Kingdom. Little did we know it, but we would build four incredible buildings, open them and dedicate them all in just over two and a half years' time. Pretty astonishing for a church of about 250 which we were at the time.

The extension had begun in 1999 and we were anticipating an opening date in the millennial year of 2000. At the same time though we were busy building the main Childcare Therapy Centre in Slatina, Romania. As well as this, we were getting drawings prepared so as to build a large children's home in India on the site I had bought. It was a very precious time for me. To be honest though, it's only when I look back that I can really 'enjoy the time'. It took so much focus and so much concentration I kind of just saw it as normal! I think though, looking back, given the conditions and the cost, it was far from normal. We raised £750,000 in the space of those three years to build and open four buildings debt free. That's not normal at all and all from a local church with 250 people. I began to think what a church with a thousand people could achieve, but on reflection it wasn't many of the people in the church who were involved in the missions work as far as the funds were concerned. As I stated previously, we were a church where about 60- 70 percent of our funds came from outside of the church for many years. This would be something like between 50-60 percent today, mainly because the congregation has more than doubled in size since then and our project income is different.

The extension for the existing Lighthouse Christian Centre in Manchester was launched late in 1999. Most of the work we did ourselves. One of our pastors, Justin (Marks) provided us with an architect who virtually did the drawings for nothing. I was the "hands on" clerk of works as I had basically been for the main building. I negotiated everything personally from bricks to volumes of concrete, provision of hardcore and other materials, equipment, sub-contractors. I even dealt with the planning permission and the building regulations.

I personally drafted in voluntary helpers as well as some part-time workers. The steelwork was fabricated and erected by a company, of course. But we laid the foundations, the footings and the drains along with the finishes. By the time we had finished we had a good sized secondary hall with its own entrance which became the main entrance for the church. We had a small kitchen at ground level and a large store room (this caused a lot of competition as to who had what amount of space). We had a large block of WC's to serve the number of attendees we envisaged. On the first floor we had four offices including mine. We had an office for Emma, another additional office and a larger general one. Also on the first floor we serviced the office block with a small kitchenette and a toilet. The final cost of the extension was £182,000. The deposit we got from Bechtel–the water company who hired our car park was £18,200 – exactly the ten percent I had asked for from the Lord. How utterly mind-blowing is that? What I also forgot to mention is that during the process of building the new Extension we managed to clear the existing loans off that we had on the main building. About £12,000 on one and about £8,000 on the other.

Whilst all of this was being done, I was busy in Romania too. We had a nightmare over the site because of the pastor of the church there on our site. In the end we had to split the site and pay him a sum of money towards his new church building £4,000. Plus legal costs. This deal was brokered by Rev Brian Edwards between The Romanian Pentecostal Church and LIM. At least we had the clearance we needed to get on with our vision of providing a Centre which would give specialist care to children from the government homes. We also put a multi-sensory room in the Centre which was a real hit with the children and produced remarkable results with them.

I was also out in India again at the time and work was about to start on the children's home, we had about £23,000 set aside for this, but we knew by the time we finished it, the cost would be more like £45,000. For us this was a bargain considering the lives we could change. A builder was selected and plans were drawn up to begin the work in 2001, some three months after the Extension was to be opened in Manchester.

Back to Manchester UK then! We had to really go some to finish the building on time. We had decided on a date in November, 2000. We had to be ready before this because a couple in our church were to be married on just before the official opening. Well, we worked through the night to make sure the work was finished on time. My office was the last room to be finished and as we were to be signing the register in there, it needed to be done nicely. Someone took over the wallpapering for me at 4am in the morning when I had just about had it. Phil and Emma (my PA) who were getting married in a matter of hours were busy helping us. We just about pulled it off. The place did look stunning to be fair. We had the wedding and this itself had a missions feel to it as Phil and Emma first started dating after they returned from mission when they were on a team together in Romania. Phil and Emma are another amazing couple in The Lighthouse, having come to the Lord in their teens here, they got baptised, were married and have both been serving God in The House here for many years. They now have three wonderful children, Ben, Abigail and Ollie. Phil is now a Trustee for LIM and teaches on our discipleship course "Footsteps".

The official opening of the Extension took place on Saturday the 4th of November. About 500 people came including one of our local MPs who was a staunch supporter and who used our nursery for all her children. Pastor John Glass, our General Superintendent unveiled the special plaque and in the evening we had a Celebration at which John preached and my Father-in-law shared too. It was a great day, but to be honest my thoughts were now in Romania where the next instalment of special openings would take place.

In Romania the Centre was coming on now in leaps and bounds. The problems we had experience with our friend Pastor Sovack had cost us a lot of time and a lot of money too. This building was the most difficult we've ever built. It took three planning permissions, about £200,000 ($300,000), most of which came through our charity shops, plus a whole pile of hassle all along the way. Early in 2001, we not only finished the building, but we opened the Childcare Therapy Centre too. It was a wonderful facility and even early on you could tell it was going to be very successful. On Saturday 27th April 2002, we officially opened the New Centre. The media were there and the National Television station too. We conducted interviews that went out across the country on prime time TV. This was indeed good publicity but we knew now we had to live up to that good publicity. All sorts of organisations and representatives attended the official opening and it was a very memorable occasion. The builders were there too and I have to say they were great to work with. They even had a surprise for me. They made a commemorative plaque and I unveiled it on the day. That was their doing–not mine. It is of course there to this day, though the Centre's use had to change with the seasons. That's another story which I'll cover just a bit later in the book. The couple who we had running the Centre for us were an incredibly dynamic couple. He had caught my eye some years ago as a very progressive thinking Romanian who had a very evident call of God upon his life. I knew him since he was seventeen. Eventually I brought him to the UK to The Lighthouse to study at a nearby Bible School in Tyldesley, (where I had met Pastor Jenson Jeberaj–my Indian connection). He stayed for about two and a half years and then married a beautiful young woman who he'd known most of his life. They both became like a son and daughter to both Mags and myself. We were very close and even took short holidays together in Romania at Christmas time. They managed the Centre for the next seven years, until one of the biggest, maybe even the biggest bombshell went off. In fact it would be nuclear! It was a very, very tragic moment and it's why I have refrained from naming the couple.

The Casa Lumini Centre as it was called (translated literally House of Light–not Lighthouse as we had intended!) became very well known within the country. We had a programme for children in the morning and in the afternoon we had children with special needs. The children in the morning were actually called 'normal' and the children in the afternoon 'children with deficiencies'. Enough said! Anyhow we raised funds along the way and bought a minibus and later a lady donated funds to buy another one, which we still have to this day. A Mercedes nine seater. These buses picked up and dropped off the children, both the morning group and the afternoon group. As you can imagine along with all our staff and personnel it was quite an operation. We employed many people and we had several income streams being generated in order to keep the programme running.

The Centre manager also became a pastor in Romania after training in the UK for the two and a half years. He married his fiancée in Romania and a lot of people flew over to be part of their happy day. I led the service in the church next door. This was about three or four years back when our relationship with Pastor Sovack was reasonably okay. Eventually the young man could no longer work with Sovack for several reasons and so as not to cause division in the church he decided to take up an assistant pastor's position with a pastor I knew in a nearby village some 35 miles away. Eventually that also came to an end, mainly because the pressure to plant a new church in Slatina became too great. It was so, so needed. The churches for me in Slatina were totally irrelevant to where the people were, especially the young people. We did many missions in Slatina which were incredibly fruitful only to find young people who had made genuine decisions to follow the Lord were put off at their first visits to church by being handed head scarves and told to take off jewellery and make up! Just bonkers! We planted together in Slatina and before long had about fifty people in regular attendance. We even planted out to a nearby town Bals which is still just about running and is being led by a missionary from the UK. The Izvorul Viatsii (River of Life) church was for me the best hope of building a church that really ministered to all ages in Slatina. Alas, when a good leader goes down, the ripples of their demise reach even far distant shores.

With The Lighthouse Extension now successfully opened, The Casa Lumini Centre also successfully opened, now it was onto the Indian scenario. In the meantime while we were focusing on the Extension project and The Casa Lumimi project, we had also set up BACS in India. Build A Church Scheme. (I'll tell you about this in the next chapter). We had our whole site dedicated to The Lord on 18th October 2001. We also held a big graduation service for the bible college students from Erode. About 2,000 people gathered and it was quite an occasion. We laid a special plaque to commemorate the day. I also planted a Neem Tree which I am looking at as I write. It is a huge and very fine tree. The stage had been set for us to now raise funds for The Children's Home. At present the church had taken in about seven or eight abandoned children. I have often been asked about my love for these kids. People ask me "Is it because you don't have your own biological children?" The truth is I don't know. If I had my own I'm still pretty sure I would have got involved in building children's homes and investing in children and young people. I absolutely love children and especially teenagers. I think I just see potential in them all the time. I've seen many a tragedy too.

Around about this time in Manchester I had to take the funeral service of a fine healthy young man, a father of two children who hung himself. I had actually led him to the Lord about two weeks before in his own house and I know the Lord got me to get him to pray for himself, which he did. I led him through the prayer of salvation. He was very disturbed at the time. Illness of the mind is a horrible thing. Both of my parents died of dementia at around this time too. People are very ungracious I've found when it comes to how they view illness related to the mind. I simply believe when a person takes their own life it is usually for two reasons. Either desperation, i.e. they cannot face something, for instance in India, a lot of people take their own lives because of great poverty. It has reached almost epidemic levels amongst tenant farmers whose debt has become out of control. The only way out for them to prevent a life of misery is suicide. It's awful and it's tragic, but unfortunately this is how many people's lives play-out over there. The other main reason is illness. They are unbalanced in their thinking and in a moment through depression or anxiety take their lives. I really don't think it helps to talk about heaven and hell in such circumstances. The fact is Christians also take their lives from time to time. It doesn't mean they're eternally dammed. It does mean they were greatly disturbed, unable to cope and desperately unbalanced at the time.

These people need respect and help while we can give it and if it's not enough they need our understanding and compassion even in the event of it being too late to save their physical being, their soul can still be in the right place. That's my own opinion and I respect it may not be yours. I have come to this conclusion. After all God is much much bigger than our complex thinking allows for. I believe He's got it all covered.

I took the funeral service of this young man. His mother had come to Christ, his sister also and his twin sister. His grandfather also I led to The Lord on his deathbed. It for me was a victory to know he made a prayer of repentance before his life ended. The congregation of over 500 heard God's word, clearly and poignantly. At the reception afterwards I got to meet many of his friends, many of whom were notorious gang members of a very well known gang in Moss Side. It was a day of great sowing and I managed to personally witness to many of the gang members about Christ's love and His purpose. I love talking to young people and teenagers especially. I think if God spares me and I'm in my eighties I'll still be encouraging young people to live for Christ. The years 2000 and 2001 were certainly Fast and Furious! 2002 and 2003 were going to be even more full on!

Chapter Eighteen

THE BACS PROGRAMME

"Never mistake activity for achievement."

The BACS ("Build A Church Scheme") programme was and still is for me, one of the most effective and sure ways of building the Kingdom here on earth. For a donation of as little as £1,500 we were building church buildings all around the South of India. BACS enabled an individual, organisation or a local church to build a church in its name, or as a legacy to a loved one. At the time we could build a small church for £1,500 or a slightly bigger one for £2,000 or a quite large one for £2,500. As I write (early 2014) we have built 76 Church buildings in India. We are about to build our 77th, 78th, 79th and hopefully 80th soon too.

This church building programme started by default actually. I was asked to visit a small, young church just planted in the suburbs of a city in Tamil Nadu. The church was about 25-30 people maximum. It met in the pastor's home. I arrived and we went in. It turned out the pastor and his family had turfed out all their belongings and hung them all on the outside wall of the house he was living in. He had hung them there to prevent bugs and insects and even snakes getting inside, of which there were many in the area. We started the service and in ten minutes the little house had about 40-50 people packed into it with about 20 people outside. I preached simply and gave an appeal. About 40-50 people came forward for salvation, many of them Hindus with the little bindi (dot) between their eyes. An easy clue as to their current belief.

It was clear to me following that small service that so much ground could be made for the Kingdom if we could support and encourage churches like this and help them to make room for more of the harvest. We devised a plan. We would send a thousand pounds and the pastor Stephen Raj would build the church using the wall on his house as part of the church wall. This would keep costs down. It was done. We sent the money, the builder set to it and I visited some seven months later. What I saw utterly convinced me that there was great mileage to be made for the Kingdom. The little church was packed–about 120-140 people were present. Many of them again were Hindus. The chief of the village also came and during the appeal was one of the respondents I recall. About 30-40 came forward at the appeal.

I have since been back several times and can fast forward here for you. The church now has planted two more congregations and we gave them a second BACS church for one of their plants. The numbers attending the three churches is around 7-800. The initial meeting we had was in or around 2002/3. I don't know about you as a reader, but if you said you would like a further 650-700 believers attending church in just over ten years I think you'd would be over the moon to see it happen. Now, take this model and downscale it as exceptional and just halve it. Then multiply by the number of church buildings built (x 76). This would equate to about 25,000 believers! That's a modest estimate of the numbers that will have come to faith through The BACS church building programme. Whilst we should never mistake activity for achievement, this is one of our activities that will probably go down as the single most fruitful missional strategy we've ever employed.

Some of these churches are in suburbs of cities like Chennai (formerly Madras) and Trippur, Salem, Coimbatore, Kollam in Kerala. Others are in more rural or even tribal areas, especially where no churches have been. Places in Andra Pradesh, even one in West Bengal for another Christian charity working from another church base in UK. This charity, called Stepping Stones, concentrates its work in West Bengal and has a children's home too and other ministries. We are blessed to support such ministries when and where we can.

The signs and wonders we have witnessed in some of our BACS church openings have been incredible too. In Andra Pradesh in the north of the state, we opened two churches we'd built in fairly close proximity. At one of the churches we are asked to pray for the sick. The outburst of supernatural power was one of the most spectacular things I've seen. People got healed left right and centre and it was just amazing and like a sovereign act of God. He had decided that He would come and display His power here. The meeting finished and then had a new start. We prayed for so many people at that church opening.

Again in another village, in a season when we had a lot of persecution by the RSS (Hindu fundamentalists), who are often responsible for beating pastors and church leaders and even killing them–these guys were on the move in the area. I was preaching in this remote village and a number of people watched from a distance. I could see them clearly and they looked suspicious to me for sure. At the end of the preach I conducted an appeal as usual. There had been a man with his hand tucked in a sling. He was wearing a lot of orange which usually meant he was RSS. As I led the appeal a lot of people came forward for salvation. These guys continued to watch motionless. There was about twelve to fifteen of them. Then I gave a call for people who needed healing from sickness disease and other infirmities. This man with his hand in a sling came forward. He was the first in the queue. He was one of the guys stood at the back. My imagination runs riot at these times and my natural SatNav goes into overdrive as I considered all the possible scenarios. I went to pray for the people in the queue. The first man with his hand in the sling I thought could have a knife or a weapon of some sort, so I was cautious. In fact the man had a paralysed arm and slightly withered too. I took it out of the sling and began to pray for him. The power of the Lord hit him and he raised his hand to the sky praising God as he did so. The rest of the queue were totally inspired and went into real confidence in God's power to heal. Not surprisingly many got healed that evening. I'm still not convinced that there was not something amiss with those fellows though. Perhaps that's why God brought such a wonderful healing to the first person in the queue!

Other BACS missions, too many to mention here, took place all over India. On one visit alone I remember opening and dedicating six church buildings. The results speak for themselves. I still try to promote the BACS programme as a cost effective way for any church to be involved in mission that lasts. Each BACS church is an opportunity of immense growth and unlimited outreach for the sake of Christ's Kingdom.

When my father died on Saturday 7th April 2001 we built a BACS church from the gifts and donations which were given in lieu of flowers etc at the funeral. We added a bit from the family and we built a church in the Pondicherry district of Tamil Nadu in a place called Tanjoor. Unfortunately I was so ill with a throat and lung infection I could hardly speak let alone preach! I still gave it my best shot though and the church is there to this day. My mother then died exactly 12 months later of the same illness– senile dementia. It was bizarre because the time of her death was within minutes of when Dad died the year previously, effectively the same day, the first Saturday in April 2002, literally within 2-3 minutes of dad's death.

Dementia is a horrible thing to deal with and it's hard when both your Mum and Dad suffer. I promised myself, as well as Mum and Dad, that I would conduct the burial for them myself. I was doing Dad's with my Mum clinging hold of my right arm. Mags was on Mum's other arm. As they lowered dad down into the grave, my Mum said to me, "Such a shame!" I was just about to say, "Yes, Mum", when she said, "And who is it again?" "Mum", I said "it's Dad!!" "It isn't is it? Why didn't you tell me? Why didn't anybody let me know?". This is the awful reality of dealing with dementia. I had to learn to roll with things as they came up. I visited my mother a lot in the ensuing months after Dad's burial. On one occasion I was just leaving, Mags was with me. "Okay Mum, I'll be on my way now, I have to leave." "Okay dear", she said, "and who did you say you were again? What was your name?" "Mum, it's me, Paul! Your son!" "What? I haven't got a son called Paul! I've got a son called Michael ... but not Paul!" Hahaha ! I wouldn't mind but Mike was the person who visited the least

165

of any of us! He won't thank me for saying that but it's a fact. Anyhow, as I said, I learned to roll with the moment.

When it came to the crunch though to bury my Mother, it was the single most hard thing I've ever had to do. I cried like a baby in my garden the morning before the burial. I loved both my Mum and my Dad greatly, but my Mum was just ... well, just my Mum. This lady was just an awesome woman of God who always put the Lord first and foremost in all she ever did. When she was dying, I was scheduled to fly out on a strategic mission to Romania to help a recruitment drive for our DUNAMIS Youth Camp in the summer that year. (We held a camp site for about 5-600 young people and children each year). As I said, I was scheduled to go out, but I couldn't leave Mum on her deathbed. Mags was great. "Love, what would your Mum have wanted you to do? Do you seriously think she would have wanted you not to go?" That was enough for me, I went and while there I preached the gospel on my Mum's favourite verse, "Behold I stand at the door and knock". She had given her life to the Lord on the truth of this verse as a little girl when she saw it accompanied with the famous Holman Hunt painting of Christ standing at the door knocking with a lantern in his hand. It is called "Jesus The Light of The World". Someone once questioned Holman Hunt as to a mistake he supposedly made in the painting. The door had no handle upon it so as to open it. "No, there's no mistake", said Holman, "the handle is on the inside." I've preached this many many times and did so in Romania on that occasion with great passion and emotion of course too. Several people gave their lives in that little Baptist Church in a small town in the south of the country.

I've always realised there is a huge cost to mission that goes way beyond finance. Time, family, pressures, priorities all take their toll and dealing with all of that can be daunting. Many people ask me, "Pastor Paul how on earth can you be away so much and still lead a great and dynamic church? Shouldn't you be careful that you're not away too much?" Whilst I appreciate their 'concern' I quickly realise the naivety of the question too. If you're going to lead and to travel and to be away on mission, then you have to do a couple of things. 1. You have to be a strong leader and 2. You have to be a good delegator. I happen to be both of those and it has stood me in great stead. When I'm home–I'm in charge! Full stop! When I'm away the guys are in charge, full stop. But they also realise that if Mags is around she is essentially part of me and therefore the Pastoral Team. Keeping her in the know automatically keeps me in the loop. If we're both away then the Team are in charge of respective areas and discuss together matters of decision making. They are free to contact me in any case as I'm always contactable by them wherever I go. But I place them in charge and trust them.

You will soon find out whether you can trust someone or not. Trust is like an eraser, the more mistakes are made the less there is left! Having said this trust is essential and integrity in certain areas is non-negotiable. Successful delegation is delegation par excellence, and is not a science. So much is involved in delegating successfully. Perceptiveness, wisdom, good judgment, courage to take risks (delegation will always have its risks). Discernment, diligence and commitment to those we choose to delegate to.

Also understanding is vital. We need to understand that successful delegation takes time and effort. Delegating is not just 'getting rid of jobs'. That's 'dumping' and there's a big difference. Delegating means accepting that people are going to do the job differently than you would do it. Some compromise is essential here. I have absolutely no desire to know everything there is to know in The Lighthouse or in LIM. Sure there are essentials, there are possibles and there are unmentionables! It is the possibles that cover the grey areas. The only way to find out what needs reporting back is to work together, grow together and learn together. This leans on organic growth and I think it is a healthy and practical strategy that will suit many leaders who lead hybrid organisations. I have a PA but I don't want to just have a PA in name only. She needs to know me and my ways, my personality and my idiosyncrasies too. I've been really blessed in this are because the only two PA's I've had had been just so good in this respect. Emma Smith who became Emma Clare was more like a daughter to Mags and I and came on staff at the tender age of 17 shortly after she gave her life to Christ. It took a couple of years before she became my PA/ Secretary. She served with us for 15 years. She only left because she had three children and she felt it was time to spend more time with them.

My PA now, Ana Tudosie, is Romanian. She became a Christian at eight years of age at an open air baptism service I did in her village. She came to work for us as a young teenager on our children's therapy programme in Slatina at Casa Lumini. I knew she would work with us for many years as the Lord showed me this when she was about 15 years of age. Both Ana and Emma are totally loyal to Mags and myself and are incredibly brilliant at holding confidential information. Some people we've worked with have been totally brilliant but they cannot keep their counsel. In fact once they know a little 'nugget of information' it's not very long before everybody knows. Such people will never be allowed to stay in close proximity and be on the main team in any department I'm part of as this is a fundamental requirement of staff who work closely with senior leadership. They actually forfeit the right to work within that circle. It's a simple as that for us. Our closest pastoral and admin staff are the key for me and Mags. We have come to see and understand this over many years. So, now I can practice what I call, "the laying off of hands"–'Dynamic delegation'. I've written a bit more about this towards the end of the book.

Chapter Nineteen

DANGER! VISIONARY AT WORK!

"Between your dream's inspiration and its manifestation, there's going to be a lot of perspiration."

So, the months were racing by with exciting deadlines and wonderful opportunities. The Lighthouse Christian Centre had been successfully extended and was growing again. The Casa Lumini Centre was up and running in Romania. We had dedicated the site in India, and we had also built about 15 Church buildings in India under the BACS programme. Now it was time to start the building work on the Children's Home. In actual fact, this building was probably the easiest building we've ever built. I know it sounds daft, but looking back, it's almost as if it built itself! It took about ten months to build it and I distinctly remember being in the Casa Lumini Centre in Romania as it was nearing completion. I was miles away in my mind and one of the staff saw me and commented "Pastor Paul! Where are you now? You are miles away somewhere else aren't you?" I said to the observant young man. "Yes, you're absolutely right. I'm in India finishing the Children's Home." I'm afraid this rather sums me up! Being such a visionary has a downside. It takes a lot of the enjoyment out of the final completion of a project or a vision, as it moves from visionary status in your life to completed and fulfilled status. Therefore your heart and your mind shift towards what is primary now, in terms of vision future. It's a strange thing, but I've become more aware of this these days. I think now it's why I need to start to excel in training, equipping and releasing leaders. I am making this a priority in UK and in India at the moment.

Even if a visionary is successful, if he or she does not get the right people on board, that which was dynamically and powerfully created and initiated can be ruined and destroyed and laid to waste a lot quicker than in the time it took to build it. This is a huge lesson for many of us entrepreneurial leaders. I said earlier in the book, many people can be responsible for our success, but only we are responsible for our failure. If the entrepreneurial leader fails to train and equip, inspire and release others into service and also be able to have an idea about business plans, finance and management, one or two things will happen. 1. We will create what we envisaged, only to find that we had no plan for continuity and development and therefore the project, vision or dream flounders and becomes redundant. Or, 2. We will not find anyone else with the passion, heart and motivation to keep the wheels turning and therefore deliver the results the project, vision or dream was created for. For example, our dream can easily become a white elephant if there is no forward planning or forward thinking.

Often the entrepreneurial leader is the least qualified to take the project onto fruitfulness and productivity. To be honest, most entrepreneurs make poor managers. The reason is quite simple. They are visionaries and visionaries hate being tied down and tied into things. Their passion is to create and innovate new things. Management of those things on a day-to-day basis can become very frustrating. I'm speaking from experience here. I can manage okay, but to be honest, sometimes I get very frustrated. I've never really had an executive manager, I've been 'that person' as well as the senior pastor and it has saved the church a fortune over the years when really it needed one but never had the finance. I found myself doing three jobs. Lead Pastor, Director of the International Missions Charity and Executive Pastor, looking after and overseeing all the staff and the church centre. It's a role that I loved for many years and continue to play, but know in the not too distant future I will need to relinquish certain responsibilities and develop new leaders. I'm working on this right now. In truth because things are growing and developing, I have to be careful that I don't become the bottleneck for growth. Raising, appointing and employing new leaders is going to be expensive, but not doing it will be much more expensive.

I am now looking at more revenue projects that will create opportunities to bring in finance. I'm asking the Lord to help me do this in new and exciting ways. In the future a lot of my time will be spent in India. I feel this is so right, although I love the church family I have and my deep sense of belonging to The Lighthouse Manchester will always be there. In India, there is a huge appetite to learn and they have the discernment to realise who they can truly learn from. In Romania it's different and many of the older generations do not really have a heart for change and the more biblical approach to leadership. They are extremely hierarchical and autocratic. Relational leadership, in their opinion, doesn't work. (Not that they've tried it by the way!–they just 'know' it doesn't work–so in the main they stay small and compact). Sad, but true. Strong leaders do not need to be autocratic. They just need to build strong relationships! Then they need to learn to delegate and give some of their power/authority away! Now, here's another important lesson. When you give your authority away you need to understand, you can give it away far more easily than you can take it back!

I had a chap once who had been in the church for approximately 17 years. On and off, because he left twice and came back. I re-instated him as a house-group leader when he came back and he and his wife were excellent at that level. The only problem was, he really aspired to a 'higher position'. However all the service and good done by him and through him usually came with not a price tag, but a "praise tag". What I mean by this is, he always needed 'praising' or 'thanking' for what he had done. He could go into a sulk faster than a rabbit could go down a burrow if he felt he didn't get the accolades etc.

At one point I seriously needed help in pastoral ministry. I had just lost one of my assistant pastors to a stroke. It was dreadful! Peter was a really good help for several years and with help, became a probationary minister in our denomination. He was heading towards ordination when out of the blue having just returned from holiday, on a Sunday morning, he suffered a terrible stroke. It was awful! Mags and I went to see him and I remember him not being able to talk properly. Half his face had slipped down. As we left the hospital Mags cried a lot. It's hard to see someone you love reduced to being a man who cannot speak properly and communicate anymore! And this was a preacher for goodness sake! Amazingly and thanks to the Lord, Pete made an unbelievable recovery although it took a full nine months. We had been told by the doctors that what would come back would come back quite quickly and the slower the recovery the less progress he would make. Peter bucked that trend and within six months he was 75 percent there and after nine months he was 95 percent. Only those who knew what had happened would tell anything had happened. Just a slight hesitation in his words now and again that was it.

During this time, I personally had to manage the whole situation. I did ask the guys to go and speak to Pete about where we stood as a church. We paid him for six months on full salary, but it was obvious this couldn't continue. Pete wanted to come back and start pastoral duties within The Lighthouse. I really felt this would not be wise. Peter's wife Chris had struggled for a long time being "up north" and she longed to go back home, down south. I felt this was the time to do it. I spoke with our Regional Superintendent and eventually a vacancy arose in the. Broadstairs Elim Church, Kent. This was perfect! I asked two of our pastoral staff, including the brother who I had brought on staff recently to visit Pete and inform him of our plan. This would also mean his salary would reduce to two thirds after the six months and to half after nine months and then cease after 12 months in the event of him not taking up another position in our denomination. My point being, the ministry especially in a church like The Lighthouse is very stressful. I did not want Peter coming back on staff and having another stroke and then this would come back on us for sure. My two pastoral staff did not want to go and speak to Peter but felt it should come from me. I went, but it was a case of me having to sort the whole sad and sorry episode out. Even our denomination didn't help much as they seemed to have no infrastructure to help with this kind of situation and so we had no meaningful and practical advice at all. It was a case of having to manage the situation as it arose.

So, this other brother came onto staff and it was incredible. He went from Dr Jekyll to Mr Hyde within six months. It was a nightmare! On one occasion I asked him to go and visit someone for me. He point blank refused! I said "I am not actually asking you to go, I'm requesting you to go!" Again he refused. I said, "You have to go, you're his pastor!" he countered "I am not his pastor anymore! I'm not seeing this guy, I'm not his pastor anymore and I refuse to have anything to do with him." I was pretty mad and stunned all in one go to be honest, and it was the beginning of the end for him. The situation grew so bad that he started bossing people about like a sergeant major. I came to a point where I'd had enough.

I remember it well. I got up at 3am and said to Mags, "That's it!! I'm finished! I've had enough! Either he goes or I go ... and I'm staying!" Whenever I reach a stage where I'm like this, it's as good as done! I spoke to him the next day and told him I'm not happy with his level of performance and told him "I'm giving you three choices. 1) You buck your ideas up and your level of accountability and you do as you are requested to do in an appropriate manner. 2) You go part time, i.e. two or at the most three days a week." (To be honest, what he was doing I could have done in a day and a half. We had volunteers who were putting in far more energy and commitment!) No. 3 option was to "leave and go and get a job!" In the end he chose No. 3. The problem was he then took himself off the preaching rota, and I never saw him again. Only once after this he ever spoke to me to see if he could come back to visit the church. I said we would have to meet up first, as he left in such a bad way. How can you go from pastor to never coming back again? But he did. His so called 'love for the people' was really a love for his position. Once that was called into question there was nothing left.

Position is the lowest form of spiritual authority. Those who desire it tend to have religious pride and that's a "no-no" in a church like ours. At The Lighthouse we try to avoid politics at all costs. It is one of the most dangerous threats to growth, life and vitality. If you see an area of politics in your church and you are able to act, get rid of it any way you can. Even if you have to dismantle it very wisely and very slowly it will be the single best thing you'll have done to grow the church. I once appointed a salaries committee. In theory it was great. It gave transparency and offloaded any sense of autocracy. The trouble is they never met for over 18 months!! I disbanded it immediately. Those on the committee apologised but it was too late. The lesson was learned!

I love the saying "God so loved the world that he didn't send a committee". Another favourite of mine is "A committee is like four people trying to park a car!" Most of the time, committees exist for those who are bored with life, have nothing much to do with themselves, love the sound of their own voices or missed out somewhere along the line. On the rare occasion where a committee does work, you will find that it's got little to do with them being a committee but more with them being a team! I am passionate about teams but totally put off by committees. Teams have common goals and often very good relationships. In fact as someone once said "Individuals may win trophies but teams win championships." Teams are our way of getting things done and I want teams of passionate people who blend and forge new beginnings and conceive new ideas. Committees are very often groups of complete individuals with their individual agendas, which makes for incredibly and unnecessarily long meetings, and protracted issues leading to absolute frustration to decision makers. To this end I'm always looking at people, weighing up potential and scouting new ability based on passion and availability first, way before gifting. In the next chapter I will deal with the special opening day of our children's home and new vision hitting The Lighthouse UK.

Chapter Twenty

A SEASON OF ABUNDANCE

"Opportunities multiply as they are seized."

The year is 2002 and the date is Saturday, 10th of October. Our brand new Children's Home in India is finished and ready to be opened and dedicated to The Lord. It is a splendid building and will accommodate about 80 children though I asked for the numbers to be capped to 50, simply because I don't want the home to become an institution. I know that many will say that any home with more than 15 children automatically becomes an institution. I do disagree. I think it depends on who is managing and running the home and the 'regimes' employed there. This is a constant battle for me. I am forever telling staff to stop referring to our kids as orphans and the home as an orphanage. Many of the introductions I have when I first meet a new boy or girl is "Pastor Paul, this is Enoch–he is an orphan boy!" I really can't stand it and have to tell the person who introduces the boy not to do it. It is totally negative language. Children need to be brought up in positive environments. This means choosing our words carefully. Our homes are 'Children's Homes', not orphanages. Many of our children are not orphans in the truest sense of the word. They are however abandoned and much work is being done at the moment to not take children whose parents are alive unless in exceptional circumstances.

We do not want to be a boarding school for children whose parents are not willing to pay for their education or are just palming them off on us until they're at a useful age. Aunts and uncles and grandparents are the main culprits here. They send their nephews and nieces, or grandsons or granddaughters so that we feed them, clothe them and educate them and then, when they're old enough, especially the girls, they come for them promising a 'proper home', money and other things. The children (usually the girls) go and end up either in a sweat shop working for 100 rupees a day, (£1) or at their relative's house cooking, cleaning, ironing, washing etc basically as a slave. They are also taken out of education completely. The practice is illegal but it is commonplace. We have introduced affidavits (agreements) to counter this action being taken and we have asked for a payment which will be returned on the child's 18th birthday. This discourages relatives 'placing' children intending to use us just as a nursery for them. It seems to be working now and we also have the added bonus of telling the children when they're 14 or 15 that we have sponsorships available for them when they go to college and then on to university if their grades are good enough. We have partners in University College School, Frognal, London, who are brilliant with our kids and raise funds for them so they can be properly educated. It is a sure way out of poverty.

The Children's Home was opened successfully and soon filled up. We now have about 60 children and currently a great [couple in charge?] Samuel and his wife Beulah head up the home for us. Pastor Samuel is a really progressive thinker, loves the kids, listens to them and loves them to play and have fun, as well as of course applying themselves to studying and revising for their school work. The home is not called 'The Lighthouse' as we tied it into a large local church, Bethany Fellowship Trust, through which we built most of The BACS Churches in India. Bethany is also affiliated with Elim UK and is part of Elim Global. The Children's home is also called Bethany Children's Home.

We also have a children's home in Goa, India. This is called "The Lighthouse Children's Home" and comprises of two homes that we rent for a modest sum. One of the houses is our girls home, the other is our boys home. We have far more girls than boys in

176

Goa, all from a variety of backgrounds. Some of their life stories are horrific. I make sure I visit Lighthouse Goa every year and try to encourage the couple who are projects managers there every year too. They do a great job on a limited budget. The Indian Government is making it very difficult for foreigners to work 'hands on' in heading up children's projects and I think it's only a matter of time before the work in Goa will have to be integrated into an indigenous Indian charitable body.

After returning to the UK from opening the Bethany Children's Home, the next building to commence as soon as we could, would be the Bible College on the same site I had purchased for the Children's Home. Little did I know at the time, but we were about to land our biggest and largest single grant for mission.

My father-in-law had told me about a friend of his who had helped him on various occasions on mission. He was a fairly wealthy businessman–cum-property owner. He had died and left a large sum of money to be used by a Christian organisation working in the field of biblical education. Dad told me to arrange a visit to see this man's solicitors. I called them to see if I could arrange a meeting with them. Thankfully they agreed to see me. Typically, just when something great is looking like breaking, there always seems to be something that happens in order to deter you. I cricked my neck overnight two nights before I was due to go down to Cardiff to the appointment with the solicitors. I was in utter agony and went to the Physio/Chiropractor for treatment to try and get me moving. My neck was in spasm. I've never had anything like this in my life before or since it was plain weird. I told Mags whatever the case I was going and I was driving! My father-in-law offered to come with me and drive if I needed. He did come with me but I wasn't going to allow him to drive. I had some work done on it and it got me moving a bit. My stubbornness definitely kicked in on that occasion.

We set out early the next day and finally got to Cardiff well in time. The solicitor of the deceased's estate said he had very clear parameters in which he had to give the money away. He asked me about LIM. I told him we existed to help disadvantaged groups to get out of poverty through a means of education, shelter and provision of clothing, medicines were needed. Usually, children were the chief beneficiaries. I also told him we brought education to many children and young people through the Bible. He pricked up his ears at this. I explained we were building a large Bible college in Tamil Nadu, South India. He asked me what king of doctrine we would teach. I looked down at a piece of paper which he had in front of him. I could just about make out "39" which I knew would refer to the "39 Articles" which is the doctrinal statement of The Church of England. I made a comment to say, "Well our doctrines broadly follow the teachings of the 39 Articles of the Church of England." With this the solicitor immediately was enthusiastic. "Oh, wow! That's great, because that's exactly what I've been asked to use as a specific guide. We will not be allowed to give the funds for anyone who operates outside of this doctrinal statement.""Oh great" I said, sounding as surprised as him! We eventually agreed that I would send him full details of the Bible College and take it from there. He did tell me right there and then that Cardiff University had made an approach to them and that their bid looked favourable too. We made our way back up the M5 and M6, my neck now feeling as stiff as a board!

I put the proposal together and sent it off as promised. The total build was about £130,000 but I said we had some finance put aside towards it ourselves. I believed the fund to be around the £100,000 mark so had to pitch it right. I also made the point that the building could not happen without this legacy being given. We were dependent upon it. I also distinctly remember making the point that the College would be training pastors, evangelists and church leaders for decades to come and therefore the benefactors' legacy would have long-lasting benefit to many men and women in the sub-continent for years to come.

Eventually I heard back from the solicitors. We had convinced them that this project was the most suited to the deceased gentleman's chosen beneficiary. We were also told it was the sum of £92,000 and that we could draw on the amounts by providing receipts or invoices. This was fine. We were on our way. It took only eight months to build the College. All the plans had already been in place and we took the decision when we were building the Children's Home, that we would lay the foundation at the same time as laying the foundation of the Children's Home. This saved us a substantial amount of money and was a great move.

On Wednesday 19th March 2003, we opened the El Shaddai Bible College. What a fabulous facility! We also incorporated a two bedroomed apartment for visiting team members going out from the UK. I have written much of this book while staying at the apartment. It has a superb library with well over 30,000 books for students' use. It has accommodation for up to 120 students. The dining room also serves our Children's Home thereby avoiding expensive costs. It also has a 500-seater chapel with brilliant acoustics too. It is decorated to a high standard and has many classrooms as you would expect. I personally (along with the senior pastor, Pastor Samuel Innocent), planted shrubs, trees and bushes that have turned the whole campus now into a bit of an Eden to be honest. It really is a beautiful and relaxed environment.

The area which was completely empty a few years ago, is now like a small village. Since we built the college, we have purchased a further two and a half acres of land opposite. Although it is important to note, none of this belongs to LIM or The Lighthouse. It really makes me laugh when people have implied I'm 'empire building'. Would you seriously build buildings and give them away, buy land and give it away if you were empire building? It's not much of an empire if you don't own it is it? The fact is, it is Kingdom, not Empire. Even our current facility in the UK we do not own. All of the buildings, the sites, the projects ultimately have to serve the vision. Nothing else matters! The Kingdom of God may include buildings, lands, fields and projects but it is so so much more. These will all pass away with time and space, but the Kingdom will remain. To know this is comforting. It puts into perspective lease agreements, title deeds, trust deeds and policies and the like.

From the end of 2000 to the beginning of 2003 was literally astonishing in terms of what we saw God do. We even managed to put a superb seven bedroomed apartment on the top floor of The Casa Lumini Centre. It was and still is a superb facility and was built in order to create Casa Noastra, ("our home") in Romania. The vision was to take 14 abandoned children from the government orphanages and put them in a family home run by Christian

179

parents. We were helped greatly by Unilever in Port Sunlight, Brighton College and West St Baptist Church in Crewe to enable this to happen. It cost about £20,000 to do all the work but was a superb home. The children were selected carefully and prayerfully. Most had already been attending the morning sessions at the therapy centre so we had a head start. Two twins were chosen first, Danny and Vasile. They were only 7 or 8 when they first came to Casa Noastra. I have known them both personally since they were four years of age. Ionela and Marius came next and then siblings Alexandra, Mihaela and Claudio, Bobi, Iuli, two sisters Lily and Ionela (now Ella), Ana, Myno and Mada. Ana and her sister Myno (Mynodora) were in a single parent family in the small church plant and faced extreme poverty so we took them in.

As time went by, Ana left to get married. Also Lily did too and Myno went back to her mother as their circumstances had improved and Myno began looking after her little brother. We still are in touch with her as she prepares to go to university in Bucharest. Marius and Ionela eventually went to Italy to live with their grandparents leaving just nine children. We took another child into our home a few years ago in 2010. Juli was five when we took him and he had nothing on his feet. Mags and I picked him up with Ramona our Director and Jayne Harris, one of our trustees at the time. Juli is still in our home to this day. He is a lovely young boy and can be very sweet though obviously very mischievous too as with most boys his age. The home went through massive disruption and turbulence as the couple running it lost their way spiritually altogether. The young man concerned (I referred to earlier) became immoral and totally unaccountable. I found this out during one of our youth camps in Romania and what I found out was appalling and simply unbelievable. (I'll cover some of this in a later chapter). In the end it cost him and his wife their vocation, their status, their relationships, their credibility, respect and their family too. A very, very costly shortcoming that led to whole-scale dishonesty, deceit and self-delusion. It cost the life of one church and jeopardised another, and virtually the lives of all our children too along with the childcare programme on the ground floor of the main centre. We were to have to spend the next few years more 'hands on' with the kids to convince them they were loved and secure and would not be going back into government homes.

Today Casa Noastra still exists in a different town altogether, as Mags and I felt we needed the kids to be in a strong, vibrant church. That certainly narrowed our options down. In the end, the family home moved to Turnu Severin, a strategically historical town on the banks of the river Danube, still in the south, but nearer Timisoara in the west of the country. Our director, Ramona's father, is the pastor of Vesta Buna which is a Pentecostal Church of about a hundred and twenty people, but it is very strong, with lots of young people. Pastor Matica is a very good man and one of the few pastors that I believe to be sincere and genuine. He together with his hard working and industrious wife Aurelia have paid a very heavy price to birth and keep the church running for many years.

Shortly after the millennium year of 2000 we purchased our own 5 acre site in the Carpathian Mountains in the South of Romania. This was a very expensive move for us financially but incredibly fruitful. I would estimate that approximately 3-3,500 different young people have attended the Dunamis Youth Camp in Romania over the past twelve years or so. We have probably seen about 1,600 young people and boys and girls make commitments to Christ too in that time so in terms of financial cost, I believe it was very much worth it all.

As you can tell, this period of time was just so full of fruitfulness. I think it was Pastor Bill Hybels who said "The local church is still the hope of the world." I think The Lighthouse is living proof of how a local church can affect so many people's lives all over the world. The Lighthouse has always punched well above its weight. I think we've always led the church like it was a thousand strong even when it was just a couple of hundred people as this was our heart and vision and I think we always live in a way that reflects how we see things. I love that saying "We see things the way we are, not the way they are". I believe this of every one of us. Looking back, this was a phenomenal and supernatural season where we found God provided so much finance and sometimes in such incredible ways. While all of this building work was going on, we continued to build church buildings all over India too.

Back home the church had a really good spate of growth too which was both numerical and financial too. It was a rich season of harvest and it's not easy to say exactly how or why this happened. Some people point to the amount we raised and gave to mission. At one point we were giving nearly £250,000 a year into our missions. Our centre in Romania was literally seeing miracles with the special needs children. They came to our centre not being able to walk properly, speak properly or engage in co-ordinated play. After three to four months some of them were speaking, walking, playing, laughing and enjoying the interaction with our staff and volunteers. At the time we were sending up to 120 volunteers to Romania and India. The voluntary programme was raising about £60-70,000 per year into the projects. Medical students from the Open Day at Nottingham University were visiting the Centre regularly.

We had a lot of support from organisations while the Therapy Centre was running. We ran it and managed it for about seven years. We also managed to get so many children fostered and adopted into Romanian families. One young six month old baby called Stefan was discovered in an orphanage by Jayne Harris, while on a visit with Mags. He was swaddled in bandages from below his head down. Jayne took off all the bandaging to reveal he had been born without arms and legs. Jayne and Mags were both horrified. Jayne as a midwife and a paediatric nurse took Stefan to her heart. Since then, through the efforts of all Stefan's supporters he has had artificial limbs provided. A wonderful guy Ken McCrea, a prosthetics specialist, has spent the past decade fitting artificial limbs to children in Romania and India. Stefan has had many "fit outs" in his life. He is now 15 years of age as I write and has been reunited with his parents and sister. It is a wonderful success story of The Lighthouse's work overseas. We continue to support Stefan and his family.

SECTION FOUR

"The 4x4 Years"

Chapter Twenty One

MIRACULOUS MISSIONS

M uch of what we have accomplished in mission has normally been of a practical, almost humanitarian kind.
Usually to do with helping young people fight poverty, abuse,
being abandoned or catering for children with special needs. The
fact is however, that along the way we have seen some incredible
and miraculous things happen.

In between the years 1996 and 2006 we saw some incredible
incidents of healing in Romania. I remember one week we did a
series of missions in several villages in the South of the country.
I remember very clearly preaching in a village called Maruntei.
We had a very large team that had driven over to Romania for
two weeks. It took about three to three and a half days to drive
over there, so we needed three weeks in total to spend two weeks
over there. As I'm writing now, I've actually driven over there
approximately 30 times now in the 22 years I've been visiting the
country. In Maruntei a typical Romanian village, we had a crowd
of between 350 and 400 people listening attentively. As I was
reaching the point of the appeal, about 25 minutes into my preach,
the local orthodox priest turned up with a small group shouting
and waving his fists. Actually he was drunk. He was telling all the
people not to listen to anything I was saying and that if anyone
converted to this 'new religion' then he would not bury them,
i.e. attend to their funeral when they died! Then the small group
began to hurl rocks and stones at me. I had a very large stocky

member of the team who stood in front of me to shield me from the missiles "Keep preaching" he said to me, "Just keep preaching pastor!" Well I did exactly that and was very energised by what was happening as I realised that it was a massive threat from the enemy. I even gave an appeal. Many of the crowd signalled their desire to give their lives to Christ and I did something I've never done before. I appealed to someone to open their home up so we could start a church in the village. A lady came forward and we used her home to start a church there. To my knowledge it is still going. The next village along Movileni we also did a mission. I remember quite a number giving their lives to Christ there too. Then we went to another village called Balanesti. A church started here in a lady's home through our initial missions work. Striesti, Strejesti and Sherbonesti were all towns where we preached the gospel to good effect with signs following.

Dragasani is a village where we conducted a powerful mission in the park which was in the centre of the town. We had amplified music and preaching from myself and a very effective speaker from the gypsy community, Ernie Burton. He was at The Lighthouse for some time before moving on, as most gypsies/travellers do. We held large open air meetings in Scornicesti (birthplace of Ceasescu) and Bals where over five hundred people listened attentively to the songs and the message. A church was planted here and it is still going to this day, though it is very small and lacks good and experienced leadership, though this could be said of so many churches in the south of Romania.

In India also, we had too many missions to count. Because of the BACS programme, (mentioned in chapter eighteen) we got to do so many village/town missions that literally must run into the 160 plus figure! The largest was in Erode city, a busy textile city in Tamil Nadu near to our Children's Home. We booked the CSI football ground. CSI is the "Church of Southern India" and would be the equivalent of the CoE or Church of England in India. I've preached in a few of their churches and received a very warm welcome too. The football ground was ideally located in the city and was capable of holding a gathering of many thousands of people.

We decided to get the churches together and hold a four night gospel mission. We got the television companies involved too. I got our worship band back at Lighthouse UK together and had to give them a name for the publicity. Not having a clue what to call them I decided on the name 'John 3:16' which I hoped would at least get people asking the right questions. I got about half of the existing worship team at The Lighthouse to come along and believe God for an incredible mission. It turned out to be the most amazing gospel mission I've ever done. Unfortunately at the time it coincided with a new law that was introduced into the state of Tamil Nadu. It was an "anti-conversion law" which was aimed primarily at the Christians in an attempt to stop so many people coming to faith in Christ. The law was introduced days before our visit and we had to make the call whether to go for it or not. I prayed and pondered very hard but decided we should not back off. After all, we were on private land, not government land. We stuck to our task.

The next opposition came in the form of the weather. The monsoon rains came early and localised flooding became a real problem. The first night we prayed really hard before driving to the site at 7.30pm. The team–John 3:16, and all the host team–had gone ahead. I was in my hotel room alone, praying and basically wearing the carpet out with my pacing. I was very nervous to be honest. Not about preaching on the night or the occasion, but just whether people would turn out. All the advertising had been done on television, thousands of leaflets had been distributed, huge posters had been positioned city wide. Interviews had been done with the host churches. It was now down to whether they came or not. Especially, because of the weather, there was a big doubt.

When I arrived at the site, there were about two thousand people congregated, which was very poor in such a large ground. We got everyone together to pray. As we prayed somehow our number grew to about three thousand, then four thousand. Then we noticed something really amazing happened. All around us the skies had cleared. Dark clouds that were hovering above had dispersed and a fine night began to be in evidence. Our service began and the worship team did a great job, as did all the team. I preached and about 1,000 responded to the appeal for salvation. The counselling and ministry team sprung into action and in the end, a successful start was experienced for The Erode City Mission, as we called it.

The next night, approximately double this number turned up. About eight thousand and it was a wonderful night with easily 2000 people plus, responding to the appeal. It was obvious now though that the team the hosts had prepared was woefully inadequate to deal with the response and this has always been my biggest criticism of large scale mission. I can't help but feel it's like growing a crop of for example, apples in an huge orchard and waiting for the time for the fruit to be ripe for picking but only recruiting a handful of harvesters to pick the fruit. The inevitable will happen. Fruit will be lost because of the inadequate number of fruit pickers. It cannot just wait and wait and wait. Once it's ripe it has to be picked then. Otherwise it can be lost and spoiled. The harvest is spoiled! If that didn't happen on the second night you can bet it did on the next two nights as on the third night some 14,000 people turned up and up to 24,000 on the last night. How many came forward I cannot say. Certainly in the thousands. How many were counselled and prayed for? Possibly two thousand tops! And this took hours. Nevertheless it was a successful mission for sure, but the Christians were far from prepared and ready for the harvest. About four thousand decision cards were filled in and collected, along with contact details so as to follow them up. In reality it should have been at least double that with a much bigger team on board. Even to this day, pastors from the different churches tell me how much their individual churches grew and increased in number. I'm grateful and blessed at least by this.

On one night (I think it was the third), I did an interview with reporters back at the hotel. They questioned me about the gospel and the numbers of people giving their lives to Christ, and about what I felt about the anti-conversion law recently introduced. I knew it was a bit of a trick question but I dealt with it in terms of true conversion being a matter of personal decision and something that cannot be forced or indeed prohibited. People would always choose which pathway to take, it was a basic human right. I told them clearly, accepting Christ as our personal Saviour is not something I can ever do for someone else.

Each evening I took a newspaper onto the stage with me and preached from the newspaper using the Bible. I felt the Lord inspire me with this strategy and I believe it worked 'big time'. The first night I drew from a tragic story of people who had died in the city by drinking from a well source that had become toxic. It was an ideal introduction to the pure water Jesus offered to all who would drink of Him, The Living Water. The second night I preached on the problem with many lepers refusing the cure they were being given because halfway through their treatment the symptoms of the medicine put them off! Naaman who was healed by strict instruction from God's word had to believe and take the correct action even though it went against all his known logic and reasoning.

One of the most bizarre and unpredictable things that happened on this mission occurred just a day or two into the mission. It was unreal. I was standing on a balcony very high up in the hotel looking down on a patch of land below, I think it was a school playing field. I heard a voice say "Jump, jump, quickly just jump–do it! Do it now!" It came with an almost unbelievable urge to just jump. I was not down, I wasn't low, depressed or upset at anything! I have never experienced anything like it before or since. It just was the most bizarre experience. I began to speak in other tongues and I managed to turn around slowly and went to my room. I began to pray on my knees in a dazed and pretty bewildered state. I went then and got a couple of the team to pray with me. I explained briefly what happened but told them not to share it with the rest of the team in case some got a bit scared. I include this here in the book because of one of our young men who I shared it with. He expressly asked me to make sure I put it in the book, if nothing else I think it shows the very bizarre and weird spirit world we are engaging with as we seek to serve God on the frontline. It made me think when I got back to the UK of Satan's attempt to get Jesus to throw himself off the pinnacle of the temple. As I'm writing this right now I can't forget the intensity of that moment and who would have known what would have happened had it not been for God's Spirit protecting and strengthening me! So, so bizarre!

The Erode City Mission in the end was a great success, and maybe one day we'll do a re-run. It would be much more difficult now, as India has clamped down on this kind of mission by westerners and we are having to think more clearly as to our strategies in the future.

I spent more time doing many more missions, but did them from churches I knew and was in relationship with. I had some incredibly strange ones too.

I remember being at a village, and I can name the town and the pastor but for security's sake will not do so. Anyhow, myself and a great friend were out on mission with me. We had gone to do a village mission at a place I'd been to before. I got up to preach and the Lord prompted me not to preach but to pray. I felt the turnout was very low to be honest and only about a hundred people had turned out. This particular church is right on the side of a busy road. I led us in prayer. The Holy Spirit fell down upon us like a heavy cloud. People started to speak in other tongues all over the place. This went on for 20 minutes. Then the Lord said, "Okay, you can preach now." I looked up and the place was packed!! People had come in off the street completely mesmerised by what they saw and heard. I preached quickly and very briefly as I couldn't wait to get to the appeal.

I got to it and so many people responded. Then, an incredible thing happened and one which I've never seen before or since! As I started praying for people to receive Christ (as they had come out for salvation) they started to be filled with The Holy Spirit and speak in other languages. I can't speak Tamil, but I can recognise it easily. This was not Tamil!! Whoahhhhhhhh! I got people to line up in two queues. My friend prayed over them for salvation and I prayed for them to receive the Holy Spirit. It was remarkable! I cannot think of a single person that night who didn't receive the baptism in The Holy Spirit. The only similar experience was an evening service in Mombasa, Kenya where everyone who came forward to receive the baptism in the Holy Spirit, did so. But they were all Christians who had been already led to Christ. Some of these people in this Indian village were only just becoming Christians and seemed to be receiving the Holy Spirit at the precise time of conversion just like at Cornelius' house in Acts 10. Please have a read to help you see where I'm coming from.

In Andra Pradesh we opened two BACS churches in Adelabad, a predominantly Muslim enclave of India. When we arrived there were three times too many people to fit in the church building. The evening was graced by the local dignitaries of the area. Wouldn't you know it. We closed the service, with quite a few people being led to Christ but then, boom! A rash of healings and miracles took place which were literally happening as soon as we laid hands on the sick and the needy.

I've always said, the miracles of Christ can never be explained properly, we just have to accept that there are moments when God just shows up in phenomenal ways. Sometimes, these moments are the least expected! Oh for many many more Lord, in our home towns and cities too.

One of the strangest missions took place in 2011 at the close of the year. It was not so much a mission of souls but of finance. An Indian gentleman who lives in Manchester became a good supporter of our work overseas through our charity shops. He was a very educated man, who lived simply. He did have money however. Every so often he would pop into one of our shops and give us a cash gift of between £1,000 and £2,000. On one occasion he met Mags to ask if I'd do a particular mission. Mags explained it to me. His parents who were by this time deceased, had deposited a box of gold and jewellery in a bank in Bombay (now Mumbai). The bank had written to him to explain that if he did not come and remove the deposited items they would become the bank's property by a particular date. He asked Mags if I would be willing to go and get the jewellery on his behalf and sell it in Mumbai and put the proceeds into the charity. I told Mags I'd do it just for the story! He promised to pay my return flights to India and my hotel bill. He told me I could stay five star, but I declined and told him four star was ample. He also agreed I could pay my friend's flight from Bangalore to Mumbai (who is a pastor too). I did not want to be a foreigner stuck in Mumbai for a week on my own. Solomon agreed to join me in Mumbai. I got the necessary notarised documents arranged in Manchester and made sure they were faxed and scanned and emailed to the bank manager of the particular bank and made sure the donor had given me the appropriate key.

Just before I went, I had read about King Cyrus in Isaiah 45:1-3 and it had been so strongly impressed upon my spirit. It was to prove amazing and very empowering in this unconventional mission. I reached my hotel on the Sunday and met Solomon there. We contacted a relative of the donor, an aunt, in order to enable us to have some local knowledge. We arranged to meet her and discussed the visit to the bank. The three of us went together. We met the bank manager who had been expecting us. After about a hour's delay and the payment of a small bill for administration purposes we were escorted to the vault where the appropriate deposit boxes were kept. We were shown the box where the gold and jewellery were kept, but to our dismay there was another key to the outer box and we only had the one key. The manager explained that this outer key needs to be brought by the client and it is not the bank's responsibility, but the owners. He should have given us another key (but obviously he didn't). The bank manager said to us that unless we had the 'owners key' as well as the bank's key we couldn't access the box! I promptly told the manager I would get the key. He said, "Fine, just come back this afternoon and I will escort you to the vault again ". I thanked him and said I'd return with the key. On the way out, Solomon said "Pastor, you have the key?" I answered, "No, but I know where to get one!"

We returned to the donor's aunt's apartment to discuss our way forward. I asked for a screw-driver but all she had was a broken bar of metal with a diameter of a standard pencil. It was perfect. I said clearly "this is the key". Solomon laughed and said "Ok pastor." I said "We have not come all this way to waste this moment and to waste all this gentleman's money on our hotel and flights and go back empty handed." We made our way back to the bank and I explained to the bank manager that I had the key. "Good" he said, "come this way". He led us to the vault. I gave him a look as if to say, "A moment of privacy sir–please!" He turned on his heel and said "Ok sir, I will leave you alone for a few minutes". It was amazing! I took the small bar and put it where I needed and immediately broke the locking system and took it off first time. We then used the bank key we'd been given by the owner and opened the deposit box. I was a bit disappointed to find about three gold chains and a pair of earrings and a ring. I thought it would barely cover the cost of our trip. At the time gold was at its peak and the Mumbai jewellery area was as busy as ever.

Now some may think I operated wrongly and should not have broken the lock in the bank. I beg to differ. The owner had given us his clear, documented and legal permission to access the box. The lock was not the bank's lock but the owner's. Only because of the years gone by he had forgotten there was an 'owner's lock' too. This verse of scriptures from Isaiah really began to make sense now!

"I will go before you and will level the mountains. I will break down gates of bronze and cut through bars of iron. I will give you the hidden treasures, riches stored in secret places, so that you may know that I am The Lord, The God of Israel who summons you by name." Isaiah 45:2-3 NIV

This came clearly into mind as I saw the lock, and by my past experience I knew exactly what I needed to do and how to break a tough lock with one sharp action. We left the bank with our 'hidden treasures of darkness '. Now all I had to do was sell it all at the highest price.

I spent the next two and a half days traipsing in and out of the jewellery shops in the main jewellery area of Mumbai City. What an experience! I love haggling and negotiating and I was in my element here. The offers ranged from the ridiculous to the outrageous so I had to play the game. I could tell that the diamond ring was catching attention and I was offered anything from £3,000–£5,000 ($4,500–$ 7,000) just for the ring. The gold necklaces and bangles shocked me. The bangles were apparently just pure gold and brought about £3,000 ($4,500). The gold necklaces £3,000 too. One of the pieces that was nice but not worth much in comparison I gave to the donor's Aunty as a keepsake. She had helped us immensely. (I obtained the donor's permission to do this first of course). I eventually had about a million rupees. Now I had to change it all to British pounds. I obtained a fantastic rate at a jewellers and came back to the UK with about £11,000 ($16,000 at the time).

The amazing thing is, at the time, we were recovering from a major fall of our main leader in Romania. Unbeknown to us, he had left us with whole-scale debts. He had run up a massive deficit in terms of salaries and tax which made a complete mockery of the financial reports he had been sending. We owed about £5,000 ($9,000 at the time). It was critical. Although the donor was Indian, he was happy for us to use the money raised for anything we needed. He was very clear about this. I laugh when I look back how Jesus was questioned over his temple-tax bill.

When they had come to Capernaum, those who received the temple tax came to Peter and said, "Does your Teacher not pay the temple tax?" He said, "Yes." And when he had come into the house, Jesus anticipated him, saying, "What do you think, Simon? From whom do the kings of the earth take customs or taxes, from their sons or from strangers?" Peter said to Him, "From strangers." Jesus said to him, "Then the sons are free. Nevertheless, lest we offend them, go to the sea, cast in a hook, and take the fish that comes up first. And when you have opened its mouth, you will find a piece of money; take that and give it to them for Me and you." (Matthew 17:24-27 NKJV)

Jesus paid their (alleged) temple tax bill in a most amazing way! I hope this chapter of the book will also show you today, that God has some incredible ways of providing. Even your bills can be paid through miraculous missions! Over the years I have been constantly amazed at God's provision, in times of plenty and in times of great need. Sometimes for really important things and other times for just simple extras that make all the difference in life. I love the fact that while God is so huge and so big, he's not too big to bother about the small things too. As I said very early on in the book, I love tigers but they're very hard to see in the wild. Only once had I seen this awesome spectacle. Then recently on my 53rd Birthday, on a beautiful site in the western ghats I was on Safari. I said, "Lord, as a son to a father I'm asking you, please can I ask for a special gift? Let me see the tiger again." We went on Safari deep into the jungle. We saw everything except the tiger!

Later that night, my travelling companions and I were treated to a special outdoor dinner, around the campfire on this site with a small house I often visit. After we'd finished the meal they presented me with a lovely birthday cake. Just as I was finishing cutting the cake, a noise was heard. It was a tiger close by. We shone our strong torches through the darkness to see clearly the piercing eyes of a large male tiger. He looked at us, got up slowly and walked right across the site, from right to left in full view of us all! What a gift from above! Outstanding! God's love for us is not only deep and unending, it's also very fatherly and considerate too.

Chapter Twenty Two

THE END OF THE ROAD

———❖———

"The end of the road is often a gateway to a new beginning."

This chapter has a very special title for me. It is about an experience I had on mission that will stay with me for the rest of my life! That's why it has to be in 'The Rubicon'. It's a phrase that taught me an invaluable lesson, albeit an incredibly hard one that probably only those who reach desperation point will ever really know. Someone once said "We will never know Christ is all we need, until Christ is all we've got". That is so true.

While most of this book is set out in a chronological order, sometimes I have placed things into a thematic order. We are still in the 4x4 years, which are the "off road experiences" i.e. more unusual than normally speaking. This experience happened several years ago in the late nineties but fits into this section of the book nicely.

I had held a number of outdoor baptisms in the village of Brancovanca in the Teleorman region of South Romania. We had seen some wonderful results at these occasions not least of all my PA at the time of writing, Ana Tudosie giving her life to Christ at the tender age of eight. Apparently I had baptised a man who about two years later sadly had died of a heart attack. The pastor of the village church literally begged me to visit his widow and children who he said were in the most desperate of circumstances. I responded to his request and was utterly and totally overwhelmed by what I saw. I visited a little house, with one room made of clay. In it ten children of varying ages were all sleeping in a circle around the edges of the room. You couldn't tell how many there were or whose legs arms and heads belonged to whom because they were all virtually sleeping on top of one another. The mother Angela was probably in her forties. She had been left with all these children to look after. Eight were her and her husband's children and two were her nieces.

I looked at them in disbelief! They were living in utter poverty and squalor. I heard a voice deep within say "So what are you going to do about this?" I decided there and then we would not allow this situation to continue. I promised we would be back. As I left the site I was introduced to Angela's father. He was living under a black polythene sheet held up by two sticks. He also had a growth on his stomach and was drinking a very, very potent alcoholic drink I guess to mask the pain as much as anything. There was no doubt the situation was one of the most shocking instances of poverty I've ever seen. And, it was in Europe! At the time, Justin and Jo Marks, our assistant pastors, had driven out to Romania with Mags and myself. We all decided once we got back we would launch a mission to sort this situation out.

The journey back to the UK was quite an amazing one too. We were actually stuck in a two to three mile queue at the border of Romania and Hungary at a place called Nadlac. We had a ferry to catch and the queue was going absolutely nowhere. I hate queues at the best of times and always feel they're mostly down to either an attempt to control people or just incompetence. I hate them, most times they're totally unnecessary, especially when they're not moving at all. Somebody somewhere is making people's lives a misery in most of these queues. I walked to near the front of the queue with Justin to see what was happening. The truth is nothing was happening and no-one seemed to know why or even want to know why! As we were returning to our vehicle, (the girls were in the car), I heard a voice very clearly within me say, "he who dares wins". It was strange but I knew it was a prompt from the Lord. I said to Justin, "Justin, he who dares wins". "Yes", he said, "I'm thinking what you're thinking".

"Great," I said, "let's put our LimUK T-shirts on and overtake the queue and get down to the checkpoint and see what happens." We got back to the car and explained to the girls to do the same and get their T-shirts on too. I drove down the wrong side of the road in my red Mondeo with the hazard lights flashing and every light on. As we got near the front of the queue angry motorists and truck drivers waved their fists at us and shouted expletives at us. I ignored their protestations completely. Once we could go no further a border guard pointed his gun at me, standing in the front of the car. I got out very slowly with my LIM Folder and matching LIM T-shirt as did Justin too. The guard beckoned me forward and shouted at me as if to say "Wwhat the &?8&£@/ are you playing at?" He then led us to a checkpoint office. A woman was there and asked us in fairly good English, "Where are you from?" I said "We are from England." "What are you doing here?" I began to explain as I opened the folder we were from a charity in the UK and we were here building a centre for kids in Slatina etc. She looked at me and said "Are you Christians?" I said "Actually yes we are and I'm a pastor. I'm sorry but we have to catch a ferry to England tomorrow evening". Amazingly she lightened up immediately. "Aaah okay" she said, "Diplomats! Come this way" We followed her closely. "Where is your car?" We showed her and she said, "Okay get in your car". We did so immediately, feeling God was with us in an amazing way. She then proceeded to back trucks and cars up to make space for us to drive through the queue. "Diplomat–diplomat–diplomat" she kept shouting as she forced people to reverse and manoeuvre their vehicles to let the Servants of the Lord through one of the tightest and most chaotic queues I've ever seen. Then she waved us goodbye with a "Drum bun" meaning "safe journey".

It was another great lesson for me, though I also remember how confident I was that God had given me a green light and I realise how wrong this could have gone had I not had that inner assurance. It was after all back in the days when Romania was still coming out from communism and a lot of potential was there for things to go awry.

Anyhow we got back to the UK on time thanks to our friend at the checkpoint, even though our front brakes failed in Hungary and we had to rely on our two new found friends Olaf and Angelica to put us up for the night. That's another story which was more comical than anything, but did show God's protection and grace. I'm sure He did have a chuckle though at both Jo and Mags sleeping on spider-ridden straw beds and having to sprint across the courtyard to use the outside loo!! Lots of laughs now, but not then. Justin managed half a night's sleep virtually on top of the boiler as he was too tall for the small bed next to it!

We decided to set up an emergency fund and wrote to churches and individuals–the mission was called 'October 10'. It was to build a new house on the plot of land by using materials mostly sourced in Romania but with the specialist tools and equipment from the UK. It was to prove much much harder than we first thought.

We brought together a team of volunteers. Tom a roofer and drains expert who was in the church at the time. A real grafter and an Irishman who knew his stuff through and through. Jo's brother Stuart, a fireman, a great driver and all-rounder. Stuart also helped me with the physical work setting up our second charity shop in Tyldesley. Chris, another good all-rounder who was a kind of jack of all trades. Another chap helped us who was a Romanian. We raised about £6,000 in a month for this specific mission. West St Baptist Church in Crewe were fabulous as was their leadership team and their senior pastors Geoff and Sandra Willetts. We forged a very strong partnership with them that helped us accomplish a lot of things.

We took about two and a half days to arrive in Romania as we virtually drove non-stop taking it in turns to drive and sleep. We had a great system I employed loads of times in those days driving to Romania. We would put all the gear in a Transit and on top we would put a mattress. This would become the sleeping quarters for two people while two drove and co-piloted the Transit. We arrived in good time but then our difficulties began. Most of the gear we needed we couldn't get in quantities we would need. We were told permission would not be granted easily even though we were assured before we came that this was a simple formality and the local mayor would just say "yes" and give us a paper and that was it. And so it was, but they didn't tell us the next mayor could just come and say "no", so there was no sense in doing it this way. In the end the only solution we could come up with was to buy another house nearby. We agreed to begin the search. While I was looking, along with a Romanian colleague, the rest of the guys were going to help the local church start their building project. Tom and Chris were going to oversee the marking out of the foundations and then supervise the digging out of the footings. Meanwhile we would search for a suitable home for Angela and the kids. We saw some real hovels and while I'm ever the optimist I'm afraid to say even my optimism died on the spot when I saw some of the homes 'for sale'. Actually one or two I'm not sure they could have given them away! One of them was being used as a distillery for a very potent local brew called 'twika'. You could smell it was potent too!

We saw one property on the top of a hill that I really liked. It had some outbuildings too and a large piece of land. I could see some of the kids beginning to grow crops on the land and maybe having a pig or two in the outbuildings. The cost was £4,500 for the whole thing (after hard negotiations). The biggest problem was not the price however, the problem was the family who were selling, would only sell if they could find a property in Constanta. They would move only once they found something there, but they needed the money from the sale of their house to us, in order to purchase the house in Constanta. We were told this would be impossible. Properties in the Constanta area were generally double and triple the price of those in the village here. I decided we would go and take the family to Constanta to see if we could find a property for them that they would agree to buy. They agreed to go with us. That night we exchanged all our British Pounds for Romanian Lei. It was a suitcase full of money. In those days you couldn't walk into a bank to transfer that amount of cash. They used to write down the serial number of every note you gave them. I would still have been there now! I had to exchange it by doing a deal with a guy and got into his black Mercedes (which was pretty much burnt inside out by the way) and counted the Romanian Lei. I handed him the GBP and shook hands and off we went. We had to be up at 4am in the morning and to set out before 5am. It was a six hour journey to Constanta which is a city on Romania's only coastline, on the Black Sea.

We set out with the family using our friends' PSV vehicle. Six of us went along. It took us about seven hours to get there and by the time we started to start looking seriously it was about 2pm. We saw many properties but they were as we were told, double the price at least. Even when the family selling to us were prepared to look at a smaller house, it still came out at £6,500 or £7,000. We looked in several areas but to no avail. We asked people and they pointed us to this area and that area. Eventually we realised we were actually running out of time. In an hour or so the light would go. I stopped the car and asked us to pray. We did and then started to drive down a country lane, more in desperation than expectation. Our driver was about to turn around when I distinctly heard a voice within me say "Go to the end of the road." I instructed the driver not to turn around but to keep going to the 'end of the road'. One of the most amazing and incredible things I have ever experience happened next. I said audibly as I prayed. "Lord, please give us a sign or something to show we are on the right track, anything Lord." Then as we proceeded, we saw a huge sign on our right side. It read 'Bethlehem'. Please bear in mind that we were still in the countryside and everything was quite rural. We drove on further up the road, totally stunned by the size and meaning of this 'sign'. Another sign came into view, exactly the same size as the previous one. This time it said, 'Gethsemane'! Weird is the only way I could describe it! We looked at one another and laughed. What on earth was this all about? We drove some more and a third sign read 'Golgotha'. Bizarre! The sign was as big as the other two and by now we were completely flummoxed. Actually we just looked at one another, speechless.

At this point we saw a man on the right side of the road. He had a bottle in his hand and was wobbling around a bit. He was clearly the worse for wear with alcohol. I asked the driver to stop and ask him if he knows of any houses for sale nearby. The driver said "But he's drunk! How will he know anything?" I said, "Just ask him". He did, and to my amazement it was like he sobered up in a second and pointed to the end of the road and then pointed right. I asked what he said and apparently he told us to "go to the end of the road and turn right". We did as he said and found a sign on the end house gable end. Betel Pentecostal Church (obviously in Romanian). We turned right into the small cul de sac with about 50 yards of road left and there was a sign "Casa de Vanzare"– House for Sale. We knocked on the door. The door opened and we were led into a room where there was an amazing sight. The whole family were sat on boxes and had packed as if they were moving that day. We said something like, "we've come because we saw your house was for sale". They replied "Yes, we've been expecting you." They were a Christian family who had been asking the Lord to send a buyer for their home. We showed the family we'd brought around the house and they loved it. We discussed the price £4,500 which was fine and we did the deal right there and then and prayed together. By the time we got out of the house an hour later it was pitch black. It was mission accomplished!

On the return journey an incredible thing happened as we entered Constanta. There was a roundabout and on that round-about is a very large lighthouse. I only noticed it because the light shining down on us was so bright I thought, what on earth is going on? It was like being under a massive spotlight in the night time. I looked up and as we travelled the light upon us was from the lighthouse. It was as if God quietly was saying, "See son, didn't I promise you that my light would shine upon you?" a reference to Isaiah 60:1,2 our 'vision verses'.

We returned to the village we were staying at about 2-3am in the morning tired, but very excited and blessed by all God had done. Later on when we woke and told the team of all that the Lord had done we rejoiced together. What was more, Chris, Stuart and Tom showed us what they had been up to. They had only laid the footings for the new church building while we'd been away! What an amazing two week mission. We also then were able to take Angela's family of ten children and show them their new home. They couldn't believe their eyes. We asked the local car-penter Ionel to build bunk beds for the kids (a job he'd done for us so so many times!) We had to leave for the UK, but before we did so there was another major blessing for us. Angela told us, "Thank you so much, now I can go and bring my baby back home." I asked what she meant. It turned out that she had a six month old baby girl in the orphanage at Alexandria, a nearby town. We were stunned. She went and brought the baby–Lydia–home and we paid for a year's supply of milk and food and clothing etc. Lydia is about 15 as I write and is a beautiful young lady who I see every year.

I see many of the children who are now grown up and some of them serving God. For me this small, but miraculous mission taught me things I would never forget. Especially that at 'the end of the road', there is often a gateway to a new beginning. Maybe you feel you've come to the end of your road. Maybe you feel you can go no further. I have news for you ... It could well be that you needed to come to this amazing place. 'The end of the road' could just be the place where God opens a brand new door leading to fresh exciting and new opportunities. There are amazing Red Sea experiences awaiting many who are prepared to go to 'the end of the road'. If you're there now, just trust God. He will come through for you. He will never fail you.

Chapter Twenty Three

'GLADIATOR MOMENTS'

———————◆———————

"When something bad happens, you have three choices; you can either let it define you, let it destroy you or let it develop you."

Shortly after the millennium year of 2000 we purchased our own 5 acre site in the Carpathian Mountains in the South of Romania. We had been holding our annual Youth Camp in a very small village called Bradisor. We took over a small Youth Centre there that could sleep about 200 youth. We called The Youth Camp, Dunamis. We first put the camp on around 2002/3 and it was a great success though it was very hard work. I did most of the teaching and preaching though I tried very hard to engage a few local pastors to come in and speak albeit with modest results. Around 2004/5 we had one of our best ever camps with many young people deciding to become Christians and a lot of miracles of healing and emotional and psychological healing took place. It set the scene for the future and before we knew it we did not have enough space on the site. In fact the last time we had it we supplemented the site with tents and a few of us stayed off site. We had our largest ever camp then with about 700 in attendance over the two weeks. Children first week and Young people in the last week. We received a legacy at that time for about £18,000 for LIM. We were alerted to the fact that there was a five acre site for sale further down the valley. It was a fabulous location and perfect for a future camp site with great potential to be developed and even expanded. We negotiated a price and bought it for £12,000 We used the other money to go towards purchasing a site in Slatina which we aimed to use at a later date for the new church building there. The church was doing very well and we fully envisaged a very strong church to eventually emerge. We bought a small site about half an acre maybe even smaller in Slatina at a cost of about £17,000 too.

In 2008 we were to hold our Youth Camp on our new site. The prices of land in Slatina had hit the roof! Our site we bought for £17,000 back in 2003 was now suddenly worth £75,000! It was astonishing! I had a very bad feeling about all this inflationary pricing going on in Romania and I asked our Director to find a buyer so as to sell it. He remonstrated a lot with me over this but I persuaded him it was better to sell at the top and have the cash than to miss such an opportunity. The worst that could happen is we find another site and buy with the £75,000. He reluctantly agreed and we did sell it for around that figure. Actually, very soon after, the economic crash came and the same piece of land a year later you wouldn't have got more that £12,000 for it! We had the £75k and we decided to invest it in developing the Youth Camp. We built shower blocks and a kitchen. We put toilets in, along with its own personal sump and we also fenced it around and dug a very deep, good well with its own secured pump. We also levelled the site by putting about 300 tons of sand on it.

Eventually, we just about managed to have a makeshift camp-site. A number of the guys in Romania worked incredibly hard to achieve this. A huge amount of sacrifice went into not only the physical work but also the financial giving that was required to put in the surrounding fence, the excavation of the soil and levelling of the ground, not to mention the amount of landfill we needed. It took a huge effort on all of our parts.

It was August 2008 and we had just successfully held our first week of camp. We had about 300 children on the site plus our workforce of about 50 (including the UK team of about 20 people). It was then that a massive bombshell hit us. I discovered reports that our Director had been acting in a very sexually immoral sexual way with members of his congregation. Young men were apparently involved and were, in my opinion and that of others manipulated and almost bullied into abusive situations. Our Romanian Pastor and Director had used his position of trust to abuse young men and encourage them to carry out sexual acts with him. Though these seemed to be consensual, there was no doubt in my mind and in the mind of our leadership team that these occasions were the result of his manipulative and persuasive powers. I had to take very strong action and my questioning led to a whole can of worms being opened up. Things were so serious I asked the Director and his wife to leave the site. I know I felt the Lord say to me "It will take five years to recover from this." I had interviewed all the young men I heard had been involved and it was a very sorry state of affairs. His wife, it turned out was aware this was happening, but through her misplaced loyalty had remained silent in the situation. It was another unbelievable chapter of fact being stranger than fiction. The first thing I had to do is break the news to all the UK team. This was incredibly difficult and I had to say to everyone that they needed to take a deep breath and gather themselves. We had a 'full on' week with the Youth to do, so it was important for their sake that we remained focused. We had to get ourselves together and face what was in front of us. The UK team were superb, especially considering some of them were very young at the time. The second week of Camp passed by and many were won to Christ and mightily blessed despite the giant shadow which loomed over those of us who knew what we knew!

The worst thing about this situation was that all our children in our family home (Casa Noastra) had been massively let down by these two people, who had always told us that these children were like their own and they would always be there for them. They were in the same position as us (with no children of their own biologically), so we had no reason to doubt their love for the kids was genuine and sincere. I was left to pick up the pieces, along with Jayne Harris one of our trustees who had recently moved out to Romania to live there and serve over there. Bless her! Jayne had just walked into a furnace! Ana Tudosie also was a rock in the situation. I promptly took up the reins of the family home and started to be far more 'hands on' than ever before–well as much as I could whilst still living in the UK and running a busy city church and overseas ministry. I broke the news and told all the older kids in

206

our family home what had happened. They were in shock. Some of them had been promised they would be adopted by this couple and were using the couple's surnames in preparation for that happening. They were in disbelief and to some extent denial too. The couple had also told Mags and myself that they had started the legal process of adopting several of the kids. In fact, as we were to find out later, this was not true. No such attempt had been made and in fact the local social services told us they would never have allowed this. They had their reasons.

The last week of camp was amazing. The film 'Gladiator' became my visual and spiritual inspiration and helped motivate me into the arena of spiritual conflict! God used this film in an incredible way as I realised it was time to step up and fight the enemy head on. I made some tough and difficult decisions. I realised that I had to deal with this openly and transparently and that the matter would not be hidden or covered up under any circumstances. Once I had gone public, it was another Rubicon moment. I knew (and I was right!) everyone would have a view and an opinion. It was very frustrating. Some would have had no mercy whatsoever. Others would have been more lenient. At the end of the day, they weren't dealing with it day in and day out. I was! Big difference! Immediately, I let all the church members who knew the couple back home know what had happened, (and there were many). I let the leadership of our denomination know too, and as many people as I felt should know I informed them immediately.

I actually drove over to Romania with a relative of our ex-Director (who lived in the UK) within one week of returning home, as I couldn't pick up a flight in such short notice. We addressed the church in Romania and told them he would no longer be pastor. We told them exactly the reason and made a public statement (without going into details). Many of the people who were disgusted and not happy went to the branch church. Others felt I had been merciless and un-compassionate. I had learned from previous mistakes that to cover anything up would be something that would come back to haunt us. In a few days I would have to fly out in the middle of the week along with Mags in order to take the ex-Director off the charity in Romania, as he was posturing to take over the whole charity including no doubt the assets. In reality no real deep repentance was shown, though lots of remorse and no doubt regret. But that isn't necessarily repentance. People can be overwhelmingly sorry and upset simply because they got caught, not necessarily because they behaved badly or let the Lord, their wives and families or church down. I believe looking back, this was the case at the time. He had arranged for several people to sign a document that secured his position by putting them onto the trust as officers. By doing this he had the potential to vote me off as the president *and* the other trust member who was also a pastor.

I was alerted to the seriousness of the situation and got on a plane with Mags, unbeknown to the disgraced young man. I got twenty people to sign as members of the trust as a counter-measure and took a document to the local notary to take him off the trust deed. One notary refused to do it (as they knew the young man and couldn't believe he had done anything serious enough to warrant being removed!). I went to another notary, who it turned out knew me through his mother. I explained briefly what had happened and he prepared and tabled the document for us. I had originally put in a condition in the trust deed that any officer in the charity could be removed for serious breach of trust and/ or sexual immorality. That was the end of the matter. We went back to the centre and waited for the couple to arrive at his ex-office. His wife still worked at the centre at that time, heading up our child-care therapy programme. This amazingly would be brought to an abrupt halt by the local authorities independently of us within a few weeks. In the end, the Department of Protection cited their own reasons for the closure and partly it was to do with the couple leading the project, which confirmed we had acted correctly to axe them from having anything to do with the centre. Finally we took the decision that they could no longer live at the centre, even at the apartment we had built within the centre. Matters really came to a head at this point that are not worth going into here. Basically, it was just unbelievable how self-deluded people can become when they have been actively involved in deception for some time. I tried to keep in touch, to counsel and to give some support, but the more I found out about things that he had done, the less I could take any supportive position or role. I tried to introduce other people to help, ministry colleagues etc. I think this in reality did little in terms of bringing a sense of closure to the matter.

I've put this in the book because I want to show people just how incredibly hard leadership can be at times. There are times when we have to just be strong and courageous and keep walking forward, even when the walk of faith becomes a footslog. Sometimes there is no substitute for resilient, stubborn determination and persistence. "Keeping on keeping on" is extremely hard when all your bitter disappointments have just been confirmed. Faith truly is "taking the first step, even when you can't see the stairway" as Martin Luther-King said. It was to be a march not so much of triumph, but a trudge of trial. The other reason why it had to be put in the book is because it made such an indelible impact on our lives. Today, we have some of the kids from our family home who call us mum and dad, because we had to step in and fulfil the promise that others, through selfishness, deceit and flawed character, couldn't fulfil. One of the greatest burdens though was to eventually turn out to be one of our greatest blessings. The enemy tried to crush us through it, but God would turn it around to bless us. It would however take time and great effort.

Today, I am constantly amazed at how many good, even great leaders lose their integrity and their sense of accountability through the privileged position of serving God. It's like they never did the simple calculation. "X plus Y multiplied by Z equals– being out on your backside basically!" It's as simple as that. There are fences, boundaries and lines that need to be drawn for our protection. We need to know that we cannot cross those lines. In fact we need to steer clear altogether of those lines. There is far too much to lose! We have to 'do the math' as they say in the US! Every set of stairs needs a sturdy handrail and every cliff top a fence. Actually, the fence builder loves His children, that's why the fence exists. We can play safely and securely with it there. Without it, that same place becomes a very dangerous place for us. As our General Superintendent and a good friend of mine, Pastor John Glass, often says, "Better a fence at the top of the cliff than an ambulance at the bottom."

I think times like these affect us in a variety of ways. They can make us very cynical actually and tremendously suspicious of people if we allow it. It can also make us reluctant to trust people and delegate properly. This is why we all need to understand and realise that charisma and gifting need to be subordinated by us to calling and vocation. This basically means we have to realise fully how fragile we are and how susceptible to the enemy and vulnerable to his strategies we are. The only way to keep secure and safe as sheep is to be close to the shepherd. Leaders are the enemy's prime target. Always have been and always will be. It is in the mind where we are at our most vulnerable. The ancestor of every action is a thought, so we need above all to understand the dynamics of mind, body and soul. The mind replays what the heart can't delete, so it is essential we keep renewing our minds regularly in God's word. When Jesus said,

> *"You shall love The Lord your God with all your heart and with all your soul and with all your strength and with all your mind"* Luke 10:27 NIV

There is a very special sense of strategic thinking here. In fact it was I believe a strategic statement. Our passion comes from our heart (heart and soul). When we put our heart and soul into something we really put everything into it. But our mind and our strength, that's real power and control. It's the control tower taking command. It's where the battles are won and lost.

In the end, no one wins apart from the enemy in situations like the one I've written about here. We have to focus on winning the war even if we lose a battle here and there. If you're in leadership and you've never had to deal with or confront moral failure you are truly unique. Unfortunately today, some people are not confronted over their lack of integrity or severe moral lapses. It is easier to sweep it under the carpet for some leaders and their organisations. Or, as is popular today, confess it, address it and move on without any real "time out" or disciplinary measures. I personally think this devalues and cheapens the responsibility of leadership within any organisation–church or ministry.

Following the immediate dealing with this situation, we have by God's grace continued to minister and work in Romania, sending teams, doing camps and supporting our children. Though it became much harder to do in the immediate aftermath and fallout of this. It has taken about five years to recover to a point of stability.

Our priority in Romania has been our Family Home (Casa Noastra) and although it has cost us a huge amount of finance, resources, energy and commitment, we do feel that it will have been well worth it all as we look at the lives that have been transformed and changed forever. Our children there are growing up fast and though the older ones remember this moment very vividly, they are old enough to know that people are human and people are frail. They have a much healthier view of life now than they did then. This is, after all, what helps to mature us. What was that I said earlier about "life is five percent about what happens to you and ninety five percent what you do about what happens to you"? Hmmm, time to think about that more after experiencing all the above!

Despite the huge challenges Mags and myself determined all our children in our Family Home (Casa Noastra) in Romania, would not go back into care or into a government home. We had promised the children this and we were going to do our very best to ensure this would be the case.

In reality, this was a very, very hard thing to do. It cost us a huge amount of time, effort and especially finance that, to be honest, we just didn't have. We would spend the next six to seven years paying thousands of pounds in debt just basically because of a person who lost his way morally and spiritually. The fallout was not only massive but far reaching. Nevertheless, we experienced great joy too. One of our girls, Alex got married in 2012 to a really good young man, Mihai, who is like a son to us. I walked Alex proudly down the aisle and gave her away as her father should have done, but was probably drunk somewhere or who knows where? To this day, Alex is like a daughter to Mags and I and we're very proud of her. Madalin (Mada) is in the UK with us now and has a job. Danny too. They have an apartment and both are working hard, they are honest and love the Lord. They too call us Mum and Dad. Ella is about to come to the UK as she's 18 and wants to be close to Mags and I and her brothers. Alex and Mihai will also come to the UK soon. This is actually fulfilling scripture for me. The Lord said from Isaiah:

> *Arise, shine; for thy light is come, and the glory of the Lord is risen upon thee. For, behold, the darkness shall cover the earth, and gross darkness the people: but the Lord shall arise upon thee, and his glory shall be seen upon thee. And the Gentiles shall come to thy light, and kings to the brightness of thy rising. Lift up thine eyes round about, and see: all they gather themselves together, they come to thee: **thy sons shall come from far, and thy daughters shall be nursed at thy side.** (Isaiah 60:1-4 KJV)*

This for me is almost too wonderful to write and put into words. Though this has posed great challenges for both Mags and myself we know that God has ordained that many children from around the world will end up in Manchester at The Lighthouse. Who knows where this will lead in the future. I even believe a number of our Indian children will end up here with us and maybe even Africa too!

Chapter Twenty Four

PREGNANT WITH
A BUILDING!

"Write your vision in ink, but your plans in pencil."

Back home in Manchester I had reached a point where I realised another major Rubicon was in the pipeline. I was really
fed up of being in our current premises. It was in my opinion
holding us back. I believe God allows us to get to a place where
our discomfort becomes so acute we cannot abide it any longer.
The sense of frustration and dissatisfaction literally jettisons us
into action. That's exactly what happened to us in 2007-8.

I began to seriously look for an alternative place for us to
worship. God had given me two words in my spirit. The first was
given in or around 2006 when the Lord clearly stated "I have provided myself a house." I took this to mean that there was already
a building set aside somewhere that we didn't have to build from
scratch. The other thing he clearly said was to "make room to
grow". As I pondered this for several weeks, I saw a lovely little
building for rent called "The Lighthouse." It was fairly close to
our branch church at the time in Wythenshawe. It was actually
a photographic studio. I checked it out and it had a superb feel
to it. Whilst it was no use as a place of worship, it would make
a fabulous facility to enable our office and administration side of
things to grow and develop, thereby releasing much more space

213

and room for the main church activities. We were really rammed
to capacity at the time so it would be a really a good move and
would help us transition to a larger premises later on. The same
building became our Resource Centre and we used it for all our
administration for Church, LIM and projects. We even held a few
conferences over there. We did a special opening too, which was
the start of a new journey on the road, which led us to our present
facility.

One of the disciplines I've always tried to maintain throughout
my personal life is to read a devotional in the morning before anything. I just find more than anything, the discipline itself helps me
to stay on track. This has nothing to do with my personal bible
reading plan or personal study. It is strictly devotional. Going to
God's word for something to eat and not something to preach. The
importance of this cannot be overestimated. One such morning
springs to mind more than most. I had been calling different property agencies to find out the details of buildings that were large
enough to house us and situated in appropriate localities. One such
person was a young man called Gary Chapman. Gary worked for
WHR Property Consultants. They are a large well known UK wide
company. I had been speaking to him quite a lot and Gary seemed
to understand what we needed, though you could tell most of the
others were not taking us seriously enough. I always felt our next
facility would be a shell, which we would put the interior in. God
had put this on my heart and it was going to be like a 'blank sheet
of paper' as it were. Very exciting indeed. Well, this morning, I
was doing my devotional as normal, and whose name popped up
in my reading? Yes, Gary Chapman! I read it again and again, and
yes again, just to make sure my eyes weren't playing tricks on me.
Apparently Gary Chapman was a doctor and a missionary back in
Lord knows when. Pardon my ignorance, but I has no knowledge
of this. As I read the name, a word from the Lord popped into my
heart: "Keep listening to this man, I have sent him to you." I realised God was putting the pieces together and that we were now in
a process that would eventually lead us to our new spiritual home.

There was a large, commercial unit on the main road that led
from Stretford in Manchester to the Trafford Centre. It fronted
onto the main road and would be a really hi-vis Centre. I also had

a very strong witness that this time, the church building would be on a main road. I'd also had a dream many years back where I saw this was the case too. That was always very vividly in my mind. This building really ticked the boxes. It was one of five units and was the third largest. The largest is owned by Kelloggs now and could well be one of the largest warehouses in the city, it is pretty enormous. As church buildings go, I love these warehouse style churches. I know they're not everyone's cup of tea so to speak, but I love them. They kind of 'de-religiousise' (to invent a word) church and at the same time they are so versatile and inexpensive compared to the brick buildings of the past. They are ergonomically sound, economical to run and incredibly functional. This was a fabulous facility and it was about 45,000 sq ft. It had some office space to it–about 4,000 sq ft (10% is the norm for these kind of buildings). It was perfect, apart from one thing. It was only accessible from round the back by car or pedestrian access by virtue of a small gauge train track that ran in front of it. This by far was to be our biggest problem, and then change of use from a D10 use (commercial) to C2 (community, place of worship). We felt we could overcome both aspects. Gary arranged to meet the owners, a small local building company who had built the five units. After much negotiation, we reached a deal of £1.2 million pounds for the freehold. We would need to raise a further £800,000 just initially to do the first phase of work in it. The second and last phase would cost the same again making a spend of over £3 million pounds ($5 million dollars).

I had negotiated the sale of our existing premises to one of two interested parties, both churches, for about £1.2 million. We signed a deal with The Ghanian Church of Pentecost. This was very timely as none of us knew what was around the corner–an awful recession that hit us all hard in the west, especially charitable organisations. Our HQ were terrific this time around and were really supportive, backing our venture, and ran with us on lining up the purchase of the building subject to change of use and access for pedestrians. The difficulty came in the end, not from any of the expected sources but from the owner. Whilst we were going through all the negotiations and had agreed the price, and had signed for the purchase (subject to change of use), the owner went and sold it to The ING Bank. I was totally and completely floored!! Gary Chapman explained that the owner had received an offer he could not refuse for ALL the five units from the ING bank. He explained it was "just one of those things".

The repercussions of this personally were hard for me. We had our 'All Nations Day' that year at Maxwell Hall, Salford. Nigel Tween, one of our National Leadership Team was the speaker. He did not know at all, but we had made a video of the site and the new building. We had prayed on the site, we had words given to us about it and even that 'angels were guarding it for us on each corner' etc etc. I requested that the video was not to be shown. The All Nations Day was a great success and to be fair, each and every one we've done has been a great blessing and has been instrumental in giving us snapshots of our future morning services. Those early days when we had 400 in our All Nations Day services have been surpassed now by our normal Sunday mornings which are several hundred in attendance whereas our All Nations Days now are hovering just under a thousand in attendance.

Concerning the new building, I tried in my own strength to rescue the situation. I wrote to the ING bank to see if we could do a deal. Eventually they wrote back in no uncertain terms, "*we do not want you or your church, or your organisation as owners or tenants of our property full stop.*" It was as conclusive as that. I had just been to Cardiff a couple of weeks before, ministering. I preached on being "pregnant with a church building" because that's exactly what I was going through. It was a horrendously difficult moment.

It's amazing how we connect and associate things in our life and in our past with things that seem so far removed practically speaking. As I sat and thought about what we'd just lost and how I'd communicated to the church, getting them all geared up for transition and moving to new premises. The horrible thought occurred to me that Mags and I had just had another miscarriage–a spiritual one where that which we were about to give birth to was taken from us. It was a watershed moment. Mags and I left Manchester for about three days to go to one of my favourite haunts, the Lake District. We strolled through the woodlands of our favourite place, Manesty on the shores of Derwentwater near

Keswick. We talked and talked as to what could have gone wrong. How could we have not seen it? How could we continue to lead God's people in truth when that which we had promised had evaporated into thin air? What would we tell the people? How would they react?

I decided to offer my resignation. I spoke to Justin, my main confidant in all major matters of this kind of thing. I called Justin from the Lakes. I told him exactly how I felt and that I felt I should offer my resignation as main leader of The Lighthouse. After all, how could the people be expected to trust me as a visionary? I'd obviously got something drastically wrong, hadn't I? Justin was his usual calm and stoic self. He helped me to see that it's somehow a part of the process. He also said a tremendously helpful thing. "I knew you'd feel like this, I told Jo (his wife) you would react like this. I can understand why you'd think like this, but listen. The people wouldn't want any other one to lead them but you–that's a fact." or words pretty similar to this. I know it wasn't just flattery or something said just to try to make me feel better. I know Justin and he's extremely pragmatic and if he feels you need to hang a little while, then ok, he'd let you hang a little while until you've learned what needs to be learned. I somehow tried to pick myself up, but it wasn't easy at all! It was one of the hardest times in my life. It's funny though because in little more than a week, things happened that made this just a distant memory and little more. I've dealt with this in the next chapter. I had learned the lesson a hard way personally, "write your vision in ink, but your plans in pencil". The vision was, thank God, still alive, and so was I by God's grace! Well just about!

Chapter Twenty Five

THE END OF THE ROAD II

*"Plans fail for lack of counsel, but with many advisers
they succeed." (Proverbs 15:22 NIV)*

Sometimes in life, you get the feeling that God is taking you on a 'dry run', a kind of rehearsal for something that's to come. I've had several instances where I've been acutely aware and conscious of this. Back in chapter twenty two of this book, "The End Of The Road" I recalled an incident which I now realise was a prequel of what was to come some fifteen years on. I couldn't have called this chapter anything other than "The End Of The Road II".

Following the intense and nerve wracking time of challenge that I shared in the previous chapter, I really cried out to God, as much in frustration as desperation. "What should I do now Lord? What should I do now?" A word came back instantly and I knew 100 percent it was the Lord. *"Go to the end of the road"*. That's all I heard! "What does that mean?" I replied. Nothing came back, only silence. Still I knew I had heard from God. I received a phone call from Gary Chapman very soon after this. He told me to meet him on the Monday morning at 9.30am at a building he felt would be suitable for us. It was in a brand new part of Eccles on the Trafford Park border of Manchester. I told him I would meet him there. Intrigued, I finished what I was doing quickly and got in the car and drove to the address. It was a Friday afternoon, about 3pm. I got to the site at about 4pm and it was going dark. Gary had told me about the units there and how there was one that was ideal. I came to a roundabout and drove down the road – Coronet Way. I saw FedEx's superb facility, Exova, Stearns and a Skills Centre. Then a pile of dirt was banked up where the road ended, and right next to it there was the unit he was referring to. It was the last one down the cul de sac. It was about as unappealing as one could imagine.

It was nearly dark at this time and I thought 'no wonder no one has taken this unit!!'. I called Gary, whom I had great respect for, and told him, "Gary, I've been down to the unit and it's the last one down the bottom of the road. Really, it's just not suitable, don't waste your time on Monday." He was quite unapologetic. "Paul, just meet me on site on Monday, there are a few things you need to know about this building. Just bear with me okay?" I thought about how The Lord had spoken to me already about Gary, so I quickly agreed with him. "Okay Gary, see you there Monday 9.30am". I thought to myself, "Well, whatever, I need to just be more patient and go with the flow, even though this building's a non-starter".

Monday came and I met Gary on site. In the day time, it did look a bit better, but in my eyes, it still hadn't got much going for it! Gary took me to the front door and showed me the large space. Then the toilets downstairs and the shower conveniently placed. Then we went to the small area of first floor space that there was in all these units. It was just a standard open plan office. Lots of natural light and nice views back over the Manchester ship canal to Trafford. He pointed out where the new headquarters of the BBC would be in Media City, Salford, which was less than a mile from our front door, and also Manchester United's Football Ground at Stretford could easily be seen from the building. Then I said to him, "Okay Gary, but come on, look where it is! At the bottom of a muddy lane! It's really not going to tick the boxes I'm afraid."

Gary knew I was looking for a site with a bit of a prestigious frontage, so I was surprised he brought me here, until he continued. "Yes Paul, but see the road there, where it comes to the end of the road?" "Er, yes", I said. "Well, that's not really the end of the road at all. There is going to be a main road put in by Salford City Council that will go straight past this building.

It will be the main road in and out of Media City and the BBC's new HQ!" To be honest, I was speechless! I thought of what the Lord had said–"Go to the end of the road." And I hadn't! I'd just driven up to the road, spotted it and said "Thanks, but no thanks!" I also remembered how the Lord had told me to stick with Gary, that he would be the key person, given to me to guide us as to where to go. I also remembered the Word that I'd been given, "I will provide myself a house"–was this it? Was this going to be the real deal?

The next few days I put into process the proverb "Plans fail for lack of counsel, but with many advisors they succeed" (Prov 15:22). This verse had never been so relevant and appropriate to me in my life. The building we had just lost had blurred my edges and certainly frayed my nerves if I'm honest about it. It was time to ask those around me, who I loved, knew and trusted, to help me make what was to be a monumental decision. My father-in-law, Alex Tee and Justin were my first port of call. My Dad had said it was terrific and made sense of all that had gone before. He also said a really helpful thing. "People in a city are not so bothered where the church meets, they accept they'll have to travel ". It was Paul Scanlon–founding pastor of Abundant Life church, Bradford, (now Lifechurch) who I first heard say "The Church that's alive is worth a drive" and it's something I do believe.

My concept of church is that it is by nature very diverse. There are several types of churches I believe. Amongst them are Metro Churches, (Mega Churches) typically a thousand or more (I mean in actual terms, not imaginary, by the way!), Missional churches (Apostolic) which I believe are by nature several hundred strong. Communal churches, which are smaller but are very involved in their local community at a very grass root level. These are typically 100 to 200 people in number (could be more). The next group of churches are 'relational' churches which hold together strictly on the basis of relationship. This is one of the reasons why they can fluctuate so much, but have a great influence albeit in a small area. They are typically between 40 and up to 120 in number. Then there are what I'd call small cell churches–even though they're not attached to a main church they are obviously part of the universal church, the body of Christ. These churches typically range from 15 to 35 or 40 at the maximum number before morphing into relational churches.

I didn't get this from the latest book or seminar by the way, but by nearly thirty years of experience of pastoring in the UK and being involved in leadership in all those types of churches up to Metro (Mega) Church level. At present there are no Mega Churches in Manchester though one is very close (not Lighthouse). This is strictly my opinion, but I believe it to be true. Where do I see The Lighthouse in the future? I see it as an Apostolic, Missional Church at the moment very similar to the Church at Antioch in Syria. I see it becoming a Metro over the next ten to fifteen years, a church of well over a thousand in attendance.

Back to the possible new facility. All my confidantes had expressed positive affirmation that it would be a good decision to go ahead. The next thing was to bring our HQ more into the equation. Officials from our denomination's HQ visited and they loved it. They were very enthusiastic, especially when they heard about the new road going in. We decided to share it with the local church. They loved it too especially once we'd organised a few visits there with prayer on site. Although in reality it just a shell, I could see many people were pretty excited to see how we'd design the layout and all the interior. The next huge mountain to climb was going to be change of use and negotiating the price. The former would be a whole different ball game to the latter. We were about to see an adventure play out in front of our eyes that would be both miraculous and quite strange too.

We tried to buy the building which had a valuation of about 1 million GBP, but the owners would not sell in any eventuality. We learned later that the whole of the land for all of the units in the existing complex are on land owned by Her Majesty the Queen. The name 'Coronet Way' was a clue I guess. We discussed a long term lease and in charitable law 21 years is an asset and 20 years a liability! So 21 years it was. Who thinks up these kind of things? I'd really like to know! We negotiated an annual lease of £95,000 for the whole building including the land and the security contract on site and the landscaping. The sums meant it was possible to use the £1.2 million from the sale of our existing building to do a complete interior design and build. I drew out an elevation including

221

moving our nursery over. This was to prove to be a problem. We made an offer of £95,000 pa for 21 years subject to change of use from the planning authorities. This was accepted. We also negotiated very hard on a rent-free period to start from change of use. The owners wouldn't give this at all but gave us a year from the date the offer was legally accepted. We went for it. The lease gave us the chance to turn a £1million building into a £4–£4.25 million building at an affordable cost if we leased. It gave us the opportunity to hugely enlarge our space and though in the world's eyes it would be a huge gamble I believe it was a massive step of faith to be able to build a strong Missional apostolic city church.

We went for it full steam ahead. Plans were drawn up by Justin based on what I believed we needed. I was very focused and specific in what I wanted to see. Admittedly there's an element of compromise has to be entered into on something like this, but as the chief visionaries so to speak, Mags and I were not prepared to compromise on certain aspects of the new facility. We felt we had literally laid our lives on the line to build such a strong church when it came to the physical, visible style and feel of the new centre we had the lion's share, and I think correctly too. We designed a really superb five star cafe, an eight hundred seater auditorium with a huge platform and a PA system and lighting and video package costing about 25% of the budget of 1.2 million. The eight hundred chairs we bought were a fabulous bargain at £26,000 which months after would have been £34,000, however, before I get going on the main breakdown for those who are interested in this kind of detail, (and I'm sure there are many) first we had to land the planning permission to change the building from D1 and D2 (light commercial and office accommodation) to B1, C2 and C3 classification (place of worship, public building and community activity–this was also phrased as sui-generis or multi-use classification). We drafted in a specialist planning company to deal with this called 'Indigo Planning Consultants'. Whilst not cheap they were and are one of the best. We got cracking on the application. It was to prove a minefield. The local planning authority were called 'Urban Vision' and whilst they were definitely 'Urban' they had no vision whatsoever and we found ourselves dealing with an immovable group of people who had absolutely no idea about inventive, creative use of brownfield sites. Just utterly amazing!

It was supposed to take 4-5 months to eventually obtain change of use but it ended up taking a whole year! But we got it in incredible circumstances. Once we'd made our mind up that this was God's reserved place for us to be, we were very diligent in setting out our path. I visited the premises on my own shortly after we decided on the move. I was in the open plan office overlooking Media City. I thought about the planning application for change of use. I had a few moments of doubt I must confess. Then I heard a voice from within me that I recognised instantly. "Ask me now and I will give you the planning permission." It was as simple as that. I knelt down right there and then and asked God to give it to me. I knew from that moment on we would eventually get it. The local authority in charge of the 'change of use' decisions, decided against the proposal. We met with them and they told us three times they would under no circumstances approve it. It was a commercial building to be on a main highway to Media City not the place for a church. Our planning consultants were stunned at such stubborn opposition and explained there was a chance to overturn the local authority's decision. I needed to meet up with the local councillors and ask them to support the proposal on the basis of what we would bring to the area in terms of employment, community involvement etc. I arranged to meet two of them. John and Geoff. One of the councillors on hearing I was a pastor cursed and swore at me and told me it was no #%€$#>% place for a church and especially a nursery and public building. No he wouldn't support it. Just before we left, I asked him, "Okay Geoff, if I took the nursery out of the proposal would you support it?" He made a u-turn. "Erm, yeah, I guess so, I would probably support it then no problem." He changed in the blink of an eye.

We called many prayer times in those days, that focused not only on the move, but on communicating and celebrating victorious steps towards our destination. Justin and myself returned back from this meeting going straight from there to one such prayer time. As we entered the car park at our existing building, we looked at one another. It was virtually full! It was a fairly large car park too and we felt a strong surge of the presence of God.

We went into the prayer time and told the 150-160 people there what had just taken place. We all celebrated and rejoiced together at what was to be an incredible episode in our journey. If anyone is reading this now and you're getting setbacks from your local authority, don't despair, there's another route you can go. You will need to press the right buttons at the right time and meet the right people and get people on side, but for churches in the UK who, let's be honest, are often trivialised and marginalised, we need to stand up and not take things lying down. Even apart from the obvious biblical implications and truths we know as Christians, leaders and pastors, the church is invaluable to society as agents tackling social deprivation, poverty, crime, domestic abuse, fragmentation of families and communities, unemployment, and issues affecting young people today. We are one of the biggest employers in the country, employing more youth leaders and community workers than any council, and we are the best crime prevention units on the planet. How many people in our churches have changed lives, coming out of crime, unemployment, domestic violence, marriage breakdown, drug and alcohol abuse and various addictions? The church actually prevents the loss of millions of pounds/dollars every year to the state which would ordinarily be utilised by people for a variety of means, but for the power and saving grace of God through Christ's ability to transform and change lives, using them instead to bring blessing and benefit to whole communities.

We need to let people know this is the reality and stop apologising as if we are some little bunch of happy clappers meeting in a back street singing "Kum ba yah my Lord". This is the downside of 'small, stunted growth' in church life. It is seen as insignificant and inconsequential. As if to illustrate this very point, we sent out our proposal document to all the councillors in the immediate area. It listed all our community involvement, our projects, children's and youth work, childcare, overseas missions and our charity shops, recycling projects, work with unemployed, homeless, refugees, etc. We highlighted all our achievements in the past and present and projected our proposals for the future and wrapped it into the new facility–our proposed new centre in Eccles, Salford near. Media City. We also pointed out that we already had about 100 people attending the church from Salford (80 of whom were from our Eritrean Church admittedly, but nevertheless constituted a very sizeable group of people). Along with the Eritrean church currently meeting on site, we had about 400 people in the church. We projected this to up to 1200 in the new facility at any one time with the help of a balcony being introduced at a later stage. It was an impressive document that was accurate but very positive and certainly had high impact with a number of the councillors.

The date for the appeal hearing had been set. It was the 4th of December 2008. I had been asked to speak for 4 minutes, and not a minute longer. I tried to get one of the planning consultants to do it, but Mags was adamant, I literally "had to do it!" Mags spoke to me about this several times and felt the Lord had told her to get me to do it! The trouble is I was afraid I'd mess it up. It was an old chestnut that had come back to haunt me. I was not qualified, I was not articulate or eloquent enough. I was not academic or educated highly enough nor had I had the professional experience etc etc etc. The list seemed endless as I gave myself 101 reasons why someone else would be better at this than me. It dawned on me though, that I had to take responsibility for this as the chief visionary. Plus, I couldn't ignore the words I knew God had spoken to me that morning: "Ask me now and I'll give *you* the permission". I prepared my speech thoroughly and earnestly and it lasted exactly four minutes. The local authority were refusing to give approval mainly on the basis that we did not have enough car parking for the initial 800 capacity. My argument against this was precise and simple. At our prime times (weekends) the area was like the "Marie Celeste"–(basically empty). You could park probably 800 cars on spaces available within the whole development, and I had written undertakings from neighbouring units to show they had no problem with us using their spaces during the weekend. I kept my gunpowder dry until this point and didn't show them my hand until the hearing.

The moment came when I delivered my four minute speech. Nerves gave way to a bit of righteous indignation to be honest when I found out that our 'Green Travel Plan' hadn't even been circulated to the council by the local authority, (Urban Vision), who had an obligation to distribute it to the panel present at the appeal. They simply hadn't done it! Furthermore in their long and tedious summing up of our application they were still using the initial preliminary drawing which had been amended at least four times as was mentioned by our Planning Consultants.

My time came and I was more than ready. Following my speech the time came to vote for the councillors. The only way I can describe it, is it was like a penalty shoot-out at a football match. It went down to the wire. Two of the major things went in our favour: firstly, the size of our congregation of four hundred (with the Eritrean church!) This had a big impact on several councillors. Secondly, the missional work particularly in Romania and India where we evidenced in our proposal document the work that we had achieved from our church centre in Chorlton. Several councillors were very much swayed by this and could see we were a credible and active 'organisation' which they wanted in their community. The voting went something like 1-0 to us, 1-1, then a councillor took exception to us daring to take a commercial property out of the business world and waste a premium building by letting 'the Church' use it! I mean, how dare we? 1-2. Then a councillor rebutted this saying she would love four hundred in her church and what on earth where they doing opposing this! We should be supporting churches and organisations like this!" 2-2. Eventually we won something like 7-5, with the chairman not voting as it was incidental and so he abstained. We had overcome the local authority!

On the 8th December we had our planning permission granted. A major battle had been won. Not only for us, but for others too, as several churches did a similar thing once they'd heard how we overcame an 'out of touch' administration with little creative thinking and no real vision. God had delivered on His promise. Now we had to get the people ready for physically 'crossing over our Jordan river', which was effectively for us, the Manchester Ship Canal, some three and a half miles north west of where we were at the time. We were going to have to navigate the way forward with precision and prayer.

SECTION FIVE

"The SUV Years"

Chapter Twenty Six

CROSSING OVER

*"Then you will know which way to go, since you
have never been this way before." (Joshua 3:4 NIV)*

A lot has been said about the process of transition by many
preachers and church leaders over the past few years. We
had our own personal and unique experience of this in 2009-10
when our church congregation moved their place of worship
three and a half miles North West of our then existing centre in
Chorlton, Manchester, to Eccles on the Salford-Trafford border.

I knew the physical and geographical move would present a
very real challenge. Looking back, I thank God for the incredible wisdom He gave and the specific instruction too, in order
to make this move successful and fairly smooth. A word of cau-
tion and warning here if I may. I see a lot of senior/lead pastors
share their vision but not actually communicate it well enough
or clearly enough to take the people with them. A little known
African proverb says;

*"If you want to go fast, go alone. If you want to go far, go
with others."*

Inspirational leadership doesn't come out of a book, but out
of a heart for God's purpose. Again, John Maxwell says people
buy into the leader first and the vision second. This is so true and

229

I've watched leaders and pastors launch their vision of building a new facility as if it is going to give the church a fresh injection of vision and commitment on its own. NO IT ISN'T! The first thing it's going to do is heighten and raise expectation levels and that's probably one of the hardest things to manage in life! I've led and overseen three fairly big, church building projects in Manchester now, in 1991, in 2000 when we extended the then existing centre by 35%, and in 2010 when I managed a new interior design scheme of about nearly £2 million (approx $3m) in order to have a facility worth over £4 million pounds (approx $6m). I also managed and supervised the building of our children's home in Tamil Nadu, India in 2001 (a pretty large building on an six acre complex), a very large Bible College (on the same site) in 2002 and a large three storey specialist childcare centre in Slatina, Southern Romania in 2001.

One of the greatest keys is clear, repeated and accurate communication. It sounds simple but how often this is overlooked. Pastors and leaders expect people to follow their heart and vision and then neglect to share any real detailed information with the church. Personally I wouldn't follow that vision or that leader! I have a series of leadership messages called "Be The Leader You Would Follow". Okay, I pinched the title from somewhere, but all knowledge is borrowed (smile). The contents are 70% my own experience of being personally involved in building church for nearly thirty years and the rest snippets of valuable information and truth I've gleaned from others who have trodden the tricky path before me.

The Lord had impressed upon my spirit that I had to be clear and had to repeat many times over, in various ways, the vision, the location of the new centre, and the manner and the way we were going to manage the miracle. This included how much it would cost and how we were going to raise the finance! I can't resist saying a 'hello' here! Vision is more than an idea simply plucked out of the sky. It must come with some form of strategy in order to have some kind of credibility. What I have not mentioned yet is the bombshell that hit us in 2008 that no one seemed to expect! A huge recession hit us. Europe and the USA would be rocked so much, that it has changed whole communities across the western world. Our strategy went to 'plan B' then to plan 'C'–in fact I'm glad we've got an alphabet of 26 letters! It's quite strange really because our first building project back in 1991 was also in a recession. I remember being told, "Don't worry Paul, the church has always had a resurgence in recession." That was little comfort for me when the national savings rate went down from about 10% to 1.5%! Now what was that I said earlier about "vision in ink and plans in pencil"?

At each and every step we communicated clearly the way forward. Habakkuk 2:2 became absolutely axiomatic for me for that year.

"Write down the revelation and make it plain on tablets so a herald may run with it" (Habbakkuk 2:2 NIV)

Everything I'm saying is right here. It's not enough *just* to communicate. It needs to be done *repeatedly* and it needs to be done *urgently* and of course *inspirationally* and *creatively*. Why? Because we need people! People are our major resource on earth. Of course our main source is the Holy Spirit, but our number one resource is His people. *We need people to run with it, follow it and be passionate about it*. I have a friend in Manchester UK who is well known as an evangelist, Andy Hawthorne founder and leader of The Message Trust based in Sharston, in Wythenshawe, Manchester. Andy has helped to reach thousands through The Message Trust over twenty years. The stand out thing about Andy is his passion in communicating vision. He's always 'up for it' and invokes a sense of passion for Christ and the lost. You know with Andy he's in something for the long haul. He's not a nine day wonder. Passion for me is critical. It's not everything but it can move heaven and earth in a few seconds and cause ordinary people to achieve extra-ordinary things.

Over the months, we communicated to our people every week the location and the proposed date we would be moving, and how we would develop the site, and yes, how we were going to fund it ! The move had to be done in two stages. First to another temporary venue within two miles of the new centre's location and then to our new centre. We proposed to move to our new centre once the Auditorium was completed, then we would finish the rest of the building off whilst partially using the centre. We found an excellent venue that had just become available due to a church moving out of the premises. The venue was part of Salford University Campus and was ideal for our use, though it would cost us a hefty £600 ($900) per week, i.e. just for a Sunday morning.

We decided to move out at the end of March 2009. The deal with our sale had gone through as the Church of Pentecost who bought the building had previously signed up for the deal at £1.2m ($1.8m). We had also accrued £160k ($240k) in our building fund. In the end, our expected three month stay at the University Campus was twice as long and unfortunately was the shape of things to come. During the whole design and build we experienced numerous delays, which ended up costing us at least £160k in wasted time, thereby resulting in the loss of our remaining rent free period and the loss of time spent potentially raising funds from the new centre too. They say "time is money" (whoever "they" are!) but you find out it's more than money. It's opportunity, it's a waste of resources and it puts pressure on relationships and quality ends up suffering too. Not good, but even with the best planning at times it's unavoidable because people, as they say, are people!

Regarding the move, I resigned myself to writing a bottom line of losing up to 20% of our congregation. I even surveyed the congregation, as a result of which only a couple of people said they would consider moving to another church nearby. I still set a benchmark of 20%. When we moved, for the first three months I was very pleasantly surprised. I worked out we had lost about 10-12% of our congregation, (about 25 people). In actual fact, most of these came back over the next six months after they had tried other churches. We 'lost' about ten people when all said and done. I believe this was an incredibly successful, physical transition and much of it while down to authentic vision was also down to very good, clear and repetitive communication, making it easy for people to follow.

We moved over to Peel Hall at Salford University Campus at the end of March 2009. We expected to be there three months whilst we developed the main auditorium first and the restrooms (wc's) next. Unfortunately due again to delays it was actually September by the time we moved and even then we had to improvise, but

232

that's our trademark at The Lighthouse. We had put the mezzanine in, and put some interior walls in, but the main hall had not yet been done, so we used curtaining all the way around the proposed auditorium. It gave a good, albeit temporary, feel to what the main hall would look like. We also put the stage in, which I became very unhappy about because it was just a big block. I re-designed it to accommodate a 'friendlier' lower tier for the preacher and main worship leader(s) so as to make sure the speaker / leader connected with the people.

Often, in my experience what is drawn on paper may look nice, but in reality it can cause problems and be totally unworkable on a day-to-day basis. We had to make sure we got it right and that we weren't building elements into the building that were prohibitive and impractical and would therefore make things difficult. The platform/stage was a case in point. I have a strong disliking for corridors and when Justin drew out for us the initial design I asked him to remove every corridor he possibly could. To his credit he found a way and we only have three corridors, two of which are fire exits. There is a lot of open plan space, giving it a warm, friendly feel and a totally 'unchurchified' atmosphere. Job done then. Most people who come to our church for the first time remark on this and it does have a wow factor, as it looks more like a hotel than a church. I'm happy too because we managed to get 'a champagne finish on a coca cola budget'!

On our first Sunday morning on September 2009 our guest speaker was Pastor Matt Beemer of Rhema Ministries. Matt and his wife Julie had become good friends with us. They had planted World Harvest Church in Salford some 15 years previous to our coming to Salford and had handed over the pastoral and leadership reins to others as they took up a more apostolic and missional role in Nigeria, Egypt and elsewhere. I decided I would not be the first to preach at the new building but give someone else the honour. I am not a sentimental person when it comes to Kingdom. I simply like to get the job done and get it done well! We had about 340 out including kids that first Sunday. A good number were visitors though.

We set our dates for the "Grand Opening" when the project would be finished, and re-scheduled them three times because of the delays experienced. Eventually I set it for the 11th September 2010. Yes, 9/11! Some people were a little unhappy about this, but I explained to them that it also made a statement that even though there were many 'destructive' people in the world, there were also people who are very constructive too. This was a day to rejoice.

Even though we had put loads of space in between the start of the project and the third opening date, we made it by the skin of our teeth. On the actual day of the opening, we had to unpack all the cafe furniture and assemble it. All the leather settees/sofas for the cafe and mezzanine needed to be put in place. Some painting was still going on. I was laying carpet tiles. Our young people were helping, and so was Geoff, the councillor who had initially been totally against the development and had turned around 180 degrees!

I was still laying carpet tiles at 4 in the morning. One of our team was laying a ceramic tiled floor in the kitchen. Another of our guys was finishing off the counter in the cafe, whilst others were setting all the chairs out. People would be arriving from 2pm.

On the mezzanine was what was for me one of our show-pieces, our timeline. It is the story of the church from the very beginning. It shows the little church starting way back when. The real story started in 1986 though when Mags and I came to Manchester. I had to ask our HQ for the previous thirty years history and this was very sketchy. We set out the vision we believe God had given us to build a Lighthouse in the city. In 1991 we founded The Lighthouse Christian Centre, which is now just called 'The Lighthouse'. There are virtually no words on our time-line, only dates and photos, but it tells an incredible and miraculous story stretching over 25 years at the time. I remember one of the guys who came to put it up. He was on his scaffold and he'd almost finished it. I was looking at it whilst in close prox-imity. "Hey mate!" he said in a very Mancunian accent, I don't understand what this place is but this is #%*^¥% marvellous! The guy was actually crying as he said it. It was further evidence that sticking my neck out and taking the decision to fully oversee the timeline was the correct and proper thing to do. Pastor Alex was a priceless Godsend in this task. I met with a bit of reluctance as I'm not too sure some of the leadership understood our intention or how it would look. I painted it all out in watercolour and I still have that template which Alex worked from. The timeline was a non-negotiable element for me and the guys sensed this I'm sure. I felt the Lord laid it heavily upon my heart to include it. I felt Him say, *'For the people to know the way forward, they need to be given an understanding of the past'*. This made perfect sense to me and I believe this is the function of our 'Timeline'. We will be adding a section to it in soon as it is due.

With the congregation safely crossing over our 'Jordan' (literally the Manchester Ship Canal), we set to, building the spiritual body. In 2012, our first full year in the centre, we grew to about 450. In 2013 this went to about 500 and then to 600 and beyond. Together with the satellite churches which are very much a part of Lighthouse, there would be over 1,000 people.

Our Satellite Churches are, Eritean and Ethiopian, Portuguese speaking (think Brazilian etc), Indian (Malayalam), and French-speaking African. A Romanian satellite church looks like the next one. The Indian and Eritrean congregations on their own number over 300 between them. Not all of them meet on site, in fact most of them meet in different parts of the city. We still bring them together at our All Nations Day held the last Sunday of November every year.

On the opening day, well over a thousand people came, including the Mayor of Salford and his wife. Hazel Blears, our local MP and ex-cabinet minister also attended. It was a fabulous opening, and Pastor John Glass, General Superintendent of The Elim Churches in GB and Ireland, was the speaker. One of my greatest blessings that day was the fact that my father-in-law Pastor Alex Tee could make it, as he had been very unwell. Other great men and women supported, Andy Hawthorne, Roger Sutton, Debra and Frank Green, local church leaders and ministry leaders representing the city of Manchester. It was a truly great occasion. A plaque was unveiled by Hazel Blears MP and Dave King read from the scripture and led a very prophetic prayer. Our plaque could only say one thing:

Arise and shine, for your light has come, and the glory of the Lord is risen upon you. (Isaiah 61:1 NIV)

The day went quickly and as usual with these occasions, I'm glad to get them over and done with so I can move on! I was and am thankful though for the citywide support pastors and leaders gave us that day. I also felt that even the opening day congregation was a snapshot of the future for us in days to come.

2006 Boxing day Tsunami - Cuddulore, India.
LIM gave out £23,000 worth of kerosine stoves, rice and clean water - LIM also built 26 homes. (top left and right / bottom left).

Image (bottom left) show the destruction and the devastation left in the wake of the tsunami.
One of the smaller mass graves is shown too (top centre).

Dunamis Youth Camp in the Carpathian Mountains, Romania.

237

THE LIGHTHOUSE | 2009

The building at the end of the road (top left).   Prayer team with Pastor Paul following the overturning of the city councils decision, winning the right to turn the commercial premises into a church (top centre).   First Sunday Morning Service held in the new premises heralding a brand new day for thousands of people to be blessed and transformed through God's grace and power via The Lighthouse Manchester, UK.

TODAY

Building the Church of Tomorrow Today!

Chapter Twenty Seven

BEING A PATHWAY MAKER

*"Do not choose to follow the path that others have trodden,
rather make a pathway for others to follow."*

I came to realise that being a pathway maker was a lot harder than being a pathway taker. The Lord had in effect given us a large blank sheet of paper and it was up to us what to put on it. This is still a challenge, though an exciting one. I also realised that we had entered totally unfamiliar territory. For some, this has been too much. Sadly people who journeyed with us and who worked for and prayed for our new house to emerge, found that once it did emerge, the challenge of continuing the journey was too much. I think about Elijah sitting under the juniper tree in 1 Kings 19.

Then as he lay and slept under a broom tree, suddenly an angel touched him, and said to him, "Arise and eat." Then he looked, and there by his head was a cake baked on coals, and a jar of water. So he ate and drank, and lay down again. And the angel of the Lord came back the second time, and touched him, and said, "Arise and eat, because the journey is too great for you."

Also you shall anoint Jehu the son of Nimshi as king over Israel. And Elisha the son of Shaphat of Abel Meholah

239

*you shall anoint as prophet in your place. (I Kings 19:1-
7,16 NKJV)*

I believe there are times when the journey just gets too great
for us. As I said earlier in the book, but it bears repeating, **"failure
is temporary, giving up makes it permanent"**. God recognised
it was time for Elijah's replacement to be anointed. Even though it
took about ten years from this point, Elijah was to be taken out of
'the journey'. Something I have had to come to realise and accept
is that people who are called to journey *with us*, may not *finish* the
journey *with us!*

I hate it when I lose good people, and I hate it even more when
I lose close people! It's like a bereavement to me. I am a fiercely
loyal person to those loyal to me and Mags. I genuinely find it
hard to accept that people you share, serve, plan, prepare, walk
with and believe with can one day just–walk away! It's a pastor's nightmare, but it will happen and it won't just happen once.
Along the way I've become close to people who've worked really
hard, believed so much and prayed so much to see The Lighthouse
flourish, only to decide that God has called them to leave and into
a new season. I make it my business now *never* to argue with these
people. If God has spoken, then who am I to question it? I also
give myself a good double dose of 'humble pie' to remind myself
that there are no guarantees when it comes to people. People will
and should always be free to decide for themselves. The scary
thing is though, most of these people never ask your advice. They
inform you of God's direction, and their choice. Even to this day
I find this really tough, but I'm very firm about it. I send them
with my blessing. If they just disappear without speaking I don't
run around trying to find them! I really can handle people leaving
and going, but I can never understand how people can do it just by
disappearing without a word. Maybe that says everything in itself.

Every church is different and every pastor and leader is different. I believe that's the way it should be. I don't think the model
of The Lighthouse is one to copy really, though I think it can teach
many things. It is a very daring and dynamic way of doing church
which is incredibly challenging. We don't own any buildings as
I write, we are always having to generate extra finance to fund

vision and new ministries. We don't have a savings account with tens of thousands of pounds in it. We don't have elders and deacons, just pastors and key leaders. We don't have committees but teams. But we do have a clear idea of our future. On our existing site we have all the scope we could ever ask for or dream of. We are not right in the centre of the city, true. But we are ideally suited for accessibility and strategic witness. We are now located on the main road into Media City. Only God could send us to the end of a road (a back street, cul de sac) in order to place us on a main and strategic route to the newest and largest development in the UK for many years, which is expected to cost about £1bn ($1.5bn) by the time it is completed. Once this has happened, in or around 2016, the Trafford Quays project will begin, which will bring waterside residential living from Salford Quays all the down the Manchester Ship Canal, past our Centre and underneath the M60 Ring-road for Manchester, to Worsley. Here a new golf course is planned and the developers' vision is to bring the Ryder Cup to Manchester in or around 2025. We will be located right in the centre of this new development. We firmly believe all our best days are ahead of us.

In practical terms, we aim to start to build our new entrance later this year, which will feature a beautiful, striking glass canopy from which we can advertise dynamically and creatively what is happening at The Lighthouse. We then aim to acquire the unit behind, which is three times the size of our existing unit, whilst retaining our existing unit. This will give us a total of about 80,000 sq ft, including our mezzanine areas. We have already been given the keys to this unit by the landlord, albeit temporarily when it was empty. We were told to use it free of charge for as long as it was vacant (which turned out to be six months). Whilst we had the keys of course, we went and prayed in it and put spiritual markers down. The owners offered it to us for a great price, but out of our league at the moment. But it is in the pipeline. It will easily hold 3,500 people with a great platform and mezzanine too. As I said, all our best days are before us.

Now, we are finding a new increase in people and in quality as we reach for our destiny in Christ. One of the key verses the Lord gave to us when we first came to our new location was from Joshua:

*Then you will know which way to go, **since you have
never been this way before.** But keep a distance of about
two thousand cubits between you and the ark; do not go
near it." (Joshua 3:4 NIV)*

We realised that this was completely new territory. We were
stepping into something entirely different. It was a whole new
landscape! How would we successfully navigate our way through
this new season?

Chapter Twenty Eight

THE NEW LANDSCAPE

*"Everyone may see the same sky but not everyone
has the same horizon."*

Change maybe an unpopular thing, but it's here to stay. Everything around us changes. The seasons are an annual reminder that it is part and parcel of nature and time and motion itself. To resist change in church life is like slowly preparing to die. Where there is true life, that will be evidenced by inspirational and fresh change. Not all change is good, but it is futile to be closed to the possibilities that are available through adapting and refining ourselves. We will need to do this over and over again.

The Lighthouse is going through probably the greatest moment of change in its history as we as leaders seek to re-calibrate how we orchestrate our people to reach the lost and disciple the found, then go on to release the equipped, for this surely has to be at the centre of our planning and praying. Our children's ministry changed last year from a basic 'Sunday School' that was really not reaching the kids' hearts and minds, let alone their souls. We launched "Lightforce", a radical approach to teaching kids biblical truth via an exciting and active programme including worship, dance, craft and educational but funky games. They love it, and their parents do too.

Recently we changed the Leadership structure and re-named deacons as 'Key Leaders'. Whereas before, we could only have up to 12 deacons and after that it would get messy, now we can have as many 'Key Leaders' as possible, all simply appointed by the existing pastoral team. The ministry of the church has been separated into three basic streams. 1. **Hospitality**–including Car Park Team, Catering Team, Welcome Team, Resources Team, Minibus Team, etc 2. **Youth**–including Children–Lighthforce, YPF (Young Peoples Fellowship), Youth House Groups, Design (Girls mentoring group) Flava and Mini-Flava (girls action groups) Atom (boys action group). 3. **Groups**–Life Groups, Purpose Groups and Home Groups. This is a huge area in itself.

As the church grows these three areas will be separated into four, then five etc. The vision behind it all is to create a model without any bottle-necks so it can easily be developed. A pastor is over each area and key leaders over each ministry and function. This for us was a very natural, organic progression and one which will be very releasing.

Other areas of change will be in our missions work and this is likely to be very deep and far reaching as we break from some long-standing commitments which have made some of our overseas partners far too dependent upon us. We will be opening another charity shop very soon and openings in Kenya and Ghana are looking very likely in the future. More entrepreneurial projects are in the pipeline to ensure we open up more revenue streams in the days ahead.

A new very modern expression of church has been launched at The Lighthouse, which takes place each month. This is called Excel and is building up a head of steam very nicely. It features a fast moving, multi-media element to it, with great live music incorporating our youth band, who are incredibly gifted. It also is a training ground for our youth ministries, giving opportunity to preach, share and develop their leadership skills and giftings. Excel is also becoming popular with other church youth. I would think it's the first time a church in Manchester has successfully launched such an event as part of its ministry to the city and not just its own people.

Xcellerate is a gap year programme recently launched for young people wanting to serve God and experience some kind of leadership training and various opportunities to serve. Cafe, conferencing, shop work, overseas missions, social and community projects all provide opportunity to experience life in an environment of faith and possibility. At The Lighthouse we give great opportunities for our young people to serve God. Our strapline now is "Building the church of tomorrow today!" I think this really sums up the church's passion and mission most. There is still much to be done. There is no real success without a successor, so I am fully aware that my successor needs to be prepared, trained and mentored over the next 7-8 years. I do not want to get to 62-64 without having him firmly in place. Even now, I believe a 'Joshua' is in the making. And my prayer is that my 'ceiling will become their floor'. Muhammad Ali once said, "A man who views the world the same at fifty as he did at twenty has wasted thirty years of his life!" I think that we begin to think more generationally as we get older. We realise that life becomes more about what we will leave behind after us, instead of what we will achieve in the future. Delegation is very much a part of this strategic thinking.

"The Laying Off Of Hands"

Recently, I was asked the question, "How can you travel so much and still lead a busy and demanding church ministry?" This month I've been two weeks in India, preached in five different churches, this morning Mags and I drove from our 'family home ' in Turnu Severin, in the South of Romania, after saying goodbye to all the kids there in our family home. We caught our flight to the UK from Craoiva to London, picked our car up at the airport and now I'm back home in my garden, in our summerhouse putting the final touches to this book. Tomorrow morning I have a leaders/ pastors meeting. So, what's the secret to this freedom? The answer is quite easy, (though the execution of it is anything but.) I developed a truly amazing, loyal, anointed, appointed and gifted team. Then I practised **"the laying off of hands"**. I noticed several years ago that many stunted churches were held back by the lead pastor! He was far happier doing the work of ten people than setting the work of ten people. The problem is that this creates a glass ceiling all of its own. That leader can desperately pray "Lord help our church grow" and the most common prayer "Send them in Lord, send them in!" But the main pastor isn't training, mentoring and releasing people into roles and areas of responsibility because of fear or insecurity. Fear in ministry as I've said before is the surest way to bring stagnancy to the church. Freshness isn't often seen where fear reigns. It gives way to staleness and puts the brakes on everything and momentum suffers, which is a huge element in church life. Real, genuine delegation promotes confidence and builds increased ability and personal growth. It also develops otherwise untapped potential and even allows unseen and undiscovered qualities to emerge.

Delegating is not easy. It is risky, but so is life! *People who are wrapped up in cotton wool are likely to choke on it too!* A few years back I let one of our Romanian teenagers drive our Mercedes bus while on mission. He had not long passed his test. "How do we know can we trust him?", the present house-parent said. *"By trusting him"*, I replied. We cannot fully know a person's trustworthiness unless we first begin to trust. Even then, there could be a few hiccups to begin with. Free-will is as unpredictable as anything on earth, but some people will choose faithfulness over unfaithfulness, and reliability over unreliability. We will make many mistakes when we delegate because human error and misjudgment are far more common than perfection. I like what Andrew Carnegie said, when asked how it was that he had made so many people who worked and managed for him into millionaires, especially as when as they started out, they virtually had nothing. He said, "When I dig for gold, I have to dig up tons of dirt just to get ounces of gold. But it is not the dirt that I'm looking for, it's the gold." I feel the same way when I delegate. I'm not looking for perfection or anything like it to be honest. I'm simply looking for that precious gold that is present deep within. Passion, dedication and integrity. If I find them, I'm not afraid to back them to the hilt. Even if I see weaknesses in other areas, I will still look to entrust responsibility to men and women to whom authenticity comes before ability.

As I close off this, my first ever book, (hopefully not my last), I would like to encourage every pastor, leader, Christian and person who has read The Rubicon: recognise your own Rubicons in life. Understand that these precious moments, when you come to the end of the road, are very often the way to a new beginning. They can be your Red Sea moments, your opportunity to cross your own personal Jordan. We all have a different pathway to take and make. *We may all see the same sky, but we all have different horizons.* I believe most of us have very exciting futures if we are willing to go beyond **'the end of the road'**.

I wish you every success in your future life and service to God. When Abraham was old in years, he sent his servant to look for a bride for his son Isaac. His servant went his way and prayed this prayer;

> *"Lord, God of my master Abraham, make me successful today, and show kindness to my master Abraham."* *(Genesis 24:12 NIV)*

Over the years I've not been very good at praying for myself. But I've begun to learn that there's a kind of success we all need if we're going to fulfil all that God has decreed for us. I pray that you too will know heavenly success. It may not look the same as earthly success, which is normally measured in material and financial terms. But it will include far, far, more than this. Peace, satisfaction, fulfilment and joy are things that no amount of money can buy. It will bring about transformation in lives and people's circumstances too. It will also take time. It's now 28 years since we started our journey and there is still a long way to go. It's taken 28 chapters to cover those amazing 28 years and I hope it's been a blessing to you. I read somewhere recently, it takes 13 hours to build a Toyota motor car and 6 months to build a Rolls Royce! I still believe slow growth is steady, sound growth, and quick growth is often full of uncertainty. I think growth that takes time, lasts time too. I trust you will find our story encouraging and inspirational, whatever stage you are at in your life and your service for Him.

May God bless you and yours, as you work out your own salvation, to His glory and His honour.

Yours in His grace,

"Paul & Mags"

THANK YOU'S

No book would be complete without mentioning a few people, who have walked with us, through the highs and the lows. People who we are indebted to. Our Aquila's and Priscilla's, Timothy's, Jonathan's, Deborah's, Ruth's, Martha's and Mary's (some of our best men have been women!)

Firstly my wonderful, amazing, beautiful wife Mags, for her unselfish and untiring, unwavering dedication and willingness to walk into the unknown with me. Love you deeply and always.

To my mother and father, Gladys and Percy Hallam, for their incredible example of godly devotion and sacrifice.

To my beautiful niece Samantha, the closest of my blood relatives.

To my father in law and mother in law, Alex and Winifred Tee, for their boundless love, support and example.

To our wonderful and precious kids from Romania–our sons from afar, Danny, Mada, Bobi, Vasi, Juli, Iuli, Clau, and our daughters nursed at our side, Alex, Ella and Miha.

To Phil and Emma Clare–our children in the Lord. Thank you for your love and support.

Emma and Dom, for your hearts of devotion to us and for your dedication in 'building the House'.

Justin and Jo Marks, our Aquila and Priscilla who made our journey possible in Christ. God will reward you for your humility, deference and loyalty. You are giants of faithfulness and like well-springs in the desert.

John and Liz Guard, wonderful servants of God and towering examples of faith and devotion.

Jenny Taylor, industrious, positive and fervent in all things.

Margaret and Graham Harrison. Martha's hands and Mary's heart combined.

Jeff Stoker, a complete one off, unique individual. A heart on legs!

Freddy Grimshaw, a hard working woman of excellence.

Alex and Nancy, for your amazing support, love, faithfulness and loyalty.

Dele and Dumebi, your godliness and sincerity is always refreshing, and your zeal is continually present in our midst.

Dana, you mean so much to us. You always amaze us. We love you and appreciate you continually.

Ana Tudosie, your loyalty and support to me and Mags has been resolute and rock solid. "Thank you!"

Sylwia and Dean, thanks for your endeavour, help and availability.

Richard and Petra Clare, your humility, meekness and unswerving loyalty has been incredible.

Nela Anjos, your love and support always steadfast despite your own hurts and challenges has been amazing.

Rhea, Jesse, Rachel, Faith, Hannah, Dom, Tio, Amari, Tom, Lois Amy, Joel, Eleanor Grace, Shem, our new generation of Joshua's and Deborah's.

Adele Adedeji, your long-standing, practical and unwavering support has been rock steady. You deserve great reward!

Pam Padmore, our longest serving and most faithful supporter over 28 years.

Dianne Collins, for sticking with us through thick and thin. May ALL your children one day drink deeply from the cup of salvation.

Matthew and Deborah, for staying the course.

Mehari and Weini, for working with us in international purpose and blessing.

Dr Edi and Ngozi, what can we say? Faithful, generous and loyal. Always encouraging and inspirational.

Chris and Flo, newcomers to The Lighthouse who seem like they've been with us for twenty years! Faithful close friends.

Luke and Beth, for your love, dedication and quality support. Love you guys.

To ALL our church family, every one of you. Past and present. Leaders are nothing without faithful followers. Eventually a church gets the leaders it deserves. I hope and pray we served you well. You deserve the best. We hope to serve you to the end.

All our best days are ahead of us! With much love and gratitude.

"Paul and Mags"

I paint watercolour paintings available at www.thepastorsstudio.co.uk and the proceeds go to help abandoned children in Romania, Africa and India. The painting of the front cover was painted by me to express the meaning of ' rubicon ' a place of no return and can be obtained from my website

Lightning Source UK Ltd.
Milton Keynes UK
UKOW04f0317141014

240043UK00002B/4/P